DRIVING PASSION

The Psychology of the Car

also by Peter Marsh

AGGRO: THE ILLUSION OF VIOLENCE
(with R. Ingham and others)
FOOTBALL HOOLIGANISM: A WIDER PERSPECTIVE
(with R. Harré and E. Rosser)
RULES OF DISORDER

also by Peter Collett

SOCIAL RULES AND SOCIAL BEHAVIOUR

also by Peter Marsh and Peter Collett

GESTURES: THEIR ORIGINS AND DISTRIBUTIONS
(with D. Morris and M. O'Shaughnessy)

DRIVING
PASSION

The Psychology of the Car

PETER MARSH
AND
PETER COLLETT

FABER AND FABER   BOSTON AND LONDON

Library of Congress Cataloging-in-Publication Data

Marsh, Peter E.
    Driving passion.
    Bibliography: p.
    1. Automobile drivers—Psychology.
I. Collett, Peter.   II. Title.
TL152.3.M38   1986   629.2'222'019   86-31907
ISBN 0-571-12973-0

CONTENTS

ACKNOWLEDGMENTS

We are indebted to the Rees Jeffreys Road Fund for their generous support of our research. The Fund's Chairman, Ken Summerfield, is acknowledged for his advice and kindly interest in our work and for sparking off the idea of this book in the first place. We would also like to single out the contribution made by Pat Ganahl and thank him for his hospitality and generous assistance in California. To Desmond Morris we also offer our thanks for his help with the book's outline and for his continuing flow of good suggestions.

We are also indebted to the following people and organizations for their help in many different ways:
Tony Ball, Reyner Banham, Thomas Barrett III, George Barris, Nathan Bond, Mark Bowman, Robert Brierly, Lucy Brown, Ann Campbell, Giovanni Carnibella, Rick Cole, Tony Colwell, Ian Craig, Jill Crossland, Carolyn Edwards, Norma and Seymour Feshbach, David Fisher, Ford Motor Company, Michael Foreman, John Galea, General Motors, Terry Genis, Dawn Gibb, Doris and Gerry Ginsburg, Horst Gundlach, William Haddon, Walter Hayes, Jim Hedlund, Anna Marie Heelas, Tracy Hemmings, Bill Hess, Alan Hjorth, Peter Hutton, International Association of Traffic and Safety Sciences Tokyo, Shaky Jake, Jonathan Jephcott, Bill Keifer, Francesca Kenny, Cathy Lindsay, Chuck Lombardo, Alex Lowe, Margaret Machin, Ann McKendry, Peter Manning, Tricia Marsh, Tom Maschler, Margaux Mirken, Helmut Morsbach, Motor Vehicle Manufacturers Association, Steven Muncer, Thomas O'Gara, Pacific Theaters, Barbara Peevers, Carmine Pellosie, Joe Plummer, David Power, Clive Prew, Jim

Richardson, John Roberts, Rolls-Royce, David Roscoe, Dunya and Evert Sagov-Cilliers, Dustin Schuler, John Sieg, Lyn Smith, Craig Stecyk, Alexander Stilwell, Tony Strammiello, Paddy Summerfield, Andy Swapp, Barry Sweedler, Sally Thomas, J. Walter Thompson, Transport and Road Research Laboratory and James Wren.

We are grateful for permission to reproduce lyrics from the following copyright material: 'Maybellene' by Chuck Berry © 1955 by ARC Music Corp. (reprinted by permission, all rights reserved) and Jewel Music Ltd (p. 17); 'No Money Down' by Chuck Berry © 1955 by ARC Music Corp. (reprinted by permission, all rights reserved) and Tristan Music Ltd (pp. 18–9); 'Every Woman I Know is Crazy' by William Emerson © 1955 by Conrad Music, a division of ARC Music Corp. (reprinted by permission, all rights reserved) and Tristan Music Ltd (p. 19); 'Baby Let's Play House' by Arthur Gunter, Excellorec Music Co. and Carlin Music Corp. (p. 18); and 'Wreck on the Highway' from 'The River' by kind permission of Bruce Springsteen (p. 175).

We are also grateful for permission to reproduce lines from the following poems: *she being Brand* by e.e. cummings, reprinted by kind permission of Grafton Books, a division of the Collins Publishing Group and Live Right Publishing Co. (pp. 199–200); and *Buick* by Karl Shapiro, reproduced by kind permission of Laurence Pollinger on behalf of Random House Inc. (p. 200).

The extract by D.H. Lawrence on Walt Whitman is from *Studies in Classic American Literature* by D.H. Lawrence. Copyright 1923, 1950 by Frieda Lawrence. Copyright © 1961 by the estate of the late Mrs Frieda Lawrence. Reprinted by permission of Viking Penguin, Inc. (p. 20).

DRIVING PASSION

The Psychology of the Car

1

BEYOND TRANSPORT

THREE thousand years ago, a group of inscrutable Mandarins assembled in Peking to inspect the most exciting invention since the firecracker – the car. Before them was a turbine powered machine capable of very high speeds. A proud and talented engineer stood on the running board of the prototype chassis demonstrating to his attentive audience the refinement of independent steering and the advantages of a single, direct-drive rear wheel.

Accounts of this momentous occasion filtered through to Europe by way of Persian translations of Chinese literature from the Chou dynasty. Roger Bacon, a renowned scholar of the Middle Ages, rendered these into Latin for the benefit of Pope Clement IV and in a letter written in 1270, we find the crucial reference to the early automobiles. They ran under their own power, being neither pushed nor pulled by animals, and 'cum impetu inestimabili'.

Shortly after publishing this piece of automobile history, Roger Bacon was thrown into jail for 14 years by Pope Clement's successor, Jerome of Ascoli. The document survived, however, for it was known to Father Verbiest who, three hundred years later, was appointed Astronomer Royal at the court of the Chinese Emperor, Kang-Hi, in 1620. According to the historian Robert Christophe, the Astronomer was joking one day to the Emperor about the gullibility of Bacon and his incredible story about the Chou dynasty car. 'Nothing absurd about that!' snapped Kang-Hi. 'We have records of the matter in our Imperial Library.' And so they did.

We know, of course, that the Chinese Empire of this time was very advanced and had reached a high level of scientific sophistication. We also know that if they really did invent the car they found little immediate use for it. Even today the standard means of personal transportation in Peking is the bicycle. Clearly, the original prototype never got as far as the production line. But let us stay with the original scene in the Peking square for a moment because the Mandarins, before dismissing the project altogether, would surely have asked the engineer to outline the potential benefits of his hissing contraption. Of what real use could it be to Chinese society?

The engineer would have started by outlining the principal advantage of the new machine – 'It will allow ordinary people to travel wherever they wish and whenever they choose.' He would have stressed the benefits of personal freedom and mobility, and how this could have positive social value, but he would also have been obliged to indicate what negative consequences would arise from this quest for rapid personal travel. The Mandarins would have heard for themselves that the machine made a lot of noise. They would also have smelled its choking fumes. But 'millions of miles of paved road through the beautiful countryside and between the houses? . . . frequent collisions resulting in tens of thousands of deaths and severe injuries each year? . . . children killed in the streets as they played? . . . whole cities covered in blankets of pollution? . . .' At this point the Mandarins would have interrupted. They might have executed the inventor on the spot, or at least had him locked up as a dangerous lunatic. They would have heard enough. Had they listened for a little longer, however, they might have learned why such an apparently absurd system would one day become an inherent feature of all civilized societies and why such a high price would be paid to preserve it.

Motor cars, our Chinese engineer might have foreseen, would become much more than a means of going from one place to another. They would be manufactured in all manner of shapes, sizes and colors. People would be able to choose which suited them best and expressed most eloquently their status, life style and personality. They would make love in these machines;

propose marriage or divorce. They would write poems and sing songs about them, give them pet names and care for them as if they were members of the family. They would pray in them, eat and watch movies in them, even die and be buried in them. They would love them.

'Ah!' the wise Mandarins would have said. 'Yes, now we understand.' And how different history would have been.

Three thousand years later the automobile is still grossly misunderstood. It is an easy target for sociologists, economists, ecologists and the pundits and prophets of doom. Each year, several new books add to the growing volume of abuse directed at the motoring world.

'Isn't man fantastic?' asks Angus Black in *A Radical's Guide to Self-Destruction*. 'How did we let things get to a point where 55,000 Americans are killed in cars each year; where over 80 per cent of all air pollution is automobile induced; where our land is half-eaten by roads, parking-lots, 220,000 hideous gas stations; where traffic noise makes city streets unbearable?'

Such sentiments are well matched by Alisdair Aird in *The Automotive Nightmare*: 'Who, fifty years ago, could have imagined that we would sacrifice so much of our lives to motor cars? . . . Who could have predicted that the elegant streets of Paris, which had survived centuries of war and revolution, would one day succumb to day-long traffic jams? That Tokyo's city center would be so torn apart by traffic that it could take half an hour to inch one's way the length of a single city block? Who would have guessed that one day London's planners would feel forced to surrender the city to a roads program and destroy, or at least wreck, the homes of 120,000 people?'

These questions sound reasonable. We are well aware that the average speed of many car commuters is slower than in the days of the pony and trap; we also know that people still sit in traffic jams even when alternative means of travel are readily available. One-third of the surface area of Los Angeles is covered by roads and the city suffers from chronic levels of pollution and smog, yet it is in Los Angeles that the automobile is so revered that it was once said that the only difference between its rich and poor was that they drove different makes of car. The explanation for these apparent contradictions is not to be found in economic or political analyses, but in a study of how individuals relate to their cars, and not just to any car, but to the particular car they have chosen to drive and in which they choose to be seen.

We all have a relationship with our cars. They are important to us, no matter how much we might wish to deny it. It is because the car has so much personal value that we have been, and are still, prepared to alter radically the environments in which we live in order to create societies in which the auto-mobile can feature so centrally. Some people have described our relationships with the things we drive as demented passions and infantile fantasies. Our attachments are certainly passion-ate and the car is truly a vehicle for fantasy. That is why, in fact, the entire automotive industry stays in business. To de-scribe such forces as infantile and demented, however, is to close the door on more serious inquiry into the psychological processes which have rendered the car one of the most signi-ficant objects of the age in which we live.

The car manufacturers themselves, of course, understand relationships between people and cars. Only in moments of relaxed off-the-record candor, however, do they say so. They prefer to be seen as responsible supporters of the convention-al theory of the automobile. They like to foster the idea that men and women buy their products as a result of a wholly rational evaluation of factors such as economy, reliability, safety – those central themes of the new automotive morality. At the same time they offer us vehicles which have more cylinders, more horsepower and far more ornament and para-phernalia than is required for purposes of safe and efficient transportation. It is only the very up-market specialist manu-facturers who will unashamedly confess that their customers are out to impress, to announce an image of themselves. From our point of view, none the less, the driver of the rusty Beetle and the one in the gleaming turbo-charged Porsche both make equally powerful statements about themselves. They declare themselves to be particular kinds of people, and so define themselves socially. They are what they drive, and so are we. It is this single psychological principle which allows us to understand how the car has pervaded every nook and cranny of our everyday lives.

Car Culture

Over one billion motor vehicles have been produced since the turn of the century. Nearly half of these are on the roads today, and three-quarters are passenger cars. In Britain there is one private car for every three and a half people. In the United States the ratio is halved: two to three and a half. By contrast, there is only one car for every 18,000 people in China. Despite economic recessions and increased oil prices in Europe and America, levels of car ownership are still steadily rising. In Britain in 1986, over a million and a half new cars will have ventured on to the already overcrowded roads, while in America nearly six times this number will have been newly registered at the license plate counters. In the Soviet Union, almost a million new Zaproshevs, Moskvitches and Volgas will have appeared on the streets.

The consequences of consistent increases in the car population are very evident. There are 3.8 million miles of streets, roads and highway in America, which works out at about 40 yards for every vehicle in the country. The space shrinks to twenty yards in Britain, where about a quarter of a million miles of paved road caters for 18 million vehicles. Even these modest allowances are difficult to find in reality on the Santa Monica freeway, or the M4 into London, during the rush-hour. The true impact of the motor car, however, is not to be found just by measuring the length of roads, or by calculating the costs of pollution and injury. Nor is it just a matter of considering the levels of mobility it has provided. Cars are used primarily for quite short journeys, and, because of increasing congestion, our real mobility is actually declining. The only way to understand the true role of automobiles in society is to look beneath the veneer of rational explanations.

For the automobile satisfies not our practical needs but the need to declare ourselves socially and individually. So powerfully does it fulfill this psychological role that a visitor from a different planet would have no trouble in describing the car as a central feature of an almost universal religion. The Sunday preening and cleaning of the revered icons might be seen as the weekly worship, and the motor show as the annual holy day celebration of the car. Such shows are deliberately designed to persuade people that automotive dispensations from the sin of being left behind socially can be bought by acquiring the latest model. As the psychologist John Cohen has pointed out, 'a modern motor show carries all the trappings which in any other epoch would form the basis of a religious festival. It has colors, lights, priests (salesmen), priestesses (fashion models), a ritual and a liturgy.' To this may be added Anthony Greeley's remark that no suppliant 'more eagerly awaited a revelation from an oracle than does the automobile worshiper await the first rumors about the new models'.

Our religious devotion to the automobile extends far beyond the rites surrounding the unveiling of new models. It also manifests itself in superstitions and pagan rites which we observe, such as the practice of securing good luck charms in our cars. It has long been the practice of people who work with domesticated animals to attach charms – like bells to cows and brasses to horses – in order to safeguard them from evil spirits and the covetous eyes of other people. The Italian who attaches an effigy of a bull's horn or a plastic *mano cornuta* to his key ring, the Englishman who fixes a St Christopher to his dashboard, and the taxi-driver in Corfu who hangs a piece of fishing net on his rear-view mirror are all symbolically resolving their fears about the inherent dangers associated with driving. At the same time each is also symbolically protecting his car.

Many societies have what is called a symbiotic relationship with certain animals – a relationship founded on some form of dependence in which one or both partners profit from the association. The North American Plains Indians once relied for their existence on the buffalo, which they repaid with respectful legends and affection, just as Hindus in the Indian subcontinent today worship the cows on which, in a similar fashion, their economic livelihood depends. On certain religious occasions Hindus decorate their cows with flowers, just as we once did by fitting out horses with bright trinkets and plumes in the days when we were an equine society.

The parallel between the symbiotic relationship that we once enjoyed with horses and the symbiotic relationship that we now enjoy with cars is inescapable. We have reached the stage when our entire livelihood depends on cars, and in unconscious recognition of this fact we repay our automobiles by garlanding them and making them objects of our devotions. We reveal the extent of our psychological dependence on the automobile as graphically as our predecessors symbolized all that was essential for their continued existence. While such things as ribbons of highway, garages and parking lots can be seen as consequences of the car's function as a mode of transport, there are many other features of automotive cultures which are clear testaments to aspects of the automobile which have little or nothing to do with transport.

Drive-in movie theaters are one of the most illuminating artefacts of a culture which has achieved the highest level of psychological dependence on the car. From humble origins just over fifty years ago in New Jersey, drive-ins spread across America, finding particular favor in the 'sun belt' where the climate allows for films to be screened in the open air almost throughout the year. Today, there are nearly 3,000 theaters, some catering for up to 3,000 cars at a time. Many are equipped with high-tech multiple screens and elaborate sound systems.

To the British, the phenomenon of the drive-in movie is archetypically American, a 'foreign' pastime, due in the main to differences in climate and land availability rather than to significant variation in the cultural role of the automobile. Watching a movie with the windshield wipers grinding all the time would not be much fun. In Canada, some enterprising drive-in owners decided to give away a free gallon of gas to patrons so that they could run their engines for two hours and keep warm, but the business were still not very successful. Farther south, the balmy Californian evenings and the wide open spaces allowed the automobile in America to take on a novel and important role – one which has almost nothing to do with transportation. People do not go to drive-in movies because it is more convenient; they go to drive-ins because they like sitting in their cars, where they can watch the film from their own territory, not from an impersonal seat in someone else's space. Because it is their little living room on wheels they can do what they like inside it; talk, smoke, eat, kick off their shoes, have sex or go to sleep. It is an opportunity for people to engage in a variety of social activities in their cars. The film simply provides a rationale.

Although sex, or a solution to child-minding problems, might be the attraction for some movie goers, the continuing success of the drive-in derives from the fact that ordinary people simply enjoy being in their cars, even when they are stationary. For some, it provides the opportunity to view the world, and all its dangers, in womb-like security. For others it is a chance to be seen inside a personal display of taste, affluence and power.

This aspect of the relationship between people and their cars also explains the meteoric rise of the Reverend Robert Schuller, a Californian preacher who saw that there was an opportunity to attract large congregations by establishing a drive-in church. For some, the idea of praying and singing hymns while sitting in a car might border on blasphemy. In a culture obsessed with the automobile, however, it seems no more than a logical extension of the car's function. After all, Roman Catholics in the United States have their own ecumenical highway code which, among other things, asks anyone guilty of dangerous driving to make mention of it during Confession. In Germany too, the Congress for Christian Automobilists has formulated a special set of prayers for drivers.

Schuller's magnificent 'Crystal Cathedral' in Garden Grove, Orange County, began as a drive-in movie theater. In 1956 he started holding services there, preaching from the roof of the snack bar to eight thousand people in their cars. When he instructed his congregation to 'Wear the armor of God in your daily life', few people saw the irony of the remark from the comfort of their steel-clad suits. When he asked, 'What if Jesus Christ today would walk down the rows of cars parked here? Would he condemn you for your sins?', no one seems to have viewed attending church in this way as at all deviant. They came back again and again in the same cars, and the collection plate was full on each occasion.

All this explains why the Reverend Schuller now drives himself to his multi-million dollar 'Cathedral' in a Rolls-Royce Phantom VI, bought from the most elegant of dealers in Beverly Hills. The performance pales into insignificance, however, when seen in the light of the Reverend Ike's nineteen Rolls-Royces in downtown Los Angeles, and that other charismatic, religious, car devotee, the Bagwam Shree Rajneesh, who began with the modest ambition of having a different Silver Spur for each day of the month. Thanks to his generous followers, the Bagwam surpassed his goal and left a fleet of eighty-five Rolls-Royces on his rather hurried departure from Oregon.

Compared with such typically Californian excesses, other types of drive-in, especially in Britain, seem almost mundane. When Martins Bank opened the first city-center drive-in check cashing service in Leicester in 1959, the English got quite excited about it. They felt that they were catching up in the race to have their lives dominated by cars. Typically, however, such novelty was greeted with some reservation as well. A picture in *Autocar* magazine illustrated the new development with a cashier's view of one of the first customers. The caption noted: 'The gentleman in the picture looks somewhat unhappy, but no doubt cashiers are accustomed to that.' Drive-in banks are now commonplace in both Europe and America, although their role has been largely superseded by roadside service tills. In contrast, drive-in restaurants have suffered a considerable decline since the 1950s.

The first drive-in restaurant was opened in 1936 by Elmo L. Geoghan, executive vice-president of the Bobs Big Boy chain. Two years later a rather more significant drive-in was opened by two brothers who were to introduce to hamburger-making the same method that Henry Ford had pioneered in automobile manufacture – the production line. They were, of course, Richard and Maurice McDonald. Those were the days before the advent of the minimum wage in America. The McDonalds quickly switched to self-service and the days when customers sat in their cars, being served by pretty car hops, were already numbered. Even so, there was something quite special about the drive-in fast-food restaurant, so much so that people, and Californians in particular, look back on them with a great sense of nostalgia. They were places where the young 'cruisers' would gather at weekends to show off their cars and their new girlfriends. They were the rendezvous of the rapidly growing auto-centric culture – the food was almost incidental.

Nostalgia associated with automobile dining has prompted a recent revival of the drive-in restaurant, despite changed economic conditions and regulations which make it more difficult to exploit casual labor. Tony Strammiello runs Angelo's in Orange County, once a sleepy hot-dog stand and now a mecca

for every car-freak in Southern California. It has the atmosphere
of 'Mels' in the film *American Graffiti*, and is the place where
the Friday night cruises end up, despite considerable interven-
tion by the local police, who have a habit of sealing off all the
roads in the neighborhood. It is now such a visible monument
to the car culture that it is regularly visited by TV film crews
and busloads of Japanese tourists.

For Tony, however, it is good business. He is passionate
about cars and can identify with his customers, holding his
own in the very special language of automobile enthusiasts. He
has re-created an entire 1950s image – waitresses on roller-
skates and rock-and-roll booming out to the parking lot. Such
is the obvious appeal of this kind of drive-in that a substantial
revival is to be expected throughout America. This seemingly
perverse desire to eat in cars, rather than at tables, produces a
much stronger relationship between customer and restaurateur
than is normally the case. Dean Williams, who was manager
of the now defunct Dolores Drive-In in Beverly Hills, sums up
an illuminating aspect of automobile psychology succinctly: 'I
can understand how they feel. People at a place like this are
different. It's like they are still at home because they are in their
own cars. And that builds up a lot of loyalty and good-will.'

Drive-in restaurants may have fallen victim, but only for a
time, to increasing land prices and staff wages. Drive-in movies
may flourish only where the climate allows. The use of the car
as an extension of the home, however, remains a central feature
of the automobile culture. Cars live in the home, in that most
special of rooms we call the garage. When we take to the roads,
a part of the home goes with us – a personal territory, an
environment of security. This is very clearly shown by the fact
that agoraphobics (those with a fear of going outside the home)
are usually quite content to go out in a car, but are terrified of
the prospect of travelling on public transportation. In Britain,
agoraphobics are now demanding disabled parking permits for
this very reason.

The car provides us with a shield and a feeling of invulnerability, a shelter for all manner of activities. We pick our noses
in traffic jams, but we assume that other people cannot see us.
We wind down our windows and yell at people. We make
obscene gestures and threaten total strangers, behavior we would

not normally have the courage to exhibit in other circumstances. We can do all this because we feel secure in our inviolable territory.

Relationships With The Car

The idea of the car as 'living room' is not new to the auto-manufacturers. The Ford brochure for 1949 declared: 'The '49 Ford is a living room on wheels!' A caption said: 'These pictures show, as well as pictures can, the space, comfort and smartness of the '49 Ford! There's room to spare for three people on each of these "sofa seats", trimly upholstered in new, modern fabrics. And there's "picture window" visibility . . . Yes, it's a living room on wheels, this '49 Ford!' Modern trends in car interior design, with extensive use of fabrics and carpets similar to those found in home environments, continue this domestic theme.

While the car has evolved as an extension of the home, it has also radically altered the houses in which we live. Before the mid-1930s, the garage was usually a shed or some other utilitarian outbuilding, detached from the house and often out of sight. Like the stable which it replaced, it was designed as simple protection for a rude, smelly object, but as the car came to rival the home as a symbol of prestige, its accommodation became a matter of increasing importance. Houses built after the early 1930s started to recognize this changing role of the automobile, and presented a quite new façade to the street. First, the garage was moved to the front of the plot, changing the whole balance of the frontal aspect. Later, there was a tendency to integrate the garage into the home, which of course upset not only the external appearance of the building but also the interior layout as well. The front porch, opening up on to a proper hallway, began to decline as a prominent feature. This, in turn, led to changes in living patterns almost as radical as those deriving from the newfound mobility which the car provided. In America, in particular, the garage of the suburban home took over the function of the porch and was increasingly used for exit from, and entry to, the kitchen.

In Britain, the 'town' house developed, with the first floor being given over entirely to a garage and a small utility room. The front doors to such houses, dwarfed by the blank expanse of the garage frontage, signalled quite plainly that ease of access for the car was of greater concern than for pedestrians. Elsewhere in Europe, architects such as Le Corbusier designed houses specifically so that owners could drive straight into them. Villa Stein in France was a particularly striking example – its bright-red rectangle of garage door bearing witness to Corbusier's dictum that 'the exterior is a result of the interior'. The new functionalist age also demanded that the role of the car should be clearly reflected in the design of 'machines for living in'.

American architects such as Lovelace and Dobberman extended the functionalist approach to its limits with their designs for truly 'motorcentric' homes. Here the only means of access was through a centrally placed garage, which in turn opened onto a narrow hall. Today, in many homes, it is possible to leave the comfort of the living room, pass directly through a hallway or kitchen into the garage, and head for the open roads without ever being outside at all. The car is no longer a machine but a detachable room.

Is the central accommodation of the car really just a matter of convenience? Do we have integral garages simply to protect our cars from the elements? If so, then we have gone to extraordinary lengths to avoid a bit of rust and a walk of just a few yards. We may try to justify such severe impositions on house design by referring to street-parking problems, but there are cheaper and far more elegant solutions to the question of where to keep the car. The real reason for these architectural 'advances' is the psychological desire to include the car in the family, and so to emphasize a strong, symbolic attachment.

This might sound a little overstated, but the family bond with the car is also illustrated in other ways. Consider, for example, the way we give the things we drive pet names. A recent poll in Britain indicates that over 200,000 people call their cars 'Betsy' or 'Bessie'. If you include all those who have given these names to one of their previous cars, then the figure rises to a staggering 750,000. Other popular names include 'Freddy', 'Jemima', 'Nellie' and 'Daisy'. In the United States a very high proportion of drivers, or members of their families, refer to their automobiles by name. 'Betsy' crops up again among such fanciful names as 'Pumpkin', 'Little Willie', 'White Pony', 'Prudence' and 'Yum-Yum'.

There is something very endearing about these names. So much so that one wonders why the manufacturers have not used them on their models. Perhaps a 'Ford Betsy' (a modern day tin 'Lizzie') or a 'Datsun Daisy' would gain a considerable share of the automobile market. Clearly, to those owners who have christened their cars in this way, what they drive has a very special significance for them. Like most relationships, however, a relationship with an automobile can also have its measure of hate. Those who have given their cars nicknames like 'Dagenham Dustbins' or 'Luton Trashcans' clearly feel that their love-affairs exact a high price. Affairs they clearly are, however, for objects of indifference have no name at all.

Giving pet names to cars is a particularly interesting aspect of a process known as animism. Small children often believe that inanimate objects have human powers. They might say that a broom is 'naughty', if it has fallen over and broken one of their favorite toys. We soon grow out of this way of thinking as we grow older, but we do retain some vestiges of the tendency to endow objects with animate, and sometimes human qualities. Machines, and cars in particular, are often talked of as if they were alive and had minds of their own. We speak to them, coax them, plead with them not to break down. Owners are heard talking about their cars 'knowing the way home' or, more commonly, 'not liking cold weather'.

This whole process is, in some ways, rather bizarre. At one level we know that cars are only machines, but, because of our relationship with them, we also see them as having qualities in common with ourselves. After all, it would be silly to have a *relationship* with a mere mechanical object. Therefore, we humanize them. We give them personalities which reflect the nature of our relationships with them, and naming is a particularly strong way in which to announce our attachment to something which is much more than just an object.

Naming not only individualizes and personifies a car, it also, on occasions, sets up a relationship of pseudo-dependency – rather like the relationship owners establish with their pets. This pet-like characteristic of cars has been recognized by several authors, not least by Aldous Huxley who, in his correspondence with the eminent British psychologist Charles Myers, noted that we treat both cars and pets in a very similar manner. Dogs, he suggested, provide their owners with a sense of power. We are their masters, they must obey us in return for our affections. So too with cars, for they also provide us with enlarged egos and opportunities for control and mastery. We pet them in the same way as we stroke the dog because both provide us with those special sources of gratification which derive from dominating those objects of our affections.

In many cases, terms of endearment, or temporary disenchantment, are supplied by females, either with reference to their own car or to that of their husband or boy-friend. Attachments to automobiles are by no means an exclusively male preserve. Women's magazines regularly run features about what their readers and contributors are driving and why, and what kinds of relationships they have with their cars. An article in Britain's *Honey* magazine introduces us to Athy Demetides, a schoolteacher, and her present car, a Ford Escort called 'Alby', although she is apparently 'mourning' for a Mini Traveller called 'Doris' which sadly rusted away. 'I adored her,' she says. 'I painted her black and white. I'm afraid no car will ever be the same for me.' Her friend, Sue Williams, empathizes with this sense of loss. 'I had an A-35 a long time ago. When it went, a close friend sent me a sympathy card.'

This concern by women for their cars is also illustrated in an article in *Options* entitled 'How to De-Clone your Car'. Here the idea of the car as a medium of self-expression is stressed heavily, and readers are urged to think more carefully about the messages that are given out by what they drive. In the same way that the agony columns of popular magazines give us interesting insights into changing codes of sexual behavior, these snippets about cars provide a clearer picture of the role of the car in the lives of ordinary people. They also illustrate the extremes to which people will take their relationship with the car.

Ruth Kramer Ziony, a one-time editor of *Playgirl*, reached her first mid-life crisis at the age of 35, and cast around for a suitable husband. Few men, however, seemed interested in the prospect. Since she described herself as overweight, interested in faith-healing and a regular thrower of the *I Ching*, this is not perhaps surprising. Her solution was a novel one. She decided to marry her Cadillac, called 'Seville'. She even envisaged a ceremony with the wedding march played on car horns and presided over by the most celebrated drive-in preacher, the Reverend Robert Schuller.

A similar attachment was displayed, in a more terminal way, by the multi-millionaire oil heiress Sandra West. When she died in 1977, at the age of 37, her will surprised even her Beverly Hills friends by stipulating that, in order to inherit $5 million, her brother-in-law, Sol West, was to have her buried, 'in my lace night-gown and in my Ferrari, with the seat slanted comfortably'. Perhaps out of respect for his sister-in-law's wishes, or perhaps just for the money, the burial was arranged in exactly the way she had requested. As a final touch, the car was covered over with nine feet of solid concrete.

These are extreme examples, but they serve to illustrate that automobiles are objects of attachment and passion as much for women as for men. Approximately forty per cent of all cars are bought by women. Market research in the United States also suggests that women have a significant influence over those cars bought by men. As much as eighty per cent of purchase decisions may be made directly or indirectly by women. Moreover, women make many judgments about men on the basis of the cars they drive. In New York there is a lady who buys and sells sports cars. When she wants to meet and go out with a 'Jaguar' man, she advertises a car of this make and waits for potential purchasers to come to her. The next week she might be in the mood for a 'Lotus' or a 'Mercedes' man. It's an effective and economical way of luring the right kind of temporary companion. Most women don't go to such lengths, but it is clear that many romances, and sometimes marriages, arise from the fact that the right kind of man was driving the right kind of car at the right time.

Our cultures and our private lives are dominated by our relationship with the car. In return for the powers and opportunities that automobiles give to us, we reward them with affection and elevate their status above that of mere machines. They become family members, pets and paramours – objects of love, and sometimes of hate. We don't talk about such emotions much. Perhaps we are embarrassed, but the strength of our personal relationships with cars is revealed in the way we celebrate them in the media which have always been used for declarations of love: songs and poetry.

Celebrations Of The Car

The tendency for women to evaluate men's prospects on the basis of what they drive has long been recognized by song writers. In the 1920s, for example, a little number called 'You Can't Afford To Marry Me If You Can't Afford a Ford' had everyone's feet tapping in the Vaudeville halls. In a very real sense Tin Lizzie had arrived in Tin-Pan Alley. Other songs, such as 'Take Me On A Buick Honeymoon', echoed the sentiment that to be worth marrying you had to have automotive assets and credentials. Only the song writer Irving Berlin seems to have stood out against whole-hearted celebration of the car with his cynical, or perhaps tongue-in-cheek number 'Keep Away From The Fellow Who Owns An Automobile'.

The celebration of the car in popular song is yet one more indicator of its secure cultural niche. Thousands of songs have been written about the automobile, stressing a variety of aspects and associations. While sex in cars has always featured prominently, songs have also reflected wider social changes. 'I've Got A White Man Running My Automobile' was a popular song sheet which featured on its cover a black man reclining in the rear seat of a car being driven by a white chauffeur. Cars symbolized freedom and offered an illusion of equality. But songs about cars were, above all, vehicles for fantasy. Take as an example a long-forgotten number by Patrick and Schwarzald called 'Mack's Swell Car Was A Maxwell':

> Mack's swell car was a Maxwell so he won this little
>   dear
> For his car excelled in all the tests and he left all the rest
>   in the rear

Because the Maxwell wins the race, the competition having dropped out one by one, Mack is able to marry the girl of his dreams. The contest between machines serves here as a metaphor of the rivalry between men for the objects of sexual passion.

History does not record whether the writer of the lyrics was rewarded by the Maxwell Car Company, which went out of business in 1925 after building rather dull runabouts, but many auto-manufacturers of the time certainly did cash in on the publicity. Although this form of promotion is uncommon today, the automobile continues to feature in popular music as much as it ever did. Chuck Berry was among the first to bring cars into rock-and-roll songs. 'Maybellene', recorded in 1955, with its fine synthesis of Blues and Country and Western, was such a hit that it even ousted Bill Hayley's 'Rock Around The Clock' from the Top 10. His concept of 'motivatin' ' captures the thrill of the open road and in the song even the guy in the old Ford can catch the guy in the Cadillac who has just stolen his girl:

> As I was motivatin' over the hill
> I saw Maybellene in a Coupe de Ville;
> A Cadillac a-rollin' on the open road,
> Nothin' will outrun my V-8 Ford.

The Cadillac is described as speeding along at 95 miles per hour. The Ford driver tries to overtake, but his engine overheats. Luckily, it starts to rain and the water cools his engine. He pulls away, leaving 'the Cadillac sittin' like a ton of lead'.

Chuck Berry's song has several layers of imagery, but its main theme is the duel between the working-class hero and the villain who has stolen Maybellene away. It is no coincidence that the hero is driving a Ford and the villain a Cadillac. Berry knew that his youthful audience would immediately recognize these cars as representing lower and upper classes, just as they would recognize the Ford's victory over the Cadillac as a triumph of working men's values over those in the upper echelons of society.

Berry recognized that cars could stand as short-hand expressions of life style and status. So too did Elvis Presley, for as soon as he left Memphis he bought himself a pink Cadillac, a car he had issued warnings about in 'Baby, Let's Play House':

> You may go to college
> You may go to school
> You may have a pink Cadillac
> But don't be nobody's fool

Chuck Berry also seems to have been eventually seduced away from his social roots by the lure of cars which he once saw as representing the enemy in his society. In a later song, 'No Money Down', it is the details of the dream car, not its caddish owner, which are highlighted in the lyrics:

> I want a yellow convertible,
> Fo' do' de Ville
> With Continental spare
> And wire chrome wheels;
> I want power steering
> And power brakes,
> I want a powerful motor,
> With jet off-take:

The other ingredients in Berry's recipe for an ideal car include automatic heating and air conditioning, a full-length bed, radio and television and, of course, a telephone so that Berry can talk to his girl-friend while on the move.

One important feature of 'No Money Down' is the way in which it catalogues a conventional set of desires for a better way of life, cast here in terms of the features of the Cadillac. Comfort and luxury as well as speed and power are the recipe for transforming a dull and unrewarding life. All of those features of the idealized home – the TV, air-conditioning, large bed and so on – are craved for in an automotive rather than domestic environment. Yet whatever the social and political implications of songs about cars, women are inevitably one of the prime reasons for having a vehicle in the first place. In a more contemporary song, 'Every Woman I Know Is Crazy About An Automobile', Ry Cooder complains that he can no longer attract the kind of women he really likes – 'tender, lean and tall'. The situation is so bad that now 'I'll take them knock-kneed and bow-legged, I'll even take 'em bald'. He suggests that it is the lack of a car that has led to this unhappy state of affairs. The days in which women were happy to be walked home, Cooder concludes, are long past. Now they insist on being driven, and in style as well. Poor Ry Cooder, however, is just 'standing with nothing but a rubber heel'.

The close ties between modern pop groups and cars is illustrated not only in song lyrics but also in the names of the bands themselves. Such is the ephemeral nature of the pop world that groups come and go and most sink into oblivion. Some people, however, may remember the British band 'Cortinas', a group who celebrated the Dagenham Ford which evoked such strong veneration and which now has become the object of intense nostalgia. Status-laden cars also find their way into band nomenclature. 'A Bigger Mercedes', the name of an English, black, reggae band, aptly sums up an ironic sense of unrealized ambition. The fact that people write and sing songs about automobiles underlines their importance. Few people sing about public transport. We occasionally find references to jet planes and ocean liners, but very rarely to British Rail, Amtrak or the bus to Birmingham.

References to cars in literature may be less sexy and romantic, but they are by no means less revealing. When D.H. Lawrence wrote about America in the 1920s, he chose the automobile to characterize not only significant aspects of the country's culture, but also particular individuals. Commenting on Walt Whitman, a man who himself marvelled at the new-found freedom brought about by the car, Lawrence wrote:

> He drove an automobile with a very fierce headlight, along
> the track of a fixed idea, through the darkness of this world
> . . . I, seeing Walt go by in his great fierce poetic machine,
> think to myself: What a funny world that man sees!
> ONE DIRECTION! toots Walt in the car, whizzing along it
> . . .
> ONE DIRECTION! whoops America, and sets off also in an
> automobile.

In novels, cars are described in order to provide that essential component – story background. From a writer's point of view, the creation of background is one of his most difficult tasks. It must contain sufficient detail to make the story intelligible and create an atmosphere, a context, and immediate imagery. At the same time, it must not be labored or so lengthy as to detract from the flow of action and dialogue. Backgrounds are, therefore, a valuable clue to what is perceived as being important and relevant by writers in different cultures and times. Since their inception, automobiles have figured very prominently among such literary devices, often providing insights into the temperament and social standing of the principal characters.

Scott Fitzgerald pays particular attention to cars. In *The Diamonds As Big As The Ritz*, we learn a great deal about the boys at St Midas because he tells us that they were driven to school in 'Rolls-Pierce' cars. There never was such a car in reality, but the deliberate combination of the two makes conjures up an image of rather special opulence. *The Great Gatsby* is virtually littered with cars. Gatsby's, in particular, has great significance. It is a Rolls-Royce, of course, but it's also a 'gorgeous car', carefully described as being 'cream color, bright with nickel, swollen here and there in its monstrous length with triumphant hat-boxes and supper-boxes and tool-boxes, and terraced with a labyrinth of windshields that mirrored a dozen suns'. The car has a dreamlike quality to it, reflecting the idealized world of fulfillment and glamour for which Gatsby has been striving and into which he fits so comfortably.

In *The Naïve and Sentimental Lover* by John Le Carré, the precise details of Aldo Cassidy's Bentley provide us with a particularly splendid pen portrait of the man himself:

> As if in recognition of this protective role which Cassidy unconsciously imposed on his own environment, the interior of the car was provided with many important adaptations designed to spare him the distressing consequences of collision. Not only had the walls, ceiling and doors been generously upholstered with additional layers of quilt; the steering wheel, the child-proof door handles – already deeply recessed in succulent cavities of felt – the glove compartment, brake lever, even the discreetly concealed fire extinguisher, each was separately encased in hand-stitched leather and padded with a pleasing flesh-like substance calculated to reduce the most drastic impact to no more than a caress . . .

Le Carré concludes his eloquent description of Cassidy's car by viewing it as a surrogate womb which protects the occupant from the harsh world outside.

Cars are used to define characters in books because in our normal lives that is how we make judgments about people. Cars feature prominently in the songs we sing because songs are a traditional means of expressing our feelings and passions. The psychological impact of the automobile is written large in a language that is as old as culture itself.

Psychology Of The Car

When we look at societies very different from those found in the United States or in Western Europe, we find that the car still occupies a very secure cultural niche and is uppermost in the aspirations of many of the people. In Romania the car is such a revered object that it can be confiscated as a punishment for offences which have nothing to do with its use – such as stealing chickens. In China, a boxy Shanghai saloon costs fourteen times the average worker's annual salary, yet demand for these symbols of prestige is so great that Peking folk will go to extreme lengths and engage in quite absurd bureaucratic charades to obtain one. In densely crowded Tokyo, where the car has about as much utility as a single chopstick, its role has become that of a talisman and, even more important, a vehicle for escapist dreams. This is immediately apparent from the car commercials on Japanese television, in which no concern at all is shown for engineering or performance, safety features or economy, and the images are exclusively of Westernized women in flimsy clothes, romantic beaches, exotic sex and sophistication. The Japanese sell cars in the same way as the Americans sell cigarettes.

In Hong Kong, the local Government perversely encourages car use by under-charging for its parking spaces. In a city where the average travelling speed by car is rarely more than walking pace, and where the price of one square foot of office space is over HK$6 per month, automobiles are considered to be so important that each is subsidized to the tune of HK$10,000 per year through parking charges which are cheaper than in any other major city in the world. In India the automobile has been neatly incorporated into the 3,000-year-old caste system. The domestically produced Ambassador, a straight copy of the old, British, Morris Oxford, is the 'Brahmin' of the Indian automotive hierarchy – and the arrogant manner in which this make is driven expresses its place in the order of things. Lower down, privately owned buses and trucks constitute a 'Gurkha' class and are used more as deadly weapons than as means of transport. Traditional values and a striving for Western modernity are fused together in the symbolism of the motor car in a country where a single cow straying onto the New Delhi four-lane highway can bring traffic to a halt for miles.

Yugoslavia, with its idiosyncratic brand of socialism, is a country where people make huge sacrifices for the sake of personal car ownership, always striving for a larger model than that of their neighbor. Tito possessed a fleet of twenty luxury limousines, and the self-inflicted privations of ordinary folk have enabled the domestic car market to increase twenty-fold in as many years. Imported models are those which symbolize status and there is a flourishing black market in foreign models. Even locally produced Fiats and Volkswagens are in great demand. When a dealer in Opatija announced that he was taking orders for a hundred Beetles, many hundreds of people lined for over a week outside his office, closely watched by armed police.

Attempts by the Yugoslav government to curb the popular obsession with cars have had little effect. During the oil crisis drivers were forbidden to use their vehicles for seven days in each month. Demand for new cars, however, actually increased during this period, and so did the cost of bribes needed to secure one. More firmly socialist countries, such as Poland, display just as much commitment to automotive freedom. Here, summer is officially announced in Podkowa Lesna by the blessing of thousands of cars by the Roman Catholic priest. Father Leon Kantorski conducts his service from an altar made from two Fiats. He recently pointed out to his motoring congregation that 'God is a driver of this world, who puts up road signs that cannot be changed.' Drivers respond to such homilies by sounding their horns before filing past to have their cars blessed.

Ordinary folk in Russia may have little access to automobiles, but Soviet leaders have long been fond of foreign cars. Lenin was the proud owner of a Rolls-Royce Silver Ghost and Stalin gratefully accepted a Mercedes from Hitler, before the relationship between the two became less amicable. Brezhnev drove around in a Cadillac Eldorado that Richard Nixon had brought as a gift during his visit to the Soviet Union in 1972. A few years later, he took special delight in careering through the streets of Moscow in a Mercedes convertible presented to him by the West German leader, Willie Brandt – much to the consternation of his secret service which had trouble keeping up in their sluggish Volgas. Soviet leaders, however, have traditionally set themselves against mass car ownership, fearing perhaps the social and political consequences that personal transportation might bring. A nation on wheels is a nation which is potentially less conformist.

In most oil-rich Arab countries, the Mercedes has replaced the camel as the prime means of getting around the desert. These gleaming tributes to German engineering are treated like mere runabouts. While richer Arabs display their newfound wealth with fleets of exotic American and European imports, their children buzz around in scaled-down, gas-driven toy models of Mustangs and Corvettes. Arabs are the biggest customers for specially customized limousines and sports cars from dealers such as the O'Gara Coach Company in Los Angeles or Chameleon in London. When the cars break down they are simply abandoned. Each year in Jidda the authorities haul away around 25,000 vehicles which have been casually abandoned on the highways or left ignominiously in the sand. Abu Dhabi suffers a similar problem, but there many of the abandoned vehicles are accident write-offs. This is bad news for the city's remaining 6,000 camels which have been blamed for causing a high proportion of these accidents. Being naturally camouflaged they are difficult to see on the sandy roads through tinted windshields. Now that the camels have been forced into the indignity of wearing bright-orange jackets, their owners must feel especially rueful about the rapid rise of the new ships of the desert.

In Latin American countries the car serves as a special means for the expression of individualistic temperament and simple machismo. Automobiles are relatively expensive, but in Argentina one in eight of the population owns a car. Elsewhere, vehicles are more thinly distributed. Brazil, for example, has only 85 cars for every 1,000 people. The Argentinian heirs-presumptive of the legendary Fangio maintain their leading role in the South American automobile league by driving in such a way as to make visitors from other countries very nervous. They take considerable pride in being 'the best drivers in the world', which means using the car in a patriotically aggressive manner to scare off foreigners. One American journalist was so shaken by his experiences in Buenos Aires that he wrote a feature article for the *Los Angles Times* which was almost as provocative as the continued British occupation of the Malvinas.

In some countries, the use of a car can have uncomfortable consequences. Those who drive on the Sabbath in Israel often find themselves victims of stones thrown by religious zealots. The equivalent of the Sunday afternoon drive can exact a high price in terms of smashed windshields and dented bodywork. Secular Jews seem resigned to this. For them, using a car whenever they wish has become a matter of principle, a basic right which takes precedence over Talmudic dogma.

Yet from Tokyo to Dubrovnik, and from Buenos Aires to Jerusalem, one can observe the universal nature of the automobile culture. Southern Californians may think that they have a monopoly on car obsessions, but they are mistaken. As in most things, they are just that little bit more extreme. Why then has the world-wide psychological impact of the car rarely been the subject of serious scientific inquiry? There are many weighty volumes on the subject of obsessions, patterns of self-expression and on situations which influence a person's emotions and behavior, but very few mention cars. Perhaps that is because the automobile is such a commonplace feature of our daily lives. After all, our generation has never known a time without them. Whatever the reason, it is clear that cars have not been regarded as sufficiently worthwhile or serious to warrant proper investigation. Yet you only have to cast your eyes along the magazine racks of the local newsagent to gain an appreciation of how important cars are to most people today. For there you will find more on automobiles and personal means of transportation than on sex or home-computing, and there is certainly a message in that.

Individuals relate to their cars in many different ways, using them to make a variety of statements about themselves. Conventionally it is assumed that notions of personal freedom or individual mobility lie behind the particular hold exerted by the car on people's lives. Certainly, in the first two or three decades of this century motor transportation brought new and dramatic opportunities for social and commercial interaction through increased mobility. Such concerns, however, are taken for granted today and scarcely serve to explain why the car continues to exercise so much more power as a means of self-expression than any other utilitarian object.

Another reason often put forward to explain our obsession is the fact that it is usually the second most expensive object we ever possess. Again, this is undeniably the case but, in real terms, the prices of cars are now lower than they were in, say, the 1930s and 1940s. On this basis, one would expect that people's attachment to their cars would weaken as prices fell, but the opposite has happened. The idea that car-obsession can be explained in terms of mobility and cost is quite inadequate. To understand the car properly, and particularly why it is used as such a powerful means of self-expression, we have to look at the inherent symbolism of this otherwise purely mechanical object.

The fundamental symbolism of the car is both complex and inescapable. It conjures up images of speed, excitement and vitality. At the same time it also communicates a sense of cozy seclusion – a womb-like refuge. Its potential deadlines gives it an air of aggression while its power and shape endow it with a sense of sexual potency. It is precisely because the car can communicate such a variety of messages that it has captured our imagination. As if this were not enough, we have provided the automobile with the potential for communicating a second set of symbolic messages. These are to do with style and class, status, elegance and personal taste. This combination of both types of symbols makes the car the most psychologically expressive object that has so far been devised.

2

COSTUME

UNTIL a hundred years ago humans were automotively naked. Although we already enjoyed the long-suffering assistance of animals and the temperamental benefits of steam, it was only with the arrival of the internal combustion engine that we achieved a reliable means of getting around. In the process we also acquired a means of clothing ourselves in the apparel of the machine age. The earliest motor cars looked just like horse-drawn buggies, minus the horse. They sported carriage lamps, leather dashboards and folding tops, and the driver was perched so high that he could see over the top of a horse, even though there was not one attached to his vehicle. The horse-and-buggy presented the early car designers with an obvious but imperfect model. Although they could harness their clattering engines to a recognizable contraption, they still faced numerous mechanical problems, such as where to house the engine. Initially this was solved by discreetly concealing the machinery in a body box, either under or behind the driver. This guaranteed an aesthetic continuity with the buggy, but produced the unfortunate spectacle of a vehicle with no apparent motive power.

In the case of the buggy and the carriage it had always been obvious where the motive power came from, and the aesthetic formula engraved on everyone's mind had been that of a powerful horse in front and a light buggy or carriage behind. When, therefore, the horse was removed and the engine was placed at the back of the motor car it immediately became apparent to everyone that something was missing. A few designers tried to recapture the traditional look by attaching false horses or horses' heads to the front of their motor cars, but an acceptable solution to the problem of the 'missing horse' had to wait until the French designer, Emile Levassor, broke with convention and moved the engine to the front of the car. This solved the aesthetic problem, for although the motive power was still part of the vehicle, it was now positioned in front of the driver, where the horse used to be.

Front-engine design had a profound impact on the appearance of cars and the way they were perceived. It ushered in the heroic age of motor racing, gave ordinary runabouts and town cars a look all of their own, and started a process that would eventually culminate in a full-blown exploitation of the automobile's sexual symbolism. It achieved this by doing for the motor car what the codpiece had done for men's costume during the sixteenth century: it placed the essential machinery where, in anthropomorphic terms, it ought to be, and clothed it in a prominent hood which hinted at the power beneath.

The inherent symbolism of the front-engine solution made it an instant success, so that even those designers who were unable to make the necessary alterations to their current models were forced to attach false hoods to the front of their cars. Now, instead of being called a 'carriage', the car was called a 'machine', and following the laws of fashion, everyone had to drive a front-engine motor car. Commenting on the rapid change, *The Horseless Age* observed, 'One would hardly have thought that such a revolutionary change of taste could have come about so quickly. The vehicle that does not wear a bonnet in front . . . is not *à la mode.*'

This reference to vehicles as 'wearing' a hood shows that even though people had started to construe motor cars in more mechanistic terms, they did not automatically dispose of an anthropomorphic attitude toward the motor car. The use of these terms to describe parts of the car, like 'bonnet', 'boot', 'hood', and, later on, 'skirts', showed that people regarded cars as a form of automotive costume, just as their retention of terms like 'dashboard' and 'horsepower' showed that they had not forgotten the origins of the motor car as a horseless carriage.

Early Car Habits

In the early days motoring was the preserve of the rich, and more often than not, the idle rich. The cost of purchasing a hand-crafted vehicle and paying for repairs placed the new hobby beyond the means of the middle classes, not to mention the artisans, factory workers and farm laborers, all of whom had to make do with the railways, horse-drawn transport, the bicycle or their own feet. For those who could afford them, motor cars were a curious novelty and a means of pitting oneself against the elements. Automobilists would deck themselves out in the motoring gear of the day, which usually consisted of a heavy coat, waterproofing, a scarf and goggles, and they would then belt out along the highways, raising hell and huge clouds of dust, scaring horses and scattering chickens, and generally disturbing the peace of the countryside. Naturally, the invasion of these goggled buccaneers and their noisy machinery met with resistance from country folk, who complained about the inconsiderate and haughty attitude of motorists. A great deal of their resentment was class-based because the motor-cads were usually members of polite society – or at least had been before they were bitten by the speed bug.

The image of the pioneer motorist consisted of two essential symbols: wealth and speed. Because motor cars were expensive, mere possession of one marked its owner off as a person of substance, separating him from the common lot of humanity. The motor car therefore conferred an automotive costume on its owner. Like the battledress in which he and his passengers clothed themselves, it bespoke a daring and adventurous attitude toward the world. Clad in his duster coat, peaked cap and goggles, the man at the wheel was instantly recognized as a wealthy daredevil, as someone who was prepared to brave the ravages of dust, wind and rain for the elixir of speed. His lady companion, swaddled in a long fur coat and chinchilla scarf, with her head enveloped by a 'bee-keeper' bonnet, was viewed in much the same light.

The popular identification of motoring garb with the exciting motor car set gave rise to a new breed of impostors – people

who owned no more than a bicycle but who would desport
themselves as though they were the proud owners of high-
powered runabouts. But the social cachet of the motoring fraternity also exercised a more general influence on fashion – so
much so that in her book of advice to women automobilists,
Mrs Arias was able to lament the fact that 'the popular dress
for the motor has infected much other dress, and the mere
loafer in the country or at the seaside, the idle shopper in Bond
Street, or even the lady who calls to fit on your blouse, will
enwrap her unoffending hat and face with a gauze, chiffon, or
net scarf, tied under her chin with ragged ends floating in the
air.'

Automotive Haute Couture

Open runabouts allowed the early motorists to present themselves as wild desperadoes, and the open touring cars that
appeared soon afterwards provided them with an automotive
costume that was somewhat more demure, and usually a lot
more luxurious. While runabouts and raceabouts were being
fitted with rakish lines, bucket seats, flowing fenders and other
accoutrements suggestive of speed, open touring cars were
starting to move in the direction of comfort. The most famous
development along these lines was the *Roi des Belges* body,
which incorporated a voluptuous back seat that looked like a
deep-buttoned leather settee. The story goes that when Leopold
II of Belgium was going over the design of his new motor car
with his coachbuilder, he complained about the meagre allow-
ance that had been made for his portly figure. His mistress,
Mlle de Mérode, proposed a solution to the problem by placing
two huge stuffed chairs side by side. The idea was immediately
adopted by the King and his coachbuilder. When the King's
new motor car appeared it boasted the outsize tonneau and
curvaceous lines that were later to be linked to his name, but
alas not to that of his mistress. *Roi des Belges* bodywork gave
motorists their first real taste of comfort, and the new styling
immediately became the rage among those members of the
motoring public for whom money was no object. When coach-

builders recognized the appeal of bulbous buttoned upholstery they started to introduce other features of the drawing-room into the motor car.

The opportunity to domesticate the motor car fully came with the advent of the closed limousine. Up to this point coach-builders had been discouraged from producing closed saloons because of the adverse power-to-weight ratio, but as engines became more powerful and materials lighter they were able to build automobiles that enclosed passengers in a weatherproof saloon. Passengers were now protected from the wind and rain, and this meant they no longer needed to dress specially for motoring. Coachbuilders obliged them further by creating sa-loons with tall doors so that gentlemen with silk or opera hats and ladies with billowing bonnets could enter motor cars with-out disturbing their head dress.

Before the age of the motor car, coachbuilders were involved in the construction of custom-made horse-drawn carriages for the rich. This usually involved some type of discussion between the coachbuilder, or *carrossier* as he was known, and the cus-tomer so that the carriage would be fashioned according to the tastes of the customer. Later on, the same procedures were used with cars. Once a customer had chosen a particular model, say a Rolls-Royce or a Hispano-Suiza, the chassis would be ordered from the factory by the *carrossier* who would arrange for the body to be built. The great *carrossiers* functioned just like custom tailors to the rich. They would consult with the client, measure up his requirements, order the basic materials from a factory, and then shape a product to suit his whims and fancies. Just as a gentleman regarded it as quite natural to have his shoes or shirts made to measure, so too he thought nothing of ordering a motor car that was hand-crafted. After all, a car was not only something to be driven; it was something to be worn.

Because each stage in the construction of early custom cars involved deliberation, the customer could dictate the particular model, the exterior coachwork and the interior appointments. With good taste, sound advice and a large enough bank account he could therefore determine the social impact he made on his fellows, his passengers and the public at large. While the image that owners of open runabouts had pursued was one of swaggering wealth, the impression that owners of closed limousines sought to create was one of sophisticated wealth. This they achieved by selecting a make of distinction and a coachbuilder of repute, and by ensuring that the color scheme, external fittings and interior décor were tastefully conceived. During the early part of the century, interiors were modelled on the reception- and drawing-rooms of the great houses. Ornate mirrors, drinks cabinets and vanity cases were fitted for the comfort and convenience of passengers, while sumptuous carpets and curtains, delicate marquetry and even tapestries were installed to create an atmosphere of domestic elegance, and to remind everyone of the social standing of the owner.

People who live in a small integrated community can usually take it for granted that members of that community know them and how to behave toward them. The situation is, however, quite different for those who live in a large anonymous society where they are constantly meeting strangers. In such a society the individual cannot rely on either reputation or a network of relationships to guide other people in their behavior toward him or her. Consequently city dwellers need to resort to a language of visible symbols that informs others of their status and the amount of deference they expect to receive. The most efficient system of visible symbols is of course that of dress. By adopting a certain mode of dress individuals can indicate who they are socially and how they wish to be treated, and by glancing at the attire of others they can ascertain their social standing and how they should behave toward them.

Before the invention of the motor car, the rich announced their position in society by investing in stately homes, large retinues of servants and expensive clothes. They also displayed their wealth by owning beautifully crafted carriages and stables of fine horses. By the turn of the century the motor car was starting to displace the horse-and-carriage. The real motive for this was the desire to secure a new means of exhibiting one's wealth. It was not the need to acquire a new means of transport, for indeed early motor cars were used almost exclusively for recreation and pleasure. Cars were used for short excursions into the countryside or for trips to the theater or opera. They were not used to transport goods or to take a family across the country. Nevertheless, if the owner were asked why he had purchased a motor car, he would probably have offered an argument about economic necessity or technological progress. In so doing he would have concealed his real motives, which were to fortify his self-esteem and earn himself the admiration of others.

Because we live in a society which apportions respect according to success, and because success is usually equated with money, we have come to judge others by the wealth that they appear to have at their disposal. In order to display our wealth, and earn the respect we deserve, we are therefore forced to make our spending power visible and palpable. This is achieved most efficiently by what the American sociologist, Thorsten Veblen, called conspicuous consumption, conspicuous leisure and conspicuous waste.

The arrival of the motor car created a totally new medium for the advertisement of wealth. By purchasing a car and making sure that one was noticed in it, the owner automatically presented him or herself as a member of the leisured class. Like the variegated costumes of the rich, different types of motor cars conveyed different messages. A gleaming limousine, for example a Haynes or a Peerless, had the same social impact as a top hat and tails, whereas a racy runabout like a Mercer or a Stutz Bearcat had the same effect as a hacking jacket and plus-fours. But whatever the type or make, ownership of a car signalled that someone had money and time to spend in the pursuit of conspicuous idleness. Those people who owned open tourers and closed limousines often underlined their idleness by leaving the menial task of driving to a chauffeur. In the early days chauffeurs were often dressed in full livery, and some were even accompanied by liveried footmen whose job it was to open the car doors. Later on chauffeurs acquired their own uniform, which usually consisted of a buttoned tunic, leather leggings and the peaked cap that is still worn to this day. This shift toward a more modest costume for chauffeurs reflected the realisation that the chauffeur did not need livery – the motor car, with its brightwork and shiny lacquer, was his livery. It was of course also the automotive costume of its owner. The leisurely associations of the early motor car were represented in both its upkeep and the way that it appeared in advertisements. Town cars, for example, were lavished with as much elbow grease as engine grease. Like the patent leather shoes of their owners they were constantly being polished to demonstrate that they were accoutrements of an idle existence. The same principle also gave rise, a few decades later, to the craze for white-wall tires, which were an attempt to give the car its own spats. They appeared at the same time as spats, and were equally useless. Like spats, the sole purpose of white-wall tires was to show that their owner had the wherewithal to keep his possessions clean, and, by implication, that he enjoyed the labor of others.

Spats were of course a favorite of the American gangster during the 1920s and 1930s, as were flashy cars and dumb broads. Like the flashy car, the gangster's moll served to publicize his status as a man of substance. She was not only a decoration, but a fixture that increased his social standing in proportion to her inability to do anything useful. The same was true of the gangster's cars: the more decorative and the less functional they were, the more they showed him to be a man of leisure. Where advertising was concerned, the early motor car was often represented as the conveyance of the golfer or the polo player, and therefore as a plaything of the leisured class. In later years sporting themes became more diffuse, so that cars were associated with bourgeois pastimes like tennis as well as with proletarian games like American football. But whatever their class appeal, the message about the equation between cars and leisure remained the same.

When the Model T Ford appeared in 1908 it completely revolutionized the world of automobile fashion. Up to that point the car salons had been dominated by the *carrossiers* who served as purveyors of automotive *haute couture* to the rich. However, with the arrival of the cheap and utilitarian Model T, motor car ownership was immediately extended to include the broad base of the population, so that people who hitherto had stared in admiration at the elegant conveyances of others could now gaze lovingly on their own, admittedly crude, vehicles. Of course wealthy individuals still continued to adorn themselves in the custom costumes of the *carrossiers*, but at last the common man had some form of automotive clothing.

Cars Off The Shelf

No car has ever had so great an impact as the Model T Ford.
It democratized mobility, opened up the suburbs, brought the
farmer to town, emptied the churches on Sunday, gave the
underprivileged a toe-hold on the running-board, and moved
courtship off the front porch and into the back seat. In these
and a thousand other ways the Model T changed people's lives
irreversibly.

Between 1908 and 1927 Henry Ford produced 15 million Model
Ts, each with as much decoration and individuality as an army
boot. Because the 'Tin Lizzie' or 'Flivver', as it was known, had
been conceived as a utilitarian means of transport, decoration
was kept to a bare minimum. Old Henry, whose dress sense
has been compared to that of a Baptist Deacon, was never
particularly interested in appearances. This showed itself in his
reluctance to decorate the Model T, and in his famous remark
that he was prepared to offer his customers any color they
wanted provided it was black. His sole concern was to provide
the public with a cheap automobile. He achieved this by stan-
dardizing design and introducing assembly line production,
which, in turn, enabled him to double the wages of his workers
and to reduce the price of the Model T from $850 in 1909 to
$300 in 1927.

Like an army boot, the Model T was robust and functional,
and as a means of cheap personal transportation it served its
purpose admirably. But because it was plain, and because every
Model T looked just like every other Model T, it could never
be used as a vehicle for individual expression – not, that is,
until the owner had somehow stamped his identity on it. To
fill the gap that Ford had left, a flourishing industry grew up
to satisfy the need for improvement and personalization of the
basic Model T. Some of the accessories on offer were functional
– one could buy springs and shock absorbers to improve the
quality of the ride – but many were purely decorative. Owners
could, for example, purchase nickel-plated bumpers, spare-wheel
covers and complete streamlined bodies to improve the car's
appearance. During the nineteen years that it was produced,
over 5,000 different accessories were available for the Model T.

For most of that time the trade amounted to about $60 million a year.

Henry Ford should have recognized this customizing craze for what it was, but he resolutely refused to do so until it was too late. In the end the Model T was eclipsed by other manufacturers who were prepared to give the public motor cars that satisfied their vanity and allowed them to express their individuality. Because it was completely without pretension, the Model T contained no suggestion of conspicuous consumption; and because it remained unchanged over the years, people who acquired their Model T in the 1920s found themselves with cars that were indistinguishable from those that had been produced a decade or more earlier. More important, though, was the fact that the price continued to drop. This meant that Model T owners were constantly being joined by people below them on the economic scale, which of course had the effect of devaluing the car socially.

In the final analysis, therefore, the demise of the Model T was due to Henry Ford's failure to understand the psychology of the car owner. When Ford first appeared on the scene, most people were automotively unshod. Ford offered them rough footwear at a price they could afford, and because they were clearly impressed, he naturally thought that they would come back to buy the same again. Ford was obviously right to assume that what people wanted was cheap personal transportation, but he was wrong to suppose that that was *all* they aspired to, or that they would come back for more of the same. By the time Ford had reduced the price of the Model T by half, and launched his original customers into a spiral of downward social mobility, even those who could not afford anything better were prepared to try something different. By the mid-1920s the public had started to tire of the strait-jacket that the Model T imposed on their tastes, and they were ready to transfer their custom to an automotive tailor who could offer them a more expressive costume.

In Britain dissatisfaction with rough practical cars came later – partly because assembly line production arrived much later than in America, and partly because cheap cars like the Bullnose Morris were sturdier than the Model T. Probably the most famous of the British cars of the 1920s was the diminutive Austin Seven, which

looked and sounded like a runaway baby carriage. When the
Austin Seven and the Bullnose Morris disappeared, their place
was taken by cars like the Morris Minor and the Triumph Super
Seven. If they did nothing else these sit-up-and-beg motor cars
evidenced the British love of pets, because they looked – and in
many cases were treated – like a member of the family.

Changing Gear

As Americans became disenchanted with the Model T they
turned to General Motors. General Motors was headed by the
dapper Alfred Sloan, a man who, in terms of temperament and
philosophy, was the total opposite of Ford. Ford was a nuts-
and-bolts manufacturer who didn't give a damn for Art, or for
History which he regarded as bunk. Sloan, on the other hand,
was an instinctive salesman who understood the emotive power
of outward appearances. He was interested, not in low-cost
transportation, but in mass-producing automobiles that would
be 'as beautiful as the custom cars of the period'. In 1925 Sloan
and his sales executives made a decision that was to change
the fortunes of the corporation and alter the entire course of
automobile history: they decided to produce annual models
rather than to make gradual changes to their existing models.
Looking back, this decision seems fairly unremarkable, but at
the time it was extremely important because it marked the point
at which mass-produced cars became articles of fashion.

The decision to embark on a program of annual models was
influenced by the fact that the first generation of motor car
owners were starting to trade in their old cars. Sloan recognized
that General Motors could secure a major portion of this market
and accelerate the process by producing new models which
induced what he euphemistically called 'a certain amount of
dissatisfaction with past models'. Sloan also realized that the
most effective way to make people dissatisfied with the car they
bought last year was to convince them that it was stylistically
obsolete and to offer them a replacement at a slightly higher
price. It was not necessary to offer any real advances in engineering: all that was needed was an illusion, a semblance of

improvement. This could be achieved, firstly, by producing models that simply looked different from those they were designed to replace, and, secondly, by bombarding the public with advertising which promised the prospect of upward mobility and which played on their fears of being left behind in the fashion stakes.

General Motors applied this simple formula with devastating effect. In the early 1920s Ford was producing every second car in America and General Motors had 25 per cent of the market, but by the early 1930s the situation was totally reversed, with General Motors holding half the market and Ford only a quarter. Car buyers had been lured to the products of General Motors by the promise of modernity and the possibility of improving their social standing. Because General Motors was made up of several divisions, each of which catered to a different sector of the public, the customer was offered the prospect of rising socially by buying a car from a more prestigious division. The driver of a Chevrolet could always aspire to a Pontiac, the Pontiac owner could always think about an Oldsmobile . . . and so on up the ladder to the Cadillac, which, at one stage, was lusted after by one out of every two American men. Of course, with the price of new models rising each year, not everyone managed to move up the ladder. But that did not matter because General Motors had covered all the bases, and in the process it had succeeded in creating a permeable caste system which allowed some people to enjoy the illusion of self-improvement and others to dream of rising up in the world.

This dream aspect of car ownership, the opportunity to walk round a showroom and imagine that one will some day be the owner of a better automobile, was an essential component in the success of General Motors. It appealed to a nation that had seen Abraham Lincoln rise from a log cabin to the White House, and which had since been nurtured on the optimistic fallacy that everyone can rise by their own efforts. In the old days the Model T owner knew that he was probably condemned to spend the rest of his days driving around in the equivalent of a motorized log cabin, but Sloan had changed all that: he had revised the myth of self-improvement and given people a chance to aspire to the automotive equivalent of the White House. The fact that a large number of people never acquired anything better did not matter – at least Sloan had given them a purpose and a chance to dream.

Sloan's decision to opt for annual models rather than gradual change was undoubtedly the main factor that enabled General Motors to overtake Ford and, in time, to become one of the most powerful industrial organizations on earth. But there were also other considerations. One was General Motors' special relationship with the Du Pont Chemical Company, which, in 1924, produced the first range of paints suitable for automobiles. Although General Motors, and even Ford, had experimented with polychrome lacquers before that, these tended to fade in the sun, and that is why somber black, which had proved to be durable, found such favor. When the opportunity arose, General Motors took full advantage of the new paints by indulging in an orgy of color that further reinforced its image as a creator of fashion.

By presenting its customers with a wide range of automobiles that changed from season to season, and by offering these in a dazzling variety of colors, General Motors began to assume the role that had formerly been occupied by the *carrossiers* – a role which was and still is occupied by the famous *couturiers* of Paris, London and Rome. Choice and constant change made the ready-to-wear car an article of fashion, so that people whose self-expression had previously been confined to clothing could now present themselves as *en vogue* through the medium of the automobile. Ordinary citizens no longer needed to stand passively by and watch the wealthy parading around in their distinctive cars. Now they too could play the status game and distinguish themselves from others – even if it was only from those who drove older or less expensive models than themselves.

By the 1960s the range in terms of color, engine, transmission and interior appointments had become so vast that although the customer was in a position to order a totally unique car, he was likely to suffer from nervous exhaustion while trying to make a decision. For example, the 1965 Chevrolet alone offered 46 models, 32 engines, 20 transmissions, 21 colors plus 9 two-tone combinations, and more than 400 accessories and options. According to the calculations of a Yale University physicist, the number of distinct cars that a Chevrolet customer could order exceeded the number of atoms in the universe!

Once Sloan had committed General Motors to a policy of annual models he realized that he needed an imaginative stylist to keep the wheels of fashion turning. He found what he was looking for in Harley Earl. Earl was designing custom-made cars for the movie stars in Hollywood when he was discovered by Lawrence Fisher, the President of the Cadillac division. Fisher brought him back to Detroit, where he was put in charge of a department which, for want of a better title, Sloan decided to call 'The Arts and Color Section'. As the head of this newly-formed section, Earl's task was to dream up new styling concepts and to test these out on the public.

Earl was in charge of styling at G.M. from 1929 to 1959. During that time he completely transformed the basic shape of the American automobile and the way that Americans thought about themselves. To begin with he lengthened and lowered General Motors' cars so as to give them a more graceful silhouette, and one that was more expressive of their function. But by the late 1940s he was fitting them out with wraparound windshields, rocket-exhaust tail-lights and enormous fins that made them look as though they would have been more at home on an air force runway than a residential driveway. By the 1950s Earl had placed the average American in control of a two-ton pleasure-craft that totally concealed any purpose that it might have had as a means of transport. The truth of the matter, of course, was that these glittering oversized monsters were never intended as a means of transport, but as articles of vehicular fashion. Those who bought one of Earl's cars automatically acquired a mobile symbol of their wealth and taste. The yards of chrome and the swooping tail-fins – what Earl referred to as the customer's 'visual receipts' – served absolutely no useful purpose. They did not reduce the car's drag coefficient, nor did they improve its road-holding ability or the quality of the ride. Their sole function was to show that the owner possessed the capacity to endure financial wastage.

This ability to accept ostentatious waste has always been a hallmark of wealth. For example, in the past the Chiefs of the Kwakiutl Indians would regularly engage in the seemingly irrational practice of potlatch, in which they would ritually de-

stroy their own possessions in public. The practice made sense
to the Kwakiutl Indians because they recognized that someone
who was able to withstand the destruction of his possessions
must be truly wealthy. It is this same principle which explains
the zeal and enthusiasm with which Americans embraced the
long-finned automobiles of the 1950s. These automobiles were
adored, not because they incorporated any ideals of beauty,
but because they revealed their owner's ability to squander his
earnings. They were the ordinary American's form of potlatch.

The golden, or rather the chromium, age of the American
automobile took place after the Second World War, when people were adapting to the austerity and shortages of the post-
war era. Chief among their acquisitions were clothes and cars.
In the case of women's fashion, for example, Christian Dior's
'New Look', with its dramatic lengthening of the skirt, was all
the rage. Dior recognized that women were tired of the dowdy
uniformity that had been forced upon them by the war, so he
created a style which was, in his words, a reaction against
poverty. But Dior was not alone in recognizing the connection
between the spirit of the times and the way that people wished
to adorn themselves, because just as he was lengthening skirts,
Detroit was tooling up for longer cars.

There has always been a link between the collective optimism
or pessimism with which people view the world and the amount
of material that is used in the creation of articles of fashion
whether they be clothes or cars. As the American anthropol-
ogists Kroeber and Richardson showed in their historical analysis of women's costume, skirts become shorter during periods
of economic growth and longer during periods of recession.
The same has also been true of cars: during periods of expansion
they get smaller and during hard times they get larger. For
example, the most lavish cars of all time were built during the
Great Depression. Just when unemployment was at its worst
and the soup lines in Europe and America were at their longest,
custom-built cars like Duesenbergs and Hispano-Suizas were
being fitted with enormous, over-powered engines and long
hoods which seemed to precede the rest of the car by half a
block. In contrast the swinging Sixties saw the world economy
in boom, and yet it was then that hem-lines reached their all-

time high with the miniskirt and hotpants, and cars reached their all-time extremity of compactness with the Mini and the Fiat 500.

The reason why cars and clothes act as economic barometers is that when times are bad there are additional incentives to show off one's pecuniary power because fewer people are able to do so. Wearing more expensive clothes and driving a more expensive car are signs that one has the power to withstand the difficult times which everyone else has difficulty overcoming. In good times there is far less incentive to compete in this way because more people are capable of at least some display of ostentation.

The size and cost of cars are not the only correlates of economic activity – cars also take on different colors during economic booms and recessions. During booms cars are usually painted in primary tones and bright colors like yellows, light blues and reds. Psychologists have found that these colors have an arousing effect on people's physiological state – they produce, for example, increased heart rate and breathing – and they are therefore suited to a mood of optimism and celebration. On the other hand, when the economy is in decline there is a tendency for people to select colors like greys, browns and dark blues. People choose these somber colors, not out of any desire to deepen their despondency, but because they need to ensure that their immediate surroundings do not clash with their own mood and the prevailing mood of others.

Whatever the economic climate there is always room for individual choice of color, and the color of a car can tell you a lot about its owner. The aspect of personality it reflects most accurately is the person's need for achievement. People differ markedly in their levels of ambition and in their desire to get ahead and dominate their environment. There are psychological tests which measure this achievement motive, and people's scores on these tests are a fairly good guide to the car colors they choose. Those with a high need for achievement will tend to drive cars with rather subdued colors such as beige, brown, black and silvery-grey, while those with relatively low levels of ambition will usually opt for bright colors such as red and yellow.

People with a high achievement motive are usually those who like to make the best use of available time – they tend to be in a hurry and want to get on with things. If car color really does reflect levels of motivation, we would expect to find that drivers of cars with the more somber hues would be more likely to break speed limits and to contravene other restrictions designed to slow them down. Studies conducted in America show this to be the case. Substantially more cars with high achievement colors exceeded 60 mph and ran red lights than did cars with the low achievement colors. The match between color and this aspect of personality is not, of course, perfect. But this is often due to the fact that people do not always have complete control over the color of the car they drive. They might drive a company car, for example, or have a second-hand model where there is little or no choice over its color. In these cases you need to ask them about their 'ideal' car and the color they would choose for it. Here the reflection of ambition, and its relation to the way people drive their car, is likely to be more accurate.

The car manufacturers have an awareness of the relationship between the color of a car, who is likely to buy it and how it is driven. You don't, for example, see too many brightly colored Rolls-Royces or Bentleys on offer. BMWs and Mercedes are more usually silver-grey or dull brown-beige than yellow or bright red. Aston Martin is keen on rather heavy maroons, while limousines are nearly always black. Contrast this with the more down-market models. It is here that we find the bright yellow Citroëns and red Renaults. Japanese cars are often painted in light blues and greens, and Ford has maintained some colors which might have been more in evidence in the days when the economy was so healthy that one was quite ready to accept the idea of a yellow Rolls-Royce. Colour has always been an important component of car design, and one which underlines the similarity between clothes and cars.

There are of course many ways in which the motor world resembles that of fashion, not least among these being the motor shows which are held around the world each year. These shows, which are nothing more than automotive fashion parades, provide the manufacturers with an opportunity to exhibit the models that will soon become available. They also provide an important venue for the unveiling of 'concept cars' or 'dream cars' – those super-extravagant creations which, like the more fanciful confections of the couturiers, are not intended for sale, but simply to fascinate the public, and to prepare it for fashions of the future.

3

FASHION

Car Messages

IT is almost impossible to look seriously at a car without making an unconscious thumbnail sketch of the kind of person who would own it. This impression might be difficult to put into words, but it is a very important factor in determining what we feel about particular cars and what kind of car we choose to own. When the impression we have made about the typical driver of a car matches the one we have of ourselves, or of how we would like to be, then we want to buy the car. In many cases, though, the impression will be of a very different sort of person, perhaps one we find unattractive or incompatible with ourselves. We are probably unaware of all of this, but we end up not liking the car. It may be economical, roomy, well styled and have a reputation for longevity, but somehow it does not seem right.

A simple but quite informative study of the images associated with certain cars was conducted recently in Britain by MORI, one of the major public opinion poll companies. As part of a larger survey, people were shown photographs of six familiar cars. They were also given a list of words which might describe the drivers of these cars, such as 'home-loving', 'professional', 'status-conscious', 'high self-opinion', etc. Each of the 2,000 people in the survey ticked those items which best described the driver of each of the cars. MORI tabulated the resulting figures to show, for example, how many people thought that the description 'successful in business' applied to the typical driver of a Rover.

Our own interest, however, was not in these simple, though interesting statistics, but in what lay underneath them. What was the basic set of judgments, for example, that distinguished the images of Volvo and Lotus drivers? To discover this we conducted our own analysis of the survey results. This showed that people make two major types of judgment about drivers, even though they are probably unaware of doing so for most of the time. Firstly, they divide them into two groups. The 'young', 'trendy', 'sporty' and 'aggressive' are contrasted with those who are identified as being 'conservative', 'middle-aged' and 'family' people. Drivers of cars such as Lotus and Golf are put into the former group, while the driver of the Volvo finds himself in the latter.

The second major distinction underlying people's perceptions of drivers is between 'professional', 'successful', 'status-conscious' men on the one hand, and 'warm', 'ordinary', 'friendly' people with little money on the other. Drivers of a Rover 2000 were identified with the former category while Citroën 2CV owners were clearly seen as belonging to the latter. It is interesting that cars such as the Cortina and the Metro fell almost in the middle of both types of classification.

Other kinds of stereotyping are also revealed when people are asked to think about the characteristics of drivers of various cars. A fairly new trend seems to involve the idea of there being a particular type of car for the young, ambitious, professional female. Here the 2CV again figures highly, but the Metro is seen as having a similar image. Further research has shown that these distinctions pertain to a wide range of cars. Mention a Rover 2000 or a Jeans Beetle, a Ford Tempo or an Audi 5000, and immediately a host of associations are evoked concerning the kind of person who would own such a car. Although the owners of these cars might resent such images, they would be able to recognize themselves in these stereotypes. For that is precisely why they bought the cars in the first place.

American auto manufacturers and their research divisions use what they claim is a more sophisticated way of identifying potential customers in terms of their values and lifestyle. Known by its acronym 'VALS', the approach has led to a huge amount of consumer research. It divides the population into a number of groups and distinguishes, for example, between 'Inner Directed' and 'Outer Directed' people. In the Inner Directed category we find various sub-groups such as the 'I-am-me' people – those who are narcissistic, impulsive, dramatic and inventive. They account for 5 per cent of the American population, and dominate the imported car market. Also within the Inner Directed category are the 'Socially Conscious', accounting for 9 per cent of the population, who are described as 'mission oriented, mature – some living lives of voluntary simplicity'.

The majority of the American population are, however, defined as being 'Outer Directed'. Within this category the largest group is the 'Belongers' – ageing, traditional, conventional, patriotic and deeply stable – the bastions of the Detroit car market. Various other groups such as 'Emulators', 'Sustainers' and 'Achievers' also make up a sizeable proportion of the car-buying public.

Each of the segments within the VALS system, it is claimed, has different preferences and buys different types of car. To enable the manufacturers to plan ahead and predict how many cars of which type to produce, they need to know the size of each sub-group within the population and what they are looking for. The idea is basically a very sound one, and it is also very useful from a marketing point of view. People in the various VALS groups read different newspapers and magazines, watch different TV stations and so on. By having detailed information about their media habits, marketing directors can selectively aim particular types of publicity at target groups. This in turn means that the image of the car can be fine-tuned to appeal, not to everybody, which no car ever does, but to those that are most likely to embrace the image it offers.

Whilst VALS heads in the right direction, we doubt that it is sufficiently well developed or clearly thought out to achieve its full potential. The names of the various categories are interesting – but do they really exist in this neat way? Perhaps both people and the images that cars project are more subtle and complex than this. Alternative, and perhaps more traditional, large-scale, survey techniques are, however, also employed by major manufacturers and their market research agencies to provide more reliable guidelines and to answer questions which are vital to the survival of the American automobile industry.

J.D. Power, a California-based company, uses nationwide samples to advise companies such as Ford, but also to provide useful hints to the Japanese opposition. Power was able, for example, to identify a trend back toward bigger cars following the knee-jerk reaction to the fuel crisis in the mid-1970s. Millions of drivers had traded in their enormous General Motors or Ford products for cars which were in tune with the new energy-conscious ethic. Unfortunately, there were few small American-built cars around, so the European and Japanese manufacturers had a field day. In a move little short of total panic the American car companies 'down-sized' all but the top of their ranges. By this time, however, American drivers had realized that small cars had a small image, and that was not at all in keeping with the national psyche. When people came to trade-in their compacts and econo-boxes the market was again out of tune with what they wanted. As a result, fewer new purchases were made. They hung on to their cars for longer than usual, with a consequently depressing effect on the market. People wanted something which more accurately projected an image of themselves, and they were prepared to wait rather than buy another car which communicated only their responsible concern for dwindling fossil fuel reserves.

Power frequently takes Detroit to task over the range of products they sell and the manner in which they market them. He criticizes the way General Motors builds several different models, but makes them so similar that people cannot tell the difference between them. 'All their marketing people sound like quarterly reports wired for sound. If you've talked to one, you've talked to them all.'

The general malaise of the American car manufacturers, which has led to importers gaining a significant slice of the market, is crisply summed up by Power: 'Over the last ten years, and especially over the last three or four, people have been spouting off that the car is a commodity, it's a means of transportation, it's a utilitarian vehicle; that people are much more practical when it comes to buying an automobile, much more rational in their decisions. That is misguided.'

All the costly research conducted on car imagery in Europe and America shows just how concerned the motor manufacturers are about trying to produce cars with images that will appeal to the various sections of the car-buying public. If the image is out of tune, and the messages a car communicates about its driver are unsuitable, few people will want to buy it despite its reliability, economy, comfort or anything else. People don't just drive cars, they wear them. Just as many men would find it difficult these days to walk around in flared trousers, so too they would squirm at the prospect of being seen at the wheel of an out-of-fashion car.

Creation Of Images

Images are not things which necessarily spring naturally from the cars themselves. They arise from advertising and promotion and from the corporate identity of the manufacturer. Mention Volkswagen, for example, and irrespective of the particular model, people will think of characteristics such as 'reliable', 'well-built', etc. These associations are quite resistant to change and this can be a real problem for some motor companies. Car buyers are essentially conservative people. They want cars with a degree of individuality, but also with features common to other cars on the road and with a well-known name. They want to be different but, fundamentally, they want to be the same as everybody else. It is a parallel to our attitude to clothes. We want the things we wear to say something about us, but we do not want to be seen as 'over the top' or totally out of line with contemporary fashion.

For the automobile manufacturers this poses a problem. They can either adapt their models gradually and so coax the public to accept a different model one step at a time, or they can produce a radically different car in the hope of inducing people into a totally new way of thinking about car styling. While General Motors has tended to opt for the safe route by building a whole range of nearly identical cars, Ford recently chose the more adventurous path, which culminated in the British Sierra and, shortly after, the American Tempo.

The Sierra was the first production model to be derived from the 'concept car', Probe IV. Most of the major manufacturers develop concept cars – one-off styling and advanced design exercises which are not intended for production but which give designers a chance to show off their innovative talents. They also pave the way for the introduction of more sophisticated technology. In the late 1970s Ford decided to go 'aerodynamic'. Bill Hess at Ford's world headquarters in Dearborn admitted that it was a 'marketing gamble, but with some sound technical reasons'. The Probe was presented as the 'latest in a series of concept prototypes aiming at pushing back the ultimate frontiers of vehicle aerodynamics'. The publicity blurb, contained in an expensively produced silver-grey brochure, claimed that the car was 'one of the most significant in automobile history . . . with a drag coefficient hitherto only matched by single-seat landspeed cars and jet aircraft'.

The Probe IV was truly a splendid car. Its main function was to appear at shows and in the motoring magazines in order to prepare the public for what was to come. They would never be able to buy this sleek dream machine. Instead, they could buy a car which, by contrast, was almost completely conventional – a familiar automobile which would not make the owner feel completely out of step with his peers.

The ploy didn't quite work. The Sierra, with features only vaguely reminiscent of the Probe, *did* stand out. It was streamlined, had full wheel discs and looked quite unlike the hugely popular Cortina it was designed to replace. Even the ostensible rationale for the aerodynamic shape – fuel economy, reduced wind noise, etc. – failed to overcome the essential conservatism of a sector of the market dominated by the fleet operators. While the buyer of an Audi, Porsche or Citroën might have been delighted with such new stylistic refinements, the Cortina man resisted the radical messages that the Sierra communicated. The cut of the new suit was quite different – as if from a different outfitter, but it was still a 'Ford', and this meant that 'fashionable' people were equally unwilling to be seen in it. They did not want the equivalent of a Burton or Sims label even though the style might have been very Pierre Cardin.

The problem of the Sierra eventually resolved itself as the once radical features of the car became more commonplace. The larger Granada which had a very similar body shape was

introduced with hardly a murmur. In the same way that out-
rageous fashions seen in the *haute couture* salons often become
available a year or so later in chain-stores and mail-order catalogues, thus making people feel less conspicuous when wearing these clothes, so too driving such cars no longer sets
one apart from everybody else. The balance between the
need for individuality and the desire to belong is eventually
struck.

The Ford Motor Company, however, still has the 'badge'
problem. It is not one that the up-market sophisticates want to
wear, and unlike a jacket, you can't keep your car buttoned up
so that the label doesn't show. This 'down-market' aspect of
Ford's corporate image is highlighted in the sales figures in
both Britain and America. General Motors, in contrast, for all
their conservatism, have been more successful in attracting customers with higher incomes and higher levels of education and
occupational status – people most keen to buy imports from
Europe and Japan. Buicks, Oldsmobiles and Pontiacs are among
General Motors' most successful divisions in this most lucrative
of market segments. Ford sells best to the under 25-year-old
group and the low-income sectors. American buyers of European cars are predominantly affluent and in the 25-34 age group.
General Motors' products are favored most by the more mature
and affluent groups while Japanese automobiles are particularly
favored by women and those in the young adults category. In
Britain, Ford cars are again favored by the relatively young and
those in the less affluent social classes. People in the top two
social classes account for only 18 per cent of Ford's sales, while
37 per cent of Renault's cars are bought by people in this group.
Only Vauxhall beats Ford in its dependence on the lower-in-
come segments.

Such sales figures not only reflect the images of the various
manufacturers and their products, they also perpetuate them.
In the case of Renault, for example, sales to middle-class people
are achieved because of the special 'continental' image that the
cars evoke. This image is subsequently reinforced because the
cars are seen being driven around by nice trendy middle-class
folk. They are parked in nice neighborhoods and this subtly
encourages other nice people to buy them. Fords, on the other
hand, are to be found parked on council estates or in the poorer

areas of town, thus downgrading their image even further. Spirals of image fixing work here like self-fulfillling prophecies, and breaking out of such spirals is difficult, but not impossible. Ford's jelly-mold cars were a brave attempt to steal a march on its rivals in Detroit and Coventry. Cadillac's 'youthmobile' in the form of the Cimmaron sought to wrest some of the rich, young, trendy market away from the German competitors. British Leyland's jingoistically heralded Metro was a deliberate thrust at the hatchback market so comfortably dominated by foreign companies such as Renault, Volkswagen, Fiat and Datsun. Technical and stylistic innovations, however, can never be sufficient in themselves to revamp either corporate or model images. Such changes come about not through rational but through emotional appeals. It is here that the copy-writers of the big advertising agencies have the potential to endow a car with qualities which give it cult status. Equally, they can turn the same car into an unsaleable lemon.

The basic principles of automotive image development are simple. Associated with any car there will inevitably be a picture of the typical driver (his or her lifestyle, personality, affluence) and a range of emotional qualities – levels of aggression, sex, thrill, ambition, etc. By manipulating these associations it is possible to alter the entire image, and therefore the potential sales of the car. The principle is simple. The execution, however, requires both flair and subtlety – even fortuitous accidents.

When the Mini was first introduced in Britain in 1959, the official launch scaled new heights in showy razzmatazz. The theme was 'that old black magic' and was organized by Tony Ball, who was later to preside over the million-pound launch of the Vauxhall Astra. The 'magic' of the Mini was that its small exterior dimensions left the maximum amount of room for people and luggage inside. It was 'wizardry on wheels'. Issigonis's truly functional design, with a transverse engine and wheels at the corners of the vehicle, made it a very serviceable car for urban use. Its ability to park in very small spaces, use little gas and yet out-perform many of its rivals should have made it an immediate winner. Despite all the hype, however, early sales were disappointing. Like the Sierra, the Mini was too radical – a quantum leap beyond familiar and trusted cars such as the

Morris Minor and the Ford Popular. What eventually made the
Mini such a phenomenal success was not its inherent virtues
but its adoption by the rich, avant-garde. Lord Snowdon and
Princess Margaret bought one as a runabout and soon the Chelsea mews and fast-rising Carnaby Street were packed bumper
to bumper with them. Twiggy, Lulu, Spike Milligan, Peter Sellers – these were the people who drove Minis.

British Motor Corporation was quick to realize the importance of these associations. The technical sophistication and
compact nature of the car were still heralded in the sales bro-
chures and advertisements. But an additional promotion tactic
was adopted. Eighty leading figures in public life were given
a Mini on loan for a year, free of charge. All they had to do
was to be seen driving around in it. As a result, Minis were
soon to be seen at Ascot, Henley, outside smart restaurants
and clubs, and being loaded up by Harrods' porters. The Mini,
originally conceived of by Issigonis as a new, people's car, now
became synonymous with fashion and style – with Biba and
Heals and the swinging Sixties.

Such gratuitous image enhancement is, of course, quite rare.
That is how the major advertising agencies stay in business,
each trying to separate its client's fairly unremarkable product
from the herd. The agencies succeed or fail in their task not
because of the informational content of the messages they communicate in advertisements, but in the extent to which they
are able to make subtle, but direct appeals to our emotions.
Advertisements may often *look* rational, but this aspect of their
content is simply to appease our sense of responsibility and
desire for 'facts'. Underneath this veneer lie messages which
are much more powerful inducements to buy a particular automobile, ones which make us want to be the people the advertisers have successfully led us to believe would ordinarily
drive such a car. The interesting thing about this process is that
it is often best achieved without featuring people in the advertisements at all. Using real people is a risk since some potential buyers might not like the look of them. A more successful
ploy is to hint at a particular lifestyle – successful, glamorous,
etc. – and encourage readers or viewers to place themselves,
rather than somebody else, in that context. In this regard, the
setting in which the car is placed is all-important.

Putting On The Style

From about 1910 onwards, when the car had become more than just a 'horseless carriage', artists and photographers have ruthlessly exploited every conceivable image that the car can convey. Early advertisements mixed elegance with almost sinister power. Cars were drawn in elongated perspective producing unmistakably phallic perceptions. A German advertisement of 1920 shows a classy *Fräulein* clutching a scaled-down model of an open tourer to her bosom, purring 'Mein Benz!' and throughout the decades women have stood by cars signalling their availability to the man who would buy one. Many advertisements have repeatedly communicated the sense of escape one feels in a car, others the thrill of being the owner of a voluptuous exercise in sheet-metal pressing.

A very significant advertisement from the 1920s has now become a classic among the New York agencies on Madison Avenue. It is said that Ogilvie and Mather made all their junior staff learn it by heart. It also shows how much imagery can be squeezed out of a car in a few short sentences. In this case the car is a Jordan Playboy. Beneath an indistinct picture of a cowboy galloping alongside a girl in a sports car the text reads:

Somewhere west of Laramie there's a broncho-busting, steer-romping girl who knows what I'm talking about. She can tell what a sassy pony, that's a cross between greased lightning and the place where it hits, can do with eleven hundred pounds of steel and action when he's going high, wide and handsome.
The truth is – the Playboy was built for her.
Built for the lass whose face is brown with the sun when the day is done of revel and romp and race.
She loves the cross of the wild and the tame.
There's a savor of links about that car – of laughter and lilt and light – a hint of old loves – and saddle and quirt.
It's a brawny thing – yet a graceful thing for the sweep o' the Avenue.
Step into the Playboy when the hour grows dull with things gone dead and stale.

Then start for the land of real living with the spirit of the
lass who rides, lean and rangy, into the red horizon of a
Wyoming twilight.

Today's advertisements and commercials are rather tame in
comparison. The frank appreciation of automotive imagery has
been masked by a special kind of 'techno-babble'. We are given
details of 'brake horse power', which few people understand,
and of fuel consumption achieved under conditions that no
motorist will ever experience. These are thought to be appropriate copy, fitting with the new ethic of the car. The technical
details, however, simply give us a way of rationalizing our
choice. It is no longer acceptable to say that we bought a car
because we thought it was 'sexy' or that it would improve our
image. We need more 'responsible' catch-phrases – references
to reliablity, economy, low drag coefficients – the new dialect
of 'car-torque'. In the pictures, however, the symbolic features
still shine through, and it is these which really influence our
choice.

Recently we have seen a lot of deserts and wild, almost
sinister settings in car advertisements. The message that is communicated, though not always consciously recognized, is that
the car and its driver can survive such hardships and win through
to the open road that lies beyond. It is a metaphor for economic
survival, which is why cars aimed at the executive class feature
most prominently in this way. The BMW sails past all those
other 'luxury' cars half buried in the sand of Dungeness beach.
The BMW driver is a survivor, the shrewd judge who knows
what is going to outrun the competition. It is no accident that
such imagery comes at a time of economic recession. Times are
hard and business is bad. But the message is that all things are
possible even in these difficult circumstances if you are the right
kind of person, which of course means driving the right kind
of car.

This image of the tough survivor is also exploited by the
manufacturers of 'off road' vehicles – those four-wheel-drive
macho buggies for contemporary urban cowboys. Largely an
American product, but fast catching on in Europe, these mini
trucks, pick-ups and jeep-like vehicles are rarely driven in the

rugged terrains that feature in their glossy advertisements. Few owners venture further into the wilds than the dirt tracks which lead down to the shore of Lake Tahoe or the Pacific beaches of Southern California. The large payloads might come in handy for transporting personal effects to the University Campus, but the real reason for driving these otherwise quite irrelevant vehicles is to project an image of independence, freedom and a buccaneering disregard for the petty restrictions of city life. The driver of the Ford V6 Ranger or the aptly named Subaru Brat most certainly doesn't eat quiche – and he most certainly wants his whole neighborhood to know that.

Four-wheel-drive vehicles are an advertising agency's dream. The vehicle's inherent imagery speaks for itself so that only a modest amount of amplification need be added. The pictures of hunky men are so stereotyped that they might have been rubbed from a stock sheet of Letraset. Rubber tires crunch through the rocks and gravel of the all-American scenery while the all-American woman in the passenger seat nestles provocatively into the corner. The messages are not about utilitarian vehicles, but about sports machines with custom options and gleaming paintwork – tough cars made for play. The success of these products rests solely on the ability of marketing and advertising departments to distinguish them from those things that real workmen drive – to associate them with Hollywood cowboys rather than real artisans. This has been achieved with apparently consummate ease. Pick up a copy of an American automobile magazine (*Car and Driver* is a good place to start) and you will find advertisements for 4×4 vehicles happily sandwiched between those for Saab, BMW, Audi and all those other very chic cars that appeal so much to upper-class Americans. No pictures of farmers in dungarees – just beautiful, white, sophisticated and gritty heroes.

Convertibles communicate their own distinctive messages. For many people they evoke not only the true spirit of motoring but also a sense of youthful freedom and non-conformity. And this applies equally to men and women. The woman who drives a convertible is the woman who doesn't wear a bra. She also wants to be seen, and the absence of a roof serves this purpose nicely. The man, on the other hand, wants you to see the woman he is with as well as himself. Even rather plain people somehow look much more attractive and interesting in a car specifically designed to achieve this effect.

The convertible has recently enjoyed a revival, particularly in America where for a period the major manufacturers stopped making them altogether. Competition from the so-called 'recreation' vehicles still remains, but the lure of the rag top continues, reflecting a constant appreciation of the images such a car transmits. In Britain, there are few modern replacements for those cheap and basic Triumph Heralds and Morris Minors with their flimsy canvas tops which epitomized the collegiate sense of freedom of the early 1960s. But some Fords, Talbots and other lines are available in convertible form, and the specialist converters are doing good business. The Golf GTI with soft top has its own special niche as the vehicle *de rigueur* of the Sloan Ranger set. The Fiat Bertone Strada Cabrio has a suitably Italian charisma about it and the Citroën Visa, along with its smaller 2CV cousin, might almost be classed as a convertible. Both provide a cheap source of fresh-air motoring, but they are more like cars with peel-back roofs rather than ragtops in the true sense. They project an image of fashionable utilitarianism rather than youthful escapism.

While the convertible induces feelings of healthy nostalgia and the off-road vehicle derives its image from a transformation of its ostensible function, other species of automobile take their personality from the special aspects of their shape. Some cars are 'cute', and thus have an immediate popular appeal. In this category we might include the old VW Beetle, the Citroën 2CV and even the now defunct Morris Minor. What makes them so immediately attractive is that their form is reminiscent of a young child or animal. Psychologists and ethologists have discovered that there are certain cues which trigger an innate caring response to young children and baby animals. Among such cues are a head which is large in proportion to the body, large eyes, rounded body shape, short thick extremities and round protruding cheeks. Cute cars seem to have many of these features. They are 'round' in shape, but not like the aerodynamic tear-drops, which have quite a different image. There is something about their stubbiness and the relatively large headlights which stand out underneath the curving forehead of the hood.

Because they look like babies they evoke a special kind of bond. They are objects demanding loving care and devotion, and not surprisingly it is these kinds of cars which are most often given pet names and treated like one of the family.

Other aspects of a car's shape can communicate quite different messages. Research done by psychologists in the United States has shown clearly that various combinations of hoods and trunks and the body height of automobiles directly influence perceptions of the kinds of people who drive these cars. Long hoods, for example, especially the square-shaped ones, are generally viewed as masculine and arrogant – which is why the 'medallion man' might be tempted to buy a car with such features. He should, however, note that long hoods are also associated with being 'less youthful' and, if the car also has a short trunk, 'older'. So a car with a long hood is not much use when it comes to disguising those grey streaks of hair or the wrinkles around the eyes. It might help to create an image of sophistication, but to get a really youthful image, a driver needs a car with a rounded hood. The trouble with this, though, is that it is low on masculinity, and if the driver wants to maintain a sense of sophistication, he will need low body height as well. The psychological tests show that to appear young, sophisticated and masculine one needs a car which is low and which has a long and rounded hood and a short trunk. That, of course, is precisely what a Porsche, for example, provides very nicely.

Perhaps our hypothetical driver doesn't want the kind of image provided by a Porsche because he feels unable to live up to the expectations that go along with it. Perhaps he just wants to be seen as an unpretentious, friendly person – a down-to-earth sort of chap. In this case he would do well to opt for a car which has a short rounded hood, a short trunk and a high body. This sounds like the VW Beetle with its additional cuteness. The mixture should make him seem really quite inoffensive. He could, perhaps, afford to have a more square-shaped hood which would give him a rather more manly (but not too macho) image. Here most of the standard mid- to low-range products from America, Japan or Britain should fit the bill quite well.

Understandably, the auto manufacturers will probably object to this over-simplification of their styling exercises. After all, they spend millions of pounds and many years agonizing over such things as the line of the rear-light clusters. These features, however, are very much of secondary importance to the overall impression that a car makes – to what psychologists might refer to as its *gestalt*. When one looks at a car, an image of it is not gained by mentally putting together its parts. One does not, for example, first look at the wheels and then the windshield followed by the radiator grille and so on. It is all taken in at one glance – only later does one come to appreciate the finer details. It is this first glance which turns us off or switches us on to the car – it is these first impressions which count most and which are most impervious to the persuasive rhetoric in which car salesmen specialize.

In addition to reflecting various aspects of personality, the car broadcasts messages about our status in life. A particularly direct expression about one's position in the hierarchy of the business world is made by the company car. In the United States, surveys by the American Management Association have shown that for executives, even quite humble ones, the most important aspect of a job, after pay and working conditions, is the automobile that goes with it. The same appears to be the case in Britain, judging by the amount of coverage given to company cars in the business and financial press. Even though the tax advantages of having a company car have been eroded by recent Chancellors of the Exchequer in Britain, the car a company supplies to you gives you an immediate indication of how much your work is valued relative to that of your colleagues. It also communicates to others in the business world your standing and therefore how you ought to be treated.

The company car market is of great importance to the manufacturers, for in some cases it can account for over 70 per cent of sales. It is vital, therefore, for the major car makers to produce a range of cars to fit into the various echelons of the business world. Companies such as Ford and British Leyland do this not only by manufacturing models in different sizes and styles, but also by grading each model in terms of its luxury and refinements. Those otherwise fairly meaningless letters such as L, HL, HSL, GL and so on are primarily there to serve the same purpose as things like the quality of carpet in one's office. They make fine distinctions between staff and pinpoint their exact rung on the ladder of promotion and advancement. So too do the various optional extras such as electric windows, sun roofs and, particularly in the United States, air conditioning. The car, in this sense, is the visible reflection of the otherwise concealed pay check. It is generally considered crude to tell people exactly how much you earn, even though one might wish to do so in order to make an impression. Parking the company car in one's driveway is a good way of getting around this obstacle of etiquette.

A 'perkmobile' becomes especially important during a recession. When pay rises are hard to come by and there is less mobility in the business world, companies are able to appease the higher ranks of their work force by upgrading the standard of cars that they supply to them. In America, executives get more Cadillacs and Lincolns, whereas in Britain they get more Rovers and Granadas. The real value of these perks might be quite meagre, but they keep people happy. They provide people with an illusion of going up in the world, even though their status and salary remain the same.

Whatever the state of the economy, there is always a need for companies to distinguish between executive cars and those supplied, for purely functional reasons, to the sales force. The salesman *needs* a car – it is part of the tools of his trade. For the office-bound executive, however, it is much more than a means of transport. It is a special kind of badge. This is why some British executives are reluctant to drive Fords, no matter how good or expensive the model. To many of them the image of these cars is tarnished by their humble role of transporting sales reps around the country with samples on the back seat. As they see it, it is much better to have a Rover or some other car which could never be confused with that of a mere salesman.

An even better way of gaining a status indicator, without actually having to pay for it, is to have a company car which doesn't look like one. The answer here is to drive a foreign, rather than a domestically produced automobile on the firm's account. Smaller and more innovative companies, especially those in the media, advertising and information technology fields, are finding that their senior managers want not only a car which reflects their status in the company but also one which distances them from their peers in the 'common' man-

ufacturing industries. A Porsche or a Mercedes provides a suitable amount of distinction and there is always the chance that
the neighbors will think the driver owns it. Whatever industry
a manager is in, however, there is one golden rule governing
the standard of company car that he will drive. He will always
get something less prestigious than the Chairman, Managing
Director, President or Vice-President. It is essential, therefore,
that everything is done to prevent the man at the top from
downgrading his own car, even if it seems right and proper to
do so in the interests of economy or a gloomy balance sheet.
If your boss changes his Rolls for a Jaguar, then you can be
certain that your next car will not have a Ghia badge and you
will have to wind down the windows by hand.

Marques Of Distinction

The Rolls-Royce is seen by most people as the ultimate in image
machines. It has become a legend throughout the world – a
hallmark of prestige, distinction and wealth, and the subject of
modern folk mythology. No other automobile, whatever its
price and quality, comes close to having that special character
which the British normally associate with 'good breeding'. But
the Rolls's image is changing. Increasingly, the aura of privilege
is being replaced by that of hard-won gain. It is now new
money, not inheritances, that prises Spirits, Spurs and Shad-
ows from those elegant showrooms.

From consumer research commissioned by Rolls-Royce itself
it is possible to get a clear picture of the typical RR owner. It
may strike some people as odd that Rolls actually engages in
consumer research at all, but we have to remember that whatever else, they are still in the business of selling cars in an
increasingly competitive market place. It has been found that
Rolls owners are nearly all middle-aged men, which proves the
statement: 'More than most cars, the Rolls-Royce is almost exclusively a man's car.' This, in turn, is reflected in the styling
of the cars – solid wood, dark leathers – certainly nothing that
has even the faintest hint of effeminacy. According to the survey, most Rolls owners will not allow their wives to drive the
car.

Eighty per cent of Rolls owners are company directors or senior executives in organizations with an average annual turnover of about £4 million. It is interesting that those with the most money drive Bentleys, and here we see a striking contrast between the preferences of those with 'old money' and those with new. The man who has inherited his wealth has less need to parade his affluence. The Bentley is an expensive car, sharing basic things such as body shell with the Rolls-Royce. It is, however, more of an understatement, although recognized for what it is by the cognoscenti. The Rolls, in comparison, signals not only wealth, but the manner in which it has been acquired. It announces individual achievement rather than traditional privilege. Both Rolls-Royce and Bentley owners, however, are united in their belief that such cars win instant respect and make a good impression. That is why, presumably, they chose to buy them in the first place. They also feel that Rolls-Royces and Bentleys are useful in their businesses and even give reassurance to their employees.

To gain a picture of the Rolls-Royce owner in the USA we talked to Tony Thompson, a charming English gentleman who owns the exclusive Rolls-Royce dealership in Beverly Hills. He drives a Bentley himself, which he describes as 'winning the laurel but not wearing it on your head'. He sells about 100 new, and 70 used cars a year. Given that the entire British market is only about 300 new models per year, the consumption of Rolls-Royces in Beverly Hills is very substantial – probably on a par with the oil-rich Arab states. Thompson estimates that there are over 9,000 Rolls and Bentleys in the Greater Los Angeles area. This he attributes to the fact that in America, and particularly on the West Coast, no stigma is attached to overt displays of wealth.

Californian customers tend to be considerably more affluent than their British counterparts. While in the UK the average pre-tax income of a Spirit or Spur owner would be around £85-90,000, the purchaser of the same car in Beverly Hills would have a *minimum* annual income of $375,000. The average is probably now well over $800,000. On both sides of the Atlantic, however, nobody asks how many miles to the gallon you get from a Rolls-Royce.

The Rolls-Royce is recognized as a symbol of wealth, prestige and power by car park attendants who work in the smart areas of Sunset and Wilshire Boulevards. At the chic and excruciatingly expensive Ma Maison on Melrose Avenue, they actually line them all up in a row on the street in front. Mere Mercedes and BMWs are relegated to the car park at the rear.

There are, of course, further degrees of prestige afforded by owning different models. Each year the company wisely makes minor modifications, such as replacing the old-style tachometer with a digital display. This creates increased demand from those wanting to trade in their cars and so have the latest refinements. Real class, though, comes with the Corniche – the convertible model which is the most expensive thoroughbred in the Rolls stable. One would think that the convertible feature of a Corniche would have its greatest utility in California, because of the climate. In fact, very few people drive it with the hood down. Telly Savalas is a rare exception – he says that it is good for his head. But if you wind down the hood, the distinctive shape is lost – and therefore the principal reason for having it in the first place also disappears. Many Corniche owners, one suspects, would have to consult the manual to find where the hood switch is located.

In contrast to the British Rolls, the Cadillac stands for all that is American. Since the early 1940s Cadillac has occupied a special place in the lexicography of motoring symbols. Owning a Cadillac has long represented the pinnacle of social achievement, a visible sign that one has arrived in more senses than one. Between the two World Wars, wealthy Americans would usually desport themselves in the great makes such as Packard, Pierce Arrow and Peerless, and they were equally at home in the old Cadillacs. The great makes disappeared in the aftermath of the Depression. Once these had gone and Cadillac had joined the ranks of the production-line cars, the symbolism changed, so that Cadillacs now became the costume of the *nouveau riche* – of the *arrivistes* rather than those who enjoyed established positions of wealth.

People who are busy clambering up the social ladder still imagine that those at the top share their reverence for Cadillacs. They are wrong. The last thing that someone who has always had money wants to do is to adopt the style of someone who has only just acquired it. The American upper crust distinguish themselves from their newly-arrived financial peers by driving 'sophisticated continental automobiles.' Even the Yuppies (young upwardly mobile professionals) prefer to distance themselves from those who have made their fortunes from gas stations or liquor stores. They drive BMWs – teutonic talismans of taste. Cadillac has tried to erode the social gulf by introducing its Cimmaron model: 'a new kind of Cadillac for a new kind of Cadillac driver.' The difference in lifestyles between Cadillac and BMW owners is, however, still there, and so too are the images that one associates with the cars. The Cadillac driver eats steak with lobster. The BMW owner dines out in sushi restaurants and loves Florence.

The Cadillac and the Rolls, for all their expensive luxury and refinement, are involved in a quietly waged class war, along with Bentleys and BMWs. While signalling discernment as well as mere wealth, these last two still lack the ability to endow the owner with real individuality. All four cars, however, say little about one's personal character. For some people, this is unsatisfactory. They value a sense of individuality more highly than visible indicators of their place in the social and economic order. For them the entire contemporary market is eschewed and they turn to those very special vehicles we refer to so reverently as 'Classics'.

Classic car enthusiasts pose a problem for sociologists, principally because none of the usual theories of leisure interests and associations seems to work in their case. As the sociologist Dale Dannefer has pointed out, there seem to be few social forces or aspects of socialization which account for the passionate enthusiasm of classic and old-car buffs. They are not drawn into vintage-car clubs because they seek an arena for social interaction and friendships. They join with others only because cars are a central focus of interest and excitement. Far from being institutionalized into this special world, they are under-institutionalized – their passions developing independently in most cases, rather than from the influence of their family or peers. The explanation for the passion and fanaticism of classic-car devotees lies in the cars themselves, not in the social world which surrounds them. Shows and clubs are only a means to a particular end – to an increased individual involvement in automobiles which often have little in common other than the devout reverence which is shown toward them.

A classic need not be a showy car at all, although many of them are. Nor need it be a true vintage model. It is the sense of charisma which sets it apart from all other cars, and its driver from all other drivers. How a car acquires a classic aura is not, however, always clear. They are mostly durable machines which have stood the test of time and not rusted away. But perhaps most important, they represented in their day a degree of innovation, either in terms of their styling or their engineering. Whatever the reason, cars such as the Jaguar XK 120 of the early 1950s will turn heads on both sides of the Atlantic. It will also win admiration from those who hanker for the days when cars were cars and men were men. Alfa-Romeo Spyders of the 1970s are cherished by the 'true' sports car brigade who take considerable pains to distance themselves from mere 'boy racers'. Even Morris Minor convertibles of the 1960s provide a distinct cachet and endow the drivers with attributes of honesty, caring and concern for craftsmanship. At the other end of the scale, the Bentleys, Bugattis, Mercedes and Duesenbergs of the past evoke such passion and affection that would-be owners are often reduced to incoherent drooling.

Although classic-car enthusiasts all over the world share a common passionate involvement with cars, the objects of their passion vary. The British Classic driver, for example, seeks a car which reflects that peculiarly British concern with a sense of good breeding. Indeed he talks of his car as a 'thoroughbred', hinting at a kind of pedigree which one would normally associate with dogs at Crufts or racehorses in the paddocks of Ascot. He will constantly hark back to the days when they really knew how to make cars properly – the days of craftsmen and honest artisans whose whole reason for living was to provide people like himself with a good motor.

In America, the notion of a classic car is sometimes rather different. In some cases there is little in the way of genuine concern for originality. Although the owner of a 1940s MG might boast about the car's original paintwork, some Americans would say that it needs a respray. In fact, they probably would not be very happy with the MG at all. Such people would opt

for a brand new Classic – one built to resemble something from
the past, but equipped with all those 'essentials' such as air-
conditioning, stereo, and the gadgetry of 1980s hi-tech. Cars
like the Clenet are much more appealing to Americans who
want to cut a dash, stand out from the crowd but also retain
associations with quality and durability – things which once
went hand in hand with wire wheels and hand-beaten alumin-
ium. For a price you can drive around in a car which looks like
a Duesenberg, once the favorite of princes and maharajas, but
which was, in fact, made only weeks ago in California. The
British company, Panther, sell their replicas in Los Angeles,
pointing out the just barely discernible similarity with Bugatti
Royales. Mallalieu's 'reincarnations' of Bentleys also end up on
the other side of the Atlantic. The true Classic devotee would
probably choke in the showrooms of the O'Gara Coach Company, but he would recognize the statements that his fellow
enthusiasts are trying to make.

Alongside such imitations of the old makes, American companies have produced specially customized versions of contemporary automobiles as vehicles to promote their own fashion
wares. Gucci, for example, produced a rather smart Cadillac
which matched nicely their expensive shoes and scarves. Giv-
enchy offered a crystal-blue Lincoln Continental, quickly followed by Pucci with a medium turquoise edition and Cartier
who sprayed the car a light champagne color. Other entrepre-
neurs in the United States cater to those who cannot quite afford
such glamorous symbols of new-found gains by renting out
automotive esoterica. Eddie's Exotic Limos in Los Angeles, for
example, will let you have a white Lincoln, complete with bar,
mink-upholstered seats and a jacuzzi for a mere $100 per hour.
Margaux Mirkin at Rent A Dream also provides the kind of
ritzy transportation that one certainly would not be able to hire
from Hertz or Avis.

In contrast to this peddling of fake image machines, there is
one man in the USA who has prospered by selling the real
thing. Tom Barrett, who lives out on the edge of the Arizona
desert in Phoenix, deals in cars from the past which ooze prestige and distinction. These are special cars for special people,
and just to sit in one is to suffer a temporary delusion of gran-
deur. A visit to his garages on a relatively cool summer day

with the temperature at 102 degrees, was rewarded by a host of historic cars. There sat Roosevelt's blue Lincoln, the one in which he had campaigned in 1935. Next to it was the red Mercedes sports which Hitler had given to Eva Braun. A Lanchester which once belonged to a Russian Countess in the late 1920s gleamed silver in the Arizona sun. But this was no museum. These cars were on sale like any others, only the prices were a bit higher.

TWB III, as Barrett is known to all in the automobile trade, prides himself on being the most expensive used car dealer in the world. He sells to casino owners, company presidents, bankers, lawyers and even kings. Whilst some of his cars end up in collections and museums, most go to individuals seeking the ultimate in automotive status and elegance. The owner of the very first Duesenberg ever made has the special experience of driving not only a unique car but also a very visible one. 'It's not like collecting stamps or coins, where they just sit in a room – you can't take your stamp and fly it up and down the road where everybody can see it.'

Barrett sees the people who buy his cars as being, in a very important sense, like any other purchasers of automobiles. They tend to be considerably richer, but they are also into image management and competition. 'If I have two parties and they're both multi-millionaires, and they're buddies, and I sell one of them a car – it is maybe nicer than his pal has got. Well, then the pal will come to me and say, "Gee, that's a great V16 you sold him, but what do you have that I could buy to put that so-and-so down – I can't let him get ahead of me".'

To own one of TWB III's cars is to own a focus of attention. The car may not get driven much, but it will be on show and people will know about it. 'It's a talking point when they're entertaining – "Look at my beautiful Bugatti". They may not even be able to start the thing up – might not be able to spell the name properly – but it's out there and guests will say "God, he's got a Bugatti", and that's the point of it.'

4

JEWELRY

SOMEONE who intends to use a car to increase his or her standing in the eyes of others can acquire an automobile that is expensive, an automobile that is distinctive, or one that is both expensive and distinctive. In so doing that person can either leave the car as it was when it was bought, or attempt to enhance its individuality by adding a personal touch which further distinguishes it from other cars – in other words, adorning it with a piece of automotive jewelry.

Normally one would assume that the *grandes marques* like Rolls-Royce have no need for further embellishment because they are already expensive and distinctive, but this, as it happens, is not an opinion that has been shared by Rolls-Royce owners. Lord Kitchener had his Rolls painted bright yellow so that he could be recognized in public, while Lloyd George had a drinks cabinet installed, as well as a stool to support his gouty leg – a case, presumbly, where installation of the first gave rise to a need for the second. More recently, Gerald, Lord Berners had a piano built into his Rolls-Royce, and John Lennon, who always preferred to protest lying down, had a bed placed in the back of his. Other owners have had their Rolls-Royces stretched, armor-plated and the chrome replaced with gold leaf, while inside they have added refrigerators, televisions and telephones.

Fixtures like drinks cabinets and televisions allow the owners of smart cars to pamper themselves and their passengers, but they also serve another important purpose, which is to remind passengers of the owner's inability to do without these creature comforts. A car telephone, on the other hand, has an additional advantage, because apart from impressing passengers, it also enables the owner casually to inform people who are far away that he is calling from his car. It is not simply an instrument for contacting people while on the move; it is a device for impressing them with one's ability to rise above the logistical problems that beset ordinary mortals, who are capable of either driving or talking on the telephone but not doing both at the same time. The fact that car telephones are for impressing people rather than for communicating with them is nicely illustrated by an incident that occurred when they first became popular. According to Mike Fox and Steve Smith, who relate the story, one of the first people in England to have a telephone installed in his car – a Rolls as it happened – was Jack Hylton, the showbiz king. Lew Grade, the other famous showbiz producer, heard about this new acquisition and, not to be outdone by his rival, immediately had a telephone fitted in his car. Naturally his first call was to Jack Hylton's car, but when he got through it was only to be told by the chauffeur, 'I'm sorry, Mr Hylton is on the other telephone'.

Motorized Mascots

Owners of smart cars have individualized their vehicles in a thousand different ways, but none, it seems, is governed by a more deep-seated need than a desire to gaze out across the hood at their own personal mascots. The habit of fitting mascots to the front of wheeled vehicles can be traced back to the Egyptian Pharaohs – Tutankhamun was buried with a chariot which bore a mascot of a sun-crested falcon – as well as to the widespread practice of affixing talismans to horsedrawn carriages and figureheads to ships. As far as we know the first person to fit a personal mascot to his car was John Scott Montagu, later Lord Montagu of Beaulieu. The year was 1896 and the mascot, which could hardly have been more appropriate, was St Christopher, the patron saint of travellers.

Broadly speaking, mascots fall into three categories, namely 'company mascots', which are the symbols of car manufacturers, 'organization mascots', which are the totems of, say, people of the same profession, and 'personal mascots', which are the private insignia of individuals. The most famous company mascot is the Rolls-Royce 'Spirit of Ecstasy'. Apart from a brief spell during which she rested on one knee, this standing figure has faithfully represented the make since she first alighted on a Rolls-Royce radiator in 1911.

The company mascots that appeared on motor cars during the 1930s and 1940s were designed to evoke a sense of speed, freedom, elegance, power, or some combination of these attributes. Although images of horses, greyhounds, gazelles, lions, rams and other animals were widely used, most mascots incorporated the notion of flight, either in the form of a winged human figure, a bird or a pair of wings. Packard, De Soto, Plymouth, Duesenberg and several other makes sported flying, human figures, Hispano-Suiza, Cadillac, Citroën and Humber chose birds, and just about every other car had a pair of wings on its hood. Wings are of course suggestive of air-borne travel and of freedom to go where one wishes. Although the cars of the 1930s and 1940s never managed to get off the ground, they certainly succeeded in giving their owners the kind of freedom enjoyed by winged creatures. Like the figureheads once fitted to the prows of ships, these and other symbols were also a kind of unconscious insurance policy, a protection against the very real dangers that lay ahead on the road.

The company mascot on the front of one's car was the badge of the make, and therefore of the fraternity of car owners to which one automatically belonged. But it was also an ornament, a piece of automotive costume jewelry which could be replaced with other forms of decoration. With a quick turn of the wrench, many an owner removed his company mascot and replaced it with another. Sometimes he substituted the mascot of his professional group – the Association of French Dentists had a figure of a patient with obvious toothache – but more commonly he fitted a personal mascot. Many personal mascots were produced in limited editions – the illuminated glass dragonflies and trailing comets created by the French jeweller, Rene Lalique, being the most obvious example. Others, like Lord Montagu's mascot of St Christopher, were unique.

People who are constantly in the public eye have always shown a special interest in having their own personal car mascot. Lloyd George, for example, had a winged artillery shell on his Rolls-Royce, Rudolph Valentino's Isotta-Fraschini sported a rearing cobra, and Gary Cooper's Duesenberg had a figure of a running girl. British Monarchs have also made a point of using their own mascots. Edward VII and George V had a figure of Britannia on the royal Daimlers, while George VI, who favored Lanchesters, used a gold-plated lion. However, his widow, Queen Elizabeth, the Queen Mother, has preferred a Britannia mascot – her's being mounted on a globe. Since Queen Elizabeth II succeeded to the throne Rolls-Royce has enjoyed the royal patronage, but this has not extended as far as its mascot. While they are in the royal mews, the Queen's Rolls-Royces usually bear the Spirit of Ecstasy, but whenever she is about to ride in state they are replaced with her own personal mascot, which is an equestrian figure of St George slaying the dragon.

The Queen has certainly not been alone in preferring her own mascot to that provided by the makers of Rolls-Royce, although most of the mascots with which other owners have replaced the flying lady have been chosen for less ceremonial reasons. In his youth Lord Burghley was a fit man – he won the 400 metres hurdles event at the 1928 Olympics – but in later years he suffered from an arthritic hip. In 1960 he had a stainless steel joint fitted to his hip, but ten years later this had to be replaced with a new one. When he recovered from the second operation Lord Burghley was shown the original steel joint. He immediately recognized its potential as a mascot, so he had it installed on his Rolls-Royce in place of the Spirit of Ecstasy. Engraved on his new mascot were the words, 'A devoted supporter, 1960–1970'.

Personal mascots provided motorists with a ready means of expressing their individuality as long as there was somewhere to attach them. After the Second World War, however, cars started to take on a more aerodynamic shape. Lights were blended into the bodywork, running-boards disappeared and skirts were draped over the wheels. By the time that radiators had been tucked under the hood there was nowhere for the owner of a new car to put his old mascot, except on the mantelpiece. But old habits died hard, because even though the radiator cap was no longer visible, motor manufacturers insisted on providing their own hood ornaments.

During the 1950s these ornaments assumed the aerodynamic shape that designers were attempting, with varying degrees of success, to express in their cars. Stylized jet planes, as well as chromed rockets, darts and suggestive projectiles piercing circles, became the order of the day. On most models these ornamental missiles appeared singly, but in some cases – for example, the Chevrolet and Dodge models of 1957 – they were offered in pairs, not unlike the rockets tucked under a fighter-bomber's wings. Even the 1958 Lincoln, which was free of missiles, had a hood ornament that looked uncannily like a gunsight. Looking out across the hoods of their cars, owners were treated to a gleaming armory of aggressive symbols, which, even if to their liking, were not of their choosing. Although motor manufacturers were offering cars in a giddy choice of engines, transmissions and two-tone colors, they insisted on providing their customers with a hood ornament that could be detached only with great difficulty. Like it or not, the public was forced to accept the heraldic imagery of the car producers, as well as everything that this imagery stood for.

The desire among motorists to individualize the front of their cars showed itself during the Bug Deflector Craze, which occurred during the 1950s. The ostensible purpose of bug deflectors was to keep the windshield clean by deflecting the stream of air round the sides of the car, but there was just one small problem: they didn't actually work. People who fitted these strange winged plastic shapes to their cars didn't know this; they all believed that they had found a contraption that would keep their windshield clean – not because they had considered the mechanics of airflow or done a little experiment of their own, but because they automatically assumed that other people must have sound practical reasons for attaching similar deflectors to their cars. The utilitarian arguments that people offered for attaching bug deflectors to their car were nothing more than rationalizations for the fact that they wanted to choose their own ornaments. If this meant attaching a plastic bauble that failed to do what it was supposed to do, this was of little concern to motorists, because at least they had found a way of personalizing their cars and distinguishing them from those of other drivers.

In the end the Bug Deflector Craze went the way of all crazes, its death brought about by the fact that there were so many deflectors that they were no longer distinctive. However, at the peak of the craze there were literally thousands of people driving around with totally useless deflectors on their cars – all of them secure in the belief that their investment was saving them from the trouble of having to clean their windshields.

Just about the time that the Bug Deflector Craze was beginning to sweep through America, a rather strange incident, involving windshields, took place in Washington State. This showed how the automobile can become the focus of a collective delusion. The event was the start of the windshield-pitting epidemic of Seattle.

In late March 1954 several newspapers in Seattle carried stories about windshields being damaged in a city to the north. Initially it was suspected that vandals had been responsible, but when the police investigated they were unable to find any evidence to support this theory. By 14th April newspapers were reporting similar damage in towns outside the State capital, and by that evening the epidemic had reached Seattle itself. On that day and the next the Seattle Police Department received reports about damage to the windshields of over 3,000 automobiles. People complained that their windshields had suddenly become scratched and pitted, and that mysterious bubbles had appeared in the glass.

Motorists immediately began to take precautions, either by leaving their cars in the garage or by covering their windshields with newspapers, and speculation about the cause of the damage was soon rife – some people suggested that the bubbles were produced by sand-flea eggs hatching in the glass, others that the pitting was a result of an H-bomb test that had been conducted earlier that year. On the evening of the 15th the Mayor of Seattle declared that the damage was too great for the police to handle and he appealed to the Governor and to President Eisenhower for help. The Governor responded by appointing a committee of investigation. After the committee had conducted its inquiries it concluded that there was no evidence to show that windshields in Seattle were in a worse state than anywhere else. As several people had suspected, the incident had been a popular delusion: motorists had been encouraged to look at rather than through their windshields and what they noticed had simply confirmed their irrational fears.

After the epidemic had run its course, two sociologists, Professors Medalia and Larsen, made a special study of what had happened. They came to the conclusion that the whole incident could be traced to people's worries about a recent H-bomb test. They showed that a great deal of anxiety had been expressed about possible radioactive fall-out in the area before the epidemic began, and suggested that the windshield panic was a collective way of dealing with this anxiety.

What is especially interesting about this case from a psychological point of view is not that people projected their worries on to a new object of concern, but that they chose to involve their cars. The citizens of Seattle could just as easily have developed irrational anxieties about their homes, or even a neurotic preoccupation with their health, but instead they chose to displace their fears on to their automobiles. The Seattle epidemic provides an important clue to the value that people attach to their cars. It shows that when they are faced with a life-threatening crisis they are more likely to displace their fears on to their automobiles than on to their homes. They may invest more of their earnings in their homes, but they invest more of themselves in their cars.

Identity Bracelets

For most of us a license plate is something that we have to be able to read at twenty-five paces in order to pass our driving test, or something we have to commit to memory in case we are stopped by the police. The actual letters and numbers that appear on our number plates are of little concern to us – they are simply a designation given to our car by the traffic authorities. However, there are people for whom license plates are an important matter, sometimes as important as the car itself. Rather than accepting the registration assigned to their car, they have gone to enormous lengths to acquire a number plate that is distinctive, or one which, quite literally, says something about them or their car.

British interest in specialized number plates goes back to
1903, when the law requiring cars to be registered first came
into effect. Earl Russell, who had helped to get the legislation
through Parliament, stayed up all night and was rewarded for
his vigil with the first number in the series – A1. This number
is now owned by Dunlop Tyres, and it is reported to be worth
well over £50,000. Today, every car in Britain – with the exception of the official state cars of the Queen – has its own
registration number. Most of the numbers issued by the Department of Transport are meaningless and inconspicuous, but
among them there are a few that are highly prized by motorists.

The trade in specialized registrations – what the dealers proudly
call 'cherished marks' – is now a flourishing industry, catering
to the vanity, whims and humor of individuals who have
hundreds, and in some cases thousands, of pounds to spend
on an unusual number. Specialized number plates are used for
all kinds of purposes. They are used to announce who one is
(Max Bygraves has MB1, Engelbert Humperdinck EH1), to inform the public of one's profession (the comedian Jimmy Tar-
buck has COM1C), or to tell other motorists what one thinks
of them (Paul Raymond of nightclub fame has FU2). Royalty
have not been above this form of self-advertisement (the Duke
of Edinburgh owns HRH1, and Princess Ann has 1ANN on her
horsebox), while various companies have taken advantage of
the publicity contained in certain combinations. A Dorset tea
merchant has T42, and a Leicester sawmill company has 1AXE.
The Rolls-Royce dealers, H.R. Owen, have RR1, which is now
reputed to be worth more than the Silver Shadow to which it
is attached.

In Britain the numbers game is big business, with motorists
spending enormous sums for the dubious luxury of having their
initials on the front and back of their car. In sheer economic
terms the mania for unusual number plates is something of an
enigma. Why are sane people prepared to spend thousands of
pounds on certain letters and numbers which, in real terms,
are worth nothing more than the metal they are printed on?
One answer is that license plates are no different from the other
valuable articles, like rare stamps or gold objects, in which
people invest large sums of money. The problem with this
explanation is that while the owner of, say, a Penny Black or

a gilded salt-cellar by Cellini can take comfort in the knowledge that he can always find a buyer, the owner of an unusual number plate seldom has the same kind of security. It would appear therefore that the main reason for the current fad in specialized number plates lies, not in people's enjoyment of speculation, but in their vanity and their desire to distinguish themselves from their fellows. Not being content with the distinction offered by their cars, motorists have sought out a way of monogramming their automotive costumes.

The fact that the monogram costs as much as a new costume only adds to its attraction. British motorists can only own license plate numbers that have been issued by the Department of Transport. This means that a British driver who wants to display his initials on his car can only do so if the Department has at some stage issued that series of letters, and if he can find someone who is prepared to sell him the registration. This is quite different from what happens in America, where the motorist is entitled to apply to the Department of Motor Vehicles for a personalized plate. Provided nobody has the plate that he wants, and provided it does not exceed a certain number of digits and letters, it is usually issued to him for a nominal fee. The only applications that are refused are those that the Department deems to be overtly sexual or offensive. The trick, of course, is to try to slip a suggestive plate past the officials at the Department of Motor Vehicles, but this is difficult because its officials are armed with dictionaries, computer listings of dirty words, and even mirrors to help them see how plates will read backwards. The department has even been known to turn down obscene combinations in other languages – recent examples of refused applications are ZERSHK, which apparently means jackass in Armenian, and KAKIMAN, which means go shit yourself in Yiddish.

American drivers use specialized license plates – or 'Vanity Plates' as they are called – to draw attention to themselves. For some motorists a vanity plate functions as a mobile billboard, saying who they are or what they do for a living, while for others it serves the role of a personal testimonial, displaying the owner's sense of humor or his ability to challenge the wits of other drivers. Plates bearing the owner's name are common – Telly Savalas has TELLY 2, and Ernest Borgnine has BORG

9 – but even more popular are those which describe the owner's profession. Some professional plates are fairly straightforward – a Californian ophthalmologist has EYE EYE, an obstetrician has STORKS, and a priest has PASTOR. Others, however, need to be decoded: CLUESO belongs to a private investigator, ME SUE4U to an attorney, 2PC ME to a urologist, and EIEIO – if you haven't already guessed – to a farmer. PSY 47 belongs to Professor Sy Feshbach, an eminent psychologist at the University of California. When drivers are not providing their name or profession, they may be using their vanity plates to exhort other drivers (WISE UP, BCALM, ENJOY), to say where they come from (IMNXNYR), to describe their automobile (IDOXLR8), or to confess their true motives for owning a vanity plate (4 MY EGO).

Although vanity plates are used to convey a wide variety of messages, inspection of their content shows that the kinds of things people say with their vanity plates are remarkably similar to the kinds of offerings that people make when they meet for the first time. When strangers meet they are usually faced with two awkward tasks – one is to find out the other person's name, the other is to determine his or her profession. The reason why strangers need to find out each other's names is that name-exchange is the first threshold that has to be crossed before they can enter a proper relationship, and of course once they have crossed this threshold they can always affect the kind of intimacy that comes from knowing the other person for a long time. The reason why strangers need to discover each other's profession is that occupation provides a rough and ready means of categorizing someone socially. In addition, once one knows what somebody does for a living it is very much easier to keep the conversation going, and to do so in an area where the other person has some expertise.

What is especially interesting about vanity plates – particularly those found in California – is that when they are not giving the owner's name they are usually offering a description of his or her profession, albeit in a roundabout way. In the normal course of events people discover these facts about each other through the accepted forms of polite conversation, but the problem with these procedures is that they require careful attention and time, and as we all know, they are fraught with all kinds of social problems, not least being the possibility of causing some embarrassment to oneself. In a society which has become impatient with the slow progress of acquaintance afforded by the normal conventions of social engagement, the vanity plate offers an instant means of announcing one's name or profession, and of discovering the name or profession of other people. The psychological attraction of vanity plates which provide personal details is that they short-circuit the normal process of acquaintance and allow people to behave as though they already know each other.

A vanity plate functions as a kind of mobile visiting card – not one that is presented to select individuals, but one which is broadcast for everyone to see. There are also plates which contain messages that are normally exchanged by people who already know each other. Some of these conversational surrogates are quite benign – IMOKRU or 1OS NE1. Others, like IM SOFT, I LUST 2, or XCYTE ME, are somewhat more suggestive. The problem with some suggestive gambits is that they will not fit into the number of letters permitted for a license plate. Shaky Jake, the famous Los Angeles pinstriper, got round this problem by illegally sporting two vanity plates on the tailgate of his vehicle. One said 'YOUR PLACE', the other 'OR MINE'.

In Britain and the United States the attraction of specialized license plates lies mainly in the opportunities they provide for self-advertisement. The same is also true of Australia, where unsubtle vanity plates are now all the rage. In Hong Kong the situation is quite different. There specialized number plates are sought for the *joss* or good luck they bring the driver. The most highly prized numbers in Hong Kong are those which are homophones of charmed expressions. For example, when 6 is spoken in Cantonese it sounds like the word for 'longevity'. By the same process 2 stands for 'easy', 3 for 'living' or 'giving birth', 8 for 'prosperity' and 9 for 'eternity'. Single numbers are the most highly prized, especially when they appear without any letters, but combinations of good luck numbers are also sought after. A number like 8222 means 'prosperity-easy-easy-easy', and 163 represents 'live all the way'. Numbers which strike a chord of reassurance are pursued with great vigour, and many a wealthy business man has parted with a small fortune in order to bring good luck to himself and his car. The record price for a number plate was in 1979, when an anonymous business man paid HK$336,000 for the number plate 6. This amounts to well over half the value of the Rolls-Royce which the number plate now adorns. The Hong Kong Government has discovered a highly lucrative source of revenue in lucky registration numbers. In the process it has succeeded in providing the superstitious Chinese with a personal amulet to put on their cars.

The most common car amulets found in the west are St Christopher medallions and fluffy dice, neither of which is ever seriously regarded as a particularly powerful defense against bad luck. However, there was one case in the United States where a member of the Assemblies of God Church went to the Federal Court to try and get her license plate changed, claiming that it was destroying her life. She explained to the Court that members of her Church were treating her as the Antichrist because her license plate bore the number 666. This, the Scriptures tell us, is the number by which the Devil shall be recognized.

Badges of Rank

Whether they are attempts at self-advertisement or cryptographic one-upmanship, most vanity plates are exercises in vanity, pure and simple. But vanity plates are by no means the most conceited form of license plate, for in some American cities there are plates which are specifically designed to announce the occupant's position in the political hierarchy. In New York, for example, the Governor has 'New York 1', the Lieutenant-Governor has 'New York 2', and so on down to the last of the favored few, who has number 2,500. In recent years fierce arguments have surrounded the issue of these numbered plates, not only because some people have felt that they deserve a lower number, but because certain individuals have acquired more than one plate. Some people have even tried to hold on to their cherished number after leaving office.

The arguments that have taken place in the New York State Assembly over the pressing issue of numbered plates show the extent to which something will be pursued once it has become an accepted symbol of status. The practice of using license plates to signify status also underlines the degree to which the automobile has become a costume to which badges of office can be attached. When President Carter stripped his White House staff of their limousines and driver privileges in 1977 he did more than reduce their ability to get around the capital: he also damaged their sense of self-importance and deprived them of a uniform that announced their political standing. People in positions of political power have always been sensitive about their chauffeured limousines, just as military men have guarded their insignia of rank. For a politician to deprive his aides of their automobiles is about as astute as trying to strip a general of his stars.

The parallel between license plates and military regalia goes further, because most States of the Union have passed legislation which allows ex-prisoners-of-war to own special license plates which show that they were incarcerated by the enemy. In addition, the Texas legislature has passed a law which entitles disabled veterans to plates which say 'Disabled Vet', and servicemen who have been awarded the Congressional Medal of Honor, to plates which say 'Congressional Medal of Honor'. Throughout the world it is common practice for military personnel and ex-servicemen to wear their medals and ribbon on ceremonial occasions. By enabling its citizens to hang their decorations on their cars, the State of Texas has succeeded in transforming every automobile ride into such an occasion.

The attraction of the vanity plate lies in its ability to make an even more explicit statement about the driver than the car does. Bumper stickers also have this advantage. A motorist can use a bumper sticker to declare his love and hates, his political allegiance, his attitude toward Richard Nixon, his favorite radio station, sport or team, even his feelings about his car or the driver in the car behind. The ubiquity of car stickers might lead one to assume that nobody pays the slightest bit of attention to them. There is evidence, however, that this is not the case. In the early 1970s Dr Heussenstamm, a psychologist, asked 15 drivers who had committed no traffic violations during the previous year to glue Black Panther stickers to their cars. Within three weeks this group of drivers had received no fewer than 33 citations from the police!

By fixing a sticker to a car – or in some cases by adorning it with an entire collage of stickers – the motorist can announce to the world what kind of person he or she is. But there is no way that other motorists can respond to someone's declarations – or at least there wasn't until motorists began to equip themselves with 'The Flasher'. The Flasher consists of a set of large cards on which are printed various messages. The messages range from 'Thank you' to 'Sit on it', and they encompass most of the things that motorists are likely to want to say to each other, things like 'Nice move', 'Would you like my telephone number?', 'Follow me', etc. Armed with the Flasher kit, the driver no longer need be incommunicado. Now he or she can address other drivers. Even if they are out of earshot, they can be propositioned or insulted, and provided that they also have a set of cards, a conversation can ensue.

Gimmicks like flasher cards expose the deep-seated need that drivers have for contact with each other; for although cars have brought people out on to the roads they have also isolated them in their mobile cocoons. Nowhere is this sense of isolation more pronounced than when one is driving in a steady flow of traffic with other motorists who are almost within arm's reach, but who, for all the contact that one has with them, may just as well be on the other side of the planet. This strange feeling of being close to other people and yet cut off from them is undoubtedly the main factor behind the current popularity of citizens' band radio. CB radio is of special interest, not only because it has provided motorists with a means of making contact with each other, but because it has given them a sense of solidarity and equipped them with a means of confounding and outwitting the law. Since the arrival of CB radio, America, and now Europe, has witnessed the birth of an entirely new language of the road. The airwaves are filled with strange coded messages, shuttling back and forth between drivers who may never meet but who know that they are part of the great clandestine fraternity of the highways.

Ever since the first cars appeared, motorists have experienced an irrepressible urge to stamp their personality on their automobile. In some cases they have tried to make their car go faster, while in others they have attempted to alter its appearance, either to suggest speed or simply to make the car look more attractive. The car accessories business is now a multi-million dollar enterprise, catering for virtually every automotive whim. It provides cylinder heads, superchargers, camshafts, manifolds and even complete engines and transmission systems for motorists seeking greater performance; it offers bolt-on scoops, air-dams, spoilers and steering-wheels to those in pursuit of the illusion of performance, and custom paints, wheels, louvres, ski racks, nodding dogs and furry dice to those who wish to make their car look unusual.

When motorists alter the appearance of their cars they usually have two requirements in mind – one being the need to make the car look different, the other being the need to make it look similar to some other cars. By fitting, say, an air scoop to the hood and a spoiler to the trunk, the owner immediately distinguishes his or her car from that of the average commuter, but this choice of accessories also expresses the owner's identification with a particular group of drivers, in this case those who inhabit the glamorous world of motor racing. The accessories that people attach to their cars are usually intended as a claim to a certain kind of social identity, in some cases without any foundation. Someone who fits a car out with a bucket seat and roll-bar may succeed in presenting himself as a race-hardened rally driver, even though he never takes his car outside the city limits, while the parking lot guerrilla who decks out his truck with a gun-rack, searchlights and outsize, macho tires may give the impression of sleeping under the stars, even though he returns home every night to be tucked into bed by his mother.

The use of accessories is motivated by the desire to be different from other drivers and, more important, by the desire to identify oneself with a particular group of drivers. There is, however, a small band of car owners who have elected to express their individuality rather than their social identification. They have chosen to avoid accessories and instead to employ techniques of embellishment that nobody else uses. The most striking cases of such idiosyncrasy are those where owners have enveloped their cars in ridiculous objects. One man has covered his car with running shoes, another with carpet, and another still with a battery of colored lights controlled by a computer. An opera singer in California has swathed his automobile in fur, and a couple in Kansas have planted grass over the entire body of their car. All of these exercises in automotive one-upmanship are designed to achieve the same end, namely, enhancing the visibility of one's car and, by association, one's own social prominence.

When people embellish their car, however modestly, they immediately lay claim to some kind of individuality over and above that already afforded by the car. Even if the modifications are copied from a manual, or the racing stripes are part of a kit, they automatically form part of the overall statement that the owner is making about him or herself. Of course the meaning of the statement may not be understood by everybody, but this does not alter the fact that when people embroider their cars they set themselves apart from other drivers who have not made the same changes to theirs.

5

UNIFORM

THROUGHOUT the world there are groups of people who assume a unique appearance in order to distinguish themselves from their neighbors. Sometimes this is achieved by etching the face and body with scars or tattoos which serve as a permanent reminder of tribal allegiance. More commonly it is done with removable forms of adornment such as headgear, dress or cosmetics. Soldiers distinguish themselves by their caps and regimental colors, the clans of Scotland by their tartans, and New Guinea warriors by their ceremonial facepaint. These kinds of regalia are the uniform of the tribe. They tell people who wear the same uniform that one is a member of their group, just as they inform those who wear something different that one is not a member of theirs. The fact that people use adornment to express their common identity is hardly surprising. What is remarkable, however, is that automobiles should be used for the same purpose.

The west coast of America has spawned more auto cults than any other part of the world. This is largely due to certain geographical and economic factors which have eclipsed alternative modes of transportation and placed the automobile at the very center of the Californian way of life. This has direct consequences, not only for the way that people get about, but, more importantly, for the ways in which Californians have used cars to define themselves as members of a group.

Hot Rod Cults

On the west coast of America transportation is almost exclusively in the hands of private individuals rather than the State
or civic authorities, and this was also the case back in the 1920s.
Even then cars were so common that a local city planner was
prompted to remark that Southern Californians had added wheels
to their anatomy. As a result one had to own an automobile in
order to move around. Those who were lucky enough to have
a job then were, however, in no position to buy a new car, let
alone one of the extravaganzas driven by the rich. Instead they
had to make do with their clapped-out Model Ts and As. It
was during this time that the foundations of hot rodding were
laid. Young men who had enough money bought used cars
and, because of the need to make a personal statement, started
to fix them up. Even for the young man who could barely afford
an automobile it was a case of you are what you drive, so he
stripped it down and beefed up the engine. Although his hot
rod was no beauty, it was fast. His car was not going to turn
heads like a flashy new model, but it could beat the pants off
cars which looked ten times better and cost a hundred times
more. The young man with the hotted-up roadster had found
a way of making his personal statement. It was a statement
fashioned by economic necessity, but one which nevertheless
gave him a sense of pride and announced to everyone that he
was the owner of a hot machine.

The people who constructed the precursors of the hot rods
were into fast cars rather than cars that looked good. They
therefore created a new set of rules which stood in stark contrast
to those of the rich. What concerned the rich was how much
money someone had invested in a car. But young men with
ordinary jobs didn't have that kind of money and they couldn't
play the rich man's game. So they created a new set of rules
in which the opulence of the rich had no place. Their game
was speed.

Although hot rodding had its roots in the fast machines of
the 1930s, it only came into its own during the 1940s and 1950s.
The people who were initially drawn to hot machines and later
to hot rods tended to be either working-class or lower middle-

class. They were the kind of people for whom neat appearances in cars were not terribly important. Hot rodders banded together and in some cases formed car clubs. Like all auto enthusiasts they spent a great deal of time talking about cars, but they also spent as much time under the hoods of their own automobiles, with grease up to their elbows.

Typically the hot rodder started with a used car. He removed the hood, bumpers and running-boards to reduce weight and fitted a higher-compression head or a new engine to increase its power. The result was a no-nonsense vehicle with its chest bared and its sleeves rolled up – a speedster stripped for action. Most cars conceal their machinery and therefore the way in which they function. Hot rodders had no truck with this kind of modesty. Instead they were devoted to vehicles that looked like what they did, and this they achieved by exposing the muscular engine and phallic pipes. In the process they created racing monsters that possessed the same kind of stylistic honesty as motor bikes, which have always been completely candid about the way they work.

Hot rods were not intended to be a pretty sight, and they seldom were. They were designed for racing rather than looks and they were noisy. With its emphasis on racing, raunchy machines and manly virtues, hot rodding had little place for women. Most hot rodders preferred the company of their male friends and valued their opinions over those of females. The guy who was interested in girls was therefore unlikely to become a hot rodder, simply because no self-respecting girl would ever be seen in one of those unsightly, monstrous machines – let alone with some wrench-slinger with grease under his fingernails. In many cases hot rodding served as a substitute for pursuit of the opposite sex.

Apart from tinkering with his automobile and talking about cars, the other major occupation of the hot rodder was racing. Hot rodders began by racing their hopped-up cars on the street. Racing was usually informal: a hot rodder might pull up beside another car at the traffic-lights and issue a challenge by revving his engine, glancing defiantly or offering a verbal taunt. Sometimes a contest was specially arranged at the drive-in, and the combatants would then proceed to a deserted street where they would either race for the hell of it or for 'pink slips' – that is, for the ownership documents of the other person's car. Later on, however, hot rod racing moved up to the dry lakes and became more organized.

Allegiance to this distinctive subculture gave the individual hot rodder a feeling of belonging and a sense of identity. But because the major medium through which he defined himself was an automobile, it also conferred other psychological advantages that can only come from using the car as a uniform. H.G. Felson's novel, *Hot Rod*, which was published in the 1950s and which enjoyed wide readership at the time, captured what it was like to be a hot rodder:

When he was behind the wheel, in control of his hopped-up motor, he was king of the road. When he was happy, his happiness reached its peak when he could express it in terms of speed and roaring power, the pull of his engine, the whistle of the wind in his ears, the glorious sensation of free flight. When he was unhappy, discontented, moody, the wheel again offered him his answer. At these times there was solace and forgetfulness behind the wheel. The motor snarled rather than sang, speed became a lance rather than a banner, and revenge against trouble was won through the conquest of other cars that accepted his challenge to race. And when he was alone on the road, his car and its speed seemed to remove him from the troubles that plagued him while his feet had contact with the earth. Once removed from bodily contact with the ground, once in motion, once in a world of his own making, he escaped his troubles and sorrows in speed.

During the Second World War thousands of troops passed through California on their way to the war in the South Pacific. Hot rodding was then the big thing, and while the troops were stationed in California they came into contact with devotees of the cult and saw the cars. While they were in Guam, Midway and Okinawa they told their buddies about this new hot rod thing and mused on the machines that they would build when they got home.

When the war ended, hundreds of young men who had been exposed to hot rod lore returned home and started to create their own fast machines. In no time at all youngsters as far away as the mid-West and the East Coast – people who had never heard of these cars before the war – were building fender-flopper hot rods and spreading the fad to the four corners of America. In 1948 *Hot-Rod Magazine* appeared on the news-stands. Hot rodding had arrived!

At the start of the 1950s there were two distinct auto cults in the USA. The hot rodders were the black-leather-jacket brigade who wore their hair long and greasy, with a pompadour fold in front. They could be a fairly mean bunch. Certainly they were not the kind of people you would ask to organize a church fête or invite to tea with your ailing aunt. While the hot rodders were prowling around, looking for cars to race, another group of auto fanatics were taking to the streets. This was the custom car clan. Custom cars had in fact been around since the 1920s – Hollywood actors such as Fatty Arbuckle and Gary Cooper had their cars personalized for comfort and show – but it was really during the late 1940s that the custom car cult moved into top gear.

Custom Car Clans

While hot rodders were interested in speed, the custom car fraternity was more concerned with appearances. They did not therefore lower their cars in the front, but in the back. By modifying a car in this way, and by removing all the chrome, a member of the custom car clan was able to produce a vehicle which looked smooth. Lowering the back made it look long and sleek, giving it something of the appearance of luxury models which sit close to the ground.

The way that a car sits in relation to the ground is determined by matters of practicality or style, and sometimes by both. Racing cars, for example, sit very low because the lower their center of gravity the greater their capacity to turn corners at high speed. Hot rods and drag racers are also built for speed, but for speed on a straight track rather than round corners, so they are raised in the back in order to accommodate large tires which increase the ratio of drive-shaft revolutions to speed. But in addition to these practical issues, there are certain aspects of lowering which are totally expressive. Most luxury cars, for example, sit fairly close to the ground. This is not because they need to corner at high speed but because a small ground clearance makes a car look sleek and aerodynamic. This particular aspect of lowering was taken up by the custom car people who tried to emulate the classy image of luxury models like the Cadillac and Lincoln.

The way that a car was raised and lowered during the 1950s automatically made a social statement to people who understood the language of car uniform. By lowering his car in the front and by jacking it up at the back in order to accommodate large tires, a young man declared his allegiance to the hot rod cult. On the other hand, by lowering it in the back he announced his membership of the custom car clan. These modifications were in part dictated by the need to ensure a certain mechanical performance, but they also served to show who one was socially. Lowering therefore took on the function of an expressive enterprise. It became a uniform, a way of indicating one's tribal membership through the medium of the automobile. Those who joined the ranks of the hot rod cult were usually from the working-class sector of Anglo society. They were the blue-collar group for whom the important things were speed and male camaraderie rather than neat looks. The custom car people, on the other hand, tended to come from the middle class. They were concerned with looking good and with driving cars which were attractive to the opposite sex.

The hot rod fraternity and the custom car clan tended to keep apart. They frequented different cafés and parked in different parts of the drive-in, or went to different drive-ins. Here was a real bifurcation of cultures with its attendant divergencies in terms of mannerisms, clothes and cars. It was just like speciation in the animal kingdom where, for example, different sub-species of birds evolve from the same species, each with their own feather patterns and song dialect. In the case of birds, speciation is usually due to ecological factors, and in a way the separation of the hot rod and the custom car had similar origins. Each sub-species needed to distinguish itself from the other, which it did by carving out a separate automotive niche which suited its way of life. In a society which is dedicated to the automobile the best way to be distinctive is to drive a distinctive car. The people who drove hot rods and custom cars achieved this by choosing a different automotive plumage.

The *aficionados* of the custom car movement were devoted to clean looks in both their dress and cars. Therefore all the clutter of a car's appearance, everything which detracted from smooth lines, had to be removed. If the elevation of the car was to be altered, it was always lowered in the back. Next, the car was 'nosed and decked' by stripping all the chrome ornaments from the hood and trunk, and by filling the holes with lead – hence the name 'lead-sled', which was used to describe custom cars of the time. New hub-caps and white sidewall tires were usually fitted, and sometimes the head and tail-lights were recessed, or 'frenched', into the bodywork. On occasion fender skirts were fitted by giving the edges of the mudguards an outward flare. Most of the youngsters who aligned themselves with the custom car clan performed sufficient of these modifications to indicate their automotive allegiance, but there was a group of customizers who modified the entire structure of their cars in order to produce a radically streamlined appearance.

The most famous of these radical modifications was the 'roof chop', which involved cutting and removing sections of the roof supports and windows so that the height of the car was reduced and the apparent size of the car increased. 'Channelling' was also popular. This involved cutting the floor and re-mounting the body of the car on the chassis so that the car sat lower to the ground. Certain zealous customizers actually went to the extreme of 'sectioning' their cars by cutting and removing a horizontal section from the body. The reward for this delicate operation was a reduction in the overall height of the car. These operations are extremely complicated. Each requires great care and skill for the resultant effect to be successful, and weeks, if not months, can be spent chopping, channelling or sectioning a car, which is why even the most ambitious custom job seldom incorporates all three modifications.

In the old days the young man who wanted to customize his car might have chopped or channelled it, but he was more likely to be content with a modified axle, borrowed hub-caps and a new paint-job. But even if the alterations he made to his own car were minor, he would certainly have appreciated the skills involved in the modification of other people's cars. The

uninformed observer, on the other hand, was unlikely to understand what all the fuss was about. Even if he noticed that
there was something unusual about a radical custom job, he
would not have recognized the artistry involved. The whole
thing was more subtle than a freemason's handshake.

In many respects the custom car fraternity was like a secret
society. On the fringes were the initiates who dabbled in the
new science, but at the center were the true devotees, the alche-
mists of customizing who knew how to take a base model off
the production line and transmute it into a noble custom car.
Only they had mastered the vast lexicon of technical terms and
the sacred language of the cult. When they spoke among themselves they understood each other, but to the uninitiated they
might as well have been talking in tongues.

During this time the hot rod and custom car cults, which
were already quite distinct, began to develop their own extreme
offshoots. The custom car cult gave rise to show cars, which
were expressly designed as art objects. They were usually trans-
ported to the shows on a trailer, and were wheeled into the
exhibition hall where they sat in all their glory while the neth-
erworld of car *aficionados* milled about them, gawping and ex-
ercising their automotive fantasies. Show cars were not meant
to be driven. They were intended to be admired for their pseudo-
mechanical inventiveness, their extravagant splendor and in
some cases their sheer whimsicality. As such they bore very
little, and sometimes no relation to the functional objects of
Detroit. They were not really cars.

While certain sectors of the custom fraternity were building
show cars, a corresponding group of hot rod freaks were em-
barking on another form of escalation, namely the quest for
speed. These were the dragsters. The dragsters evolved from
hot rodders who raced their cars on the streets, usually late at
night when the streets were empty and the police were not
around. First they moved out to strips on the dry lakes in
southern California, and then to drag strips on the outskirts of
cities all round the country. Drag racing soon became an organized affair, with rules and special competitions, but it remained a totally amateur pursuit until the early 1960s, when it
also became a professional sport with all the paraphernalia of

commercial sponsorship. By then drag racing was a long way from the street racer with his beat-up hot rod.

During this time the car culture expanded out of all recognition. Hundreds of thousands of teenagers who had been part of the post-war baby boom had just acquired their driving licenses and were eager to buy their own cars. All of a sudden young people had money; they had become a market force to be reckoned with. Madison Avenue soon caught a whiff of the oil rag and began pitching its sales-talk at the new car fanatics. Overnight dozens of magazines appeared to cater for the craze. Publications like *Hot Rod Magazine* made a fortune advertising acne creams and whetting the automotive appetites of youngsters across the country.

The teenage car business had become big business. During the early 1960s the whole mood surrounding cars began to change. Young people started to lose interest in the rough image of the hot rodders and to place more emphasis on neat looks, so much so that the hot rods were painted up and chromed. Now they wanted cars which had high performance and which also looked good. Due to the rising popularity of the new straight-strip drag racers, and the eclectic coverage of the enthusiast magazines, young people began to gravitate toward a new type of personalized automobile in which performance mattered as much as appearance. They no longer saw their automobile as a hot rod or a custom car, but as something you drove to the drive-in, the drag races and the car shows. During this era the new auto fads came into conflict with the old. The movie, *American Graffiti*, set in 1962, shows the kinds of confrontations that occurred between teenagers who were wearing the automotive uniform of the 1960s and those who were still bombing around in vehicles from the 1950s. The movie also emphasized the degree to which cars and girls completely dominated the thinking of young men at the time.

The main character in the film is a clean-cut kid who is having trouble with his girl. He drives an immaculate white Chevy Impala and she drives an unprepossessing Edsel. The Chevy is complete with tuck-and-roll upholstery and a lovingly attended paint-job which reflects every admiring glance; the Edsel, on the other hand, never turns anybody's head. Apart from

these cars, the other *dramatis automobilae* are a chopped, red
Mercury with flipper hub-caps which belongs to the Pharaohs
gang, a yellow 1932 Ford coupe owned by Milner, the local
street-racing champion, and a hotted-up black 1955 Chevy driven by a hick with a stetson. The hick arrives in town, hoping
to challenge Milner, and finds him cruising the streets. He pulls
up beside the yellow hot rod and shouts, 'That's not your car
man; that must be your Mama's car!' This fails to provoke the
desired response, so he shifts up a gear in the register of insults:
'What's that color? Looks like a cross between piss-yellow and
puke-green!' This is too much, even for our reluctant hero, so
a contest is arranged on a deserted strip of highway outside
town.

The next scene opens with the Ford and the Chevy flexing
their mechanical muscles at the starting line. At a signal from
one of the spectators, the two automobiles explode into action
and scream off down the highway in a cloud of burning rubber
and exhaust fumes. Just as the Chevy is starting to get ahead
of the Ford, it loses control, careers off the road and rolls over.
The hick manages to clamber to safety before it bursts into
flame, and the Ford is acclaimed the winner. But this is a hollow
victory for Milner, because he knows that the Chevy would
have won had it not come off the road.

This scene represents the moment when hot rods began to
give way to the hot machines of the 1960s. It was the point at
which the 1932 Ford gave way to the 1955 Chevy and when
people with faster, more modern cars supplanted guys like
Milner and everything they stood for. Early in the movie Milner
expresses the opinion that 'driving is a serious business'. For
people like him, who spent their time fixing up hot rods while
other young men were chasing girls, cars were the only serious
business. They refused to identify with the new crew cut look
and what Milner dismissed as 'that Surfin' shit'. For Milner
rock-and-roll had never been the same since Buddy Holly died.
But teenagers of the early 1960s were unimpressed with this
kind of nostalgia. They were the neophytes who refused to
wear the old automotive badges of the hot rod or the custom
car. Instead their uniform had to be both flashy and fast. But
most important of all it had to be modern.

All of a sudden cars became a standard form of uniform because youngsters had some money to spend and because there were more of them – they were the great post-war baby boom. As important was the fact that Detroit was now turning out high-performance vehicles in the shape of muscle cars. This meant that armies of youngsters with unprecedented spending power were able to acquire powerful machines which only needed a bit of exterior embellishment in order to make a social statement.

The democratization of competition racing during the 1950s had far-reaching consequences, both for the way in which young men spent their leisure time and the ways in which they gained prestige. It meant that however lackluster a young man's achievements, he could always make his mark. Even if he was a failure at school and a flop on the playing field, he still had a chance of gaining the admiration of his peers. All he needed was the money to buy and fix up a car, the ability to steer it down a straight track, and the dexterity to change gear quickly. Equipped with his machine and these meagre skills, he was automatically guaranteed a race and the possibility of success; and if success eluded him he could at least enjoy the thrill of competing in a heady atmosphere of burning rubber and screaming engines. Equally important was the fact that the races involved two cars at a time. This made each race reminiscent of a duel at High Noon, except that here the weapons were cars, and nobody was likely to get hurt.

Drag racing provided young men with a means of gaining recognition, but street racing offered them a way of staking out a real reputation. It was far more dangerous, and it was also illegal. Danger and illegality gave street racing its edge, compounding the prestige that was attached to winning, especially when spectators had gathered to witness the contest. Pre-arranged races took place late at night. The nocturnal contests on the long boulevards and freeways of Los Angeles during the 1960s have now become part of Californian folklore. As soon as word spread that a race had been arranged, scores of teenagers would arrive. Before the police had time to arrive, self-appointed stewards would block the freeway off to normal traffic, and the combatants would take up their positions in separate lanes. Someone would wave a makeshift flag and the two cars would go hurtling down the freeway, through the avenue of cheering teenagers.

In some cases street racing was motivated by the sheer love of competition, while in others it was done for money or the other person's car. Where it was linked to the prospect of financial gain there were inevitably cases of hustling. Youngsters would pretend, for example, that their car was underpowered in order to raise the stakes and therefore their earnings from contests they were assured of winning. They would disguise their cars to look like a 'sleeper' – that is an ordinary car that is not especially fast. Wearing this unexceptional automotive uniform, these car-sharps would stalk the drive-ins and streets in search of suckers who might be tempted into an ill-advised duel. But whatever its motivation, street racing derived its thrill from the youthful defiance of authority and the law. It was charged with the excitement of racing where racing was not allowed, and of competing where adults had no say.

In their desire to distance themselves from their parents, young people of the early 1960s gravitated toward different kinds of clothes, music and cars. No self-respecting adolescent would now be found wearing a suit, dancing the quick-step or, heaven forbid, driving a stock model – unless of course he was without a car and had to borrow the family saloon. Like no generation before them, teenagers of the early 1960s began to wean themselves from society. They sought greater independence and played with new ideas, and even though they did not reach the extremes of self-expression which characterized the late 1960s, they took the first important steps toward social non-conformity. The only trouble was that to be a non-conformist, you had to be a conformist; in order to reject the values of your parents you had to show that you accepted those of your peers. So, although the teen culture of the early 1960s boasted all the features of a heresy, it still exhibited those cohesive forces which bind heretics together. While teenagers did not seek acceptance from their parents, they certainly wanted it from their contemporaries, and to gain each other's acceptance they had to display remarkable orthodoxy in their taste and fashion. This applied as much to the clothes they wore and the dance steps they performed as it did to the kinds of cars they drove.

Pat Ganahl, senior editor of *Hot Rod Magazine*, has made a special study of this era, and he has offered the interesting observation that the rules which governed what teenagers did to their cars were probably stronger than those which applied to their dress code. Ganahl tells us that during the early 1960s there were definite rules about the way a young man should dress if he hoped to be accepted by his peers. For example, at one stage the big things were peg pants, white buck shoes with crêpe soles and a button-down shirt. But it couldn't be just any old button-down shirt. The collar had to be of a certain length, with two buttons in front and one at the back, and there had to be a loop at the back of the collar and a pleat down the length of the shirt. The sleeves too had to be of a certain length, rolled up one turn. But if the dress code was severe, the car code was even worse. If in, say, 1960 you owned a 1949 Ford, you would de-chrome the hood and trunk and remove the door handles. Two years earlier you would probably have installed a side piece from a Buick and painted your car two-tone, maybe dark green and light green, or white and red. But two years later you were not supposed to have a two-tone paint job any more. Instead you would have had a straight color, probably of some metallic paint.

According to Ganahl, the same principles applied to a car's hub-caps and tires. The early hub-caps looked like a bell-boy's hat or an army helmet. These were then adapted to include a single bar across the cover which produced stroboscopic reflections when the wheels were spinning. Next there was the 'flipper hub-cap', which had three bars and a star in the center. Then in 1959 Chrysler installed a hub-cap with four bars on their Lancer model, so everyone had to get hold of Lancer hub-caps. The same whimsical process occurred with tires. In 1958 you would have had wide, white side-wall tires. A few years later the side-walls had to be of medium width, and finally, about 1962, you were expected to have narrow, white side-walls. At each stage in the cycle teenagers had to abandon their old hub-caps and tires and fit new ones. To gain the respect of one's peers one had to know the latest vogue. This meant that the socially conscious teenager had to adopt the latest hair-style and clothes, but again, because he moved in a car culture, he also had to fit his car out with the latest baubles of auto fashion.

Apparently even this was not enough, because along with one's car had to go a certain demeanour of driving. The novelist Harry Crews, writing in *Esquire Magazine* in 1955, describes the situation at the time:

> I owned a 1953 Mercury with three-inch lowering blocks, fender skirts, twin aerials, and custom upholstering made of rolled Naugahyde. Staring into the bathroom mirror for long periods of time I practised expressions to drive it with. It was that kind of car. It looked mean, and it was mean. Consequently, it had to be handled with a certain style. One-handing it through a ninety-degree turn on city streets in a power slide . . ., you were obligated to have your left arm hanging half-out of the window and a very *bored* expression on your face . . .

By assuming the latest automotive uniform, and the appropriate comportment, young people were able to distinguish themselves, both from their parents and from their peers who were still caught up in the old habits. During the early 1960s cars were important to teenagers and to their parents, but in quite different ways. While teenagers were moving with the vagaries of auto fashion, their parents were busy eyeing the Jones's automobile, discussing the latest models in the showroom and swallowing whatever Detroit threw at them. When teenagers of the early 1960s left school and found a job they discarded their fixed-up high school bombs and bought muscle cars. Only later in life did they assume the automotive uniform of their parents.

Teenagers of the early 1960s were completely obsessed with cars. Those of the late 1960s, however, were quite different. For them Dylan, Vietnam, protest songs, long hair and sexual liberation were all the rage. They were also the first counter-car culture. It was now necessary to show that material possessions, cars included, were not important. What mattered instead was the way that people related to each other. At least that was the official line, because although members of the hippie movement disclaimed any interest in cars, they were often forced to make their statement through the medium of the automobile. To demonstrate that you were not interested in cars you had to drive a certain kind of car, say a Volkswagen Beetle or a beat-up van. Consequently, to make your social statement you would either leave the paintwork untouched or give your car a crazy paint-job (like the psychedelic Carnival Car which appeared in the movie, *I love you, Alice B. Toklas*). Alternatively you would deliberately ignore the dents and let the mudguards fall off. But whatever you did to your car you would ensure that you concealed any loving attention you had given it. Your car could either be a joke or a mess; never an object of pride. In the final result, therefore, hippies were forced to adopt their own automotive uniform. In a society dominated by the car, nobody, not even the members of a counter-car culture, could escape.

Auto-Tribes

In the 1950s Swedes woke up to find a new horror in their midst – the Raggare. These were gangs of youths who spent their time driving around in beat-up American cars, brushing with the police and living close to, and sometimes on the other side of, the law. Like the Teddy Boys in Britain and the Halbstarken in Germany, the Raggare sported their own uniform. In the case of the Raggare this consisted of blue jeans, a leather jacket with wide shoulders, gaudy socks and pointed black shoes. Like greasers elsewhere they also plastered their hair down with pomade. But the central focus, the unifying passion of the Raggare, was their cars. In 1960 a police officer in Stockholm described them as follows:

Their cars are in a bad condition and very often a real danger to road safety. In their cars they invariably carry a can and a hose so that they can steal gas from other cars. These young people have little interest in their own education, in reading books, or in sport or any organized activities. Their cars have become their God.

Contrary to popular belief, most Raggare were gainfully employed. Employment provided them with the necessary finance to purchase big American cars which, when set against a backdrop of diminutive European models, gave them a flamboyant and distinctive appearance. The early Raggare represented an indigenous attempt on the part of disaffected youth to distance themselves from their parents and society as a whole. Their motives, however, were not political, but expressive. They simply wanted to be different, and to appear to be different from everyone around them. In fashioning an image for themselves the Raggare borrowed liberally from what they had found in American magazines and seen at the cinema. They took style components from the hot rodders and the custom car people, and fused these into a syncretic image which had bits of James Dean, the greasers and the High School cruisers.

The Raggare are still in evidence today, although their numbers and the horror they instil in law-abiding citizens appears to have diminished. Today their apparel is far less stereotyped than it was in the early days, but their devotion to things American and their attempts to reproduce the automotive ambience of California in chilly Sweden are still as pronounced as they ever were. American cars still bind the Raggare together. Simply by possessing cars the Raggare are able to cruise together and to congregate where they want. Cars provide them with excitement and an escape from the drudgery of their working lives. But because a Raggare's car is distinctive, it is also his uniform. It is his badge of nonconformity, an automotive statement which unites him with like-minded individuals and separates him from the world of people who drive practical, family saloons.

The automotive uniform the Raggare chose was made available by the American cultural invasion that swept round the world following the Second World War. Wherever Americans went they took Coca-cola and hamburgers. They also introduced something that was entirely alien to the European experience, namely elongated chrome-infested automobiles. Ever since they were first exposed to these monsters, Europeans have been divided between those who view American cars as four-wheeled follies and those who see them as an expression of audacious design. But whatever their view, most Europeans are united in the belief that American automobiles have no place in their society. In Europe, as in America, it is quite in order to parade one's wealth on wheels, but while exhibitionism in America knows no limits, in Europe it has always been muted by the constraints of modesty. The European reluctance to own a car that might be construed as excessive therefore produced a situation in which groups who wished to distinguish themselves from mainstream society could adopt the American automobile as the symbol of their distinctiveness. This is exactly what happened with the Raggare. While the average Swede was driving his Volvo or Saab, the Raggare were gathering together under the banner of the American automobile. They colonized a symbolic gap that had been left unoccupied by the bourgeoisie and in the process acquired an automotive uniform that expressed their pursuit of freedom and independence.

Much the same happened in Japan. During the 1960s Japan witnessed the emergence of a radical student movement which was dedicated to overthrowing the state. Regiments of masked students, all wearing the same anarchist's uniform, regularly confronted the police in set-piece battles which had all the trappings of medieval Japanese warfare. But while the students were reading Lenin and making Molotov cocktails, another group of alienated youths were waiting in the wings. These were the notorious bo-so-zuku. They too sported a uniform, but with their black leather jackets and Regency hairdos they looked more like Californian hot rodders than hotheaded students. By the early 1970s the student movement had started to disband and most of its leaders had joined the big corporations. At this stage the spotlight fell on the bo-so-zuku. They became the new social devils.

In the early days the bo-so-zuku's main means of transportation and self-expression was the motor cycle, but by the 1970s many of them had acquired cars. Now, instead of zig-zagging wildly through the traffic on their motor bikes, they piled into cars and went roaring through the streets, hanging out of the doors and windows, yelling at passers-by. Like their counterparts in Sweden, the bo-so-zuku were intent upon provoking the public and drawing attention to themselves. Their nocturnal escapades, street-racing and reckless driving soon attracted the disapproval of the authorities, and on more than one occasion

the riot police were called out to quell disturbances involving
their members.

The bo-so-zuku are loosely organized into gangs. Some of
these are exclusively motor cycle gangs, others are exclusively
car gangs. But most gangs possess both types of transportation.
Here it tends to be the case that younger members begin with
a motor cycle before they graduate to owning an automobile.
Each gang has a name which is either an American derivative
like Black Emperors, Hell's Princes or Pink Panthers, or a designation involving Japanese gods, devils or animals. Individuals
announce their gang membership by wearing logos on their
jackets or by sporting stickers on their cars. Beyond this they
announce their membership of the wider fraternity of bo-so-
zuku by wearing a certain uniform and having a distinctive
hair-style, and by driving a vehicle which functions as a mobile
symbol of their allegiance to this subculture. In medieval times
Japanese foot soldiers would attach a small regimental flag to
their back so that they could be recognized in the heat of battle.
This heraldic device disappeared a long time ago, but it has
now reappeared in the form of the automobile. For the bo-so-
zuku the car offers a way of broadcasting their social identity.
It is their way of asserting themselves in the face of a society
which they feel has neglected them and cast them aside.

The emphasis Japanese society places on success within the
conventional avenues of education and the professions is certainly more extreme than in most other countries. Academic
achievement and a conforming acceptance of society's values
are highly prized, and those who do not make the grade are
constantly reminded of their failure. The education system in
Japan is organized in such a way that those who are not going
to make it to university are weeded out at an early stage, with
the result that their chances of joining the rat race are severely
diminished. The way in which success is structured in Japanese
society therefore has direct psychological consequences, not
only for the way in which individuals are viewed by others,
but also for the way in which they view themselves. Those
individuals who fall by the wayside are offered little chance of
redeeming their self-respect, and many of them gravitate toward alternative subcultures like the bo-so-zuku. The automobile plays a crucial role in this. Because cars offer an escape

and a means of self-definition, they are the natural focus for alienated teenagers who see their opportunities curtailed by a system which offers no respite from failure. Ronald Loftus, who has written on this subject, captures the problem of Japanese youth in the following way:

> Having thus failed to establish their identity through the educational system, it is doubtless true that the possession and manipulation of an automobile or motorcycle serves to bolster their threatened identity and self-esteem. If by day, in school or society, one feels frustrated and powerless, at night, behind the wheel of a speeding car, feelings of failure and inadequacy may be left behind and the 'true self' reclaimed. In Japan as elsewhere, cars and motorcycles can also be important status symbols that somehow make one's presence in the world more tangible.

Ethnic Insignia

The youngsters in America who were involved with hot rods and custom cars were invariably white – usually working-class whites in the case of the hot rods and middle-class whites in the case of custom cars. By aligning themselves with these auto cultures, young people defined themselves collectively as belonging to a particular group within mainstream *white* society. But there were several ethnic minorities, such as the Chinese, the Blacks, the Japanese and the Hispanics, who, to varying degrees, existed outside mainstream white society. Even to this day each of these minorities has remained fairly distinct, retaining its cultural identity in the midst of a society that is dominated by white values. Some minorities, such as the Chinese, have kept their language. Others have relied on the distinctiveness offered by a different patois or mode of attire. One ethnic minority has chosen the automobile as a way of announcing who they are. These are the Chicanos.

The Chicanos are of Mexican descent. Although most of them are second and third-generation Americans, they are still quite separate from Anglo society. Before the war the uniform of the young Chicano male was the zoot-suit, which consisted of a loose-fitting jacket and baggy trousers. In those days he might have joined the gang in his barrio or neighborhood. Nowadays he is more likely to become a member of a lowrider car club. Becoming a Lowrider and owning one of the street-hugging vehicles which have become the totem of the Chicanos is one of the main avenues through which a young Chicano can gain the admiration and respect of his peers. As soon as he has amassed or borrowed the necessary finance, he begins the search for a second-hand automobile that can be customized according to the aesthetic canons of lowrider culture.

The principal motive of the Lowrider is to transform a standard model off the production line into a low-slung transportation of delight. The first stage is to modify the suspension so that the car sits as low as possible. This is done by removing or cutting the springs and fitting small tires so that the frame rides no more than the height of a packet of Marlboro cigarettes off the ground. Sometimes the interior of the car is also lowered by dropping the floor pans and seats. The resultant effect is one of sleekness. When the car is stationary it looks like a contented creature in repose; when it moves it appears to glide on its belly.

A car with ordinary suspension which sits low automatically rides slow. Once a car has been lowered it must be driven slowly to avoid scraping the road. But, instead of being an obstacle, slowness is a virtue to the Lowrider because it fits in with the relaxed image that he tries to cultivate. When the Lowrider goes out cruising with his buddies they turn up the music and sit low in the seats, affecting an air of cool indifference. They crawl along the street at a snail's pace, looking out for any action and making sure that they are seen. Lowriders are never hurried or hassled; as they say, they are low and slow.

As soon as Lowriders began to lower their cars they came into conflict with the authorities. The police saw their vehicles as unsafe, and their practice of cruising as a Pachuco gang-land invasion of the streets. Perhaps even more, they were alarmed by the ethnic solidarity which this motorized uniform seemed to encourage. Ordinances specifying the minimum ground clearance were enforced, making it illegal for a vehicle's frame to be lower than the inside rim of the wheel. But Lowriders had an answer: they simply replaced their suspension systems with hydraulic lifts.

With hydraulics at his fingertips the Lowrider has a host of antics at his disposal. For example, unwary policemen can be bamboozled by the driver who instantly jacks the automobile up to a legally acceptable height. The mythology of the Lowrider is replete with tales of hydraulic trickery; like the one about the police-officer who starts to book the Lowrider for riding too low. When the officer finishes writing out the ticket he discovers, to his amazement and consternation, that the car is actually at the legal height, so he is forced to drop the charge! But if instant raising and lowering of the car plays a part in confusing officers of the law, it plays an even greater role in ostentatious displays of virtuosity.

Hydraulics can be used to 'lay' the car flat on the ground, or to acknowledge the presence of other Lowriders with a simple mechanical nod of the hood. When the vehicle is fitted with a full set of lifts it can be made to gyrate like a frenzied rock-and-roller, or it can be made to hop up and down like a jack rabbit with hiccups. But the fullest expression of Lowrider ingenuity is found in the practice of 'hopping'. As soon as Lowriders discovered the gymnastic potential of pumps they began to challenge each other to hopping competitions. Typically the duels took place on the street or in a vacant parking lot. Two Lowriders would park their cars nose to nose. If money was changing hands a suitably impartial judge would be nominated to decide on the winner. Beer cans would be piled up to measure the height of the hops. The owners would stand outside their vehicle with remote controls connected to the dashboard, and, at a signal from the judge, they would start to bounce their vehicles in unison. Up and down the cars would go, until one had managed to raise its hood above the other and win. A hopping contest is full of sexual symbolism. With its emphasis on simultaneous comparison and rigid elevation, it has all the trappings of a penis-measuring competition in the locker-room. At the same time, the sight of cars bouncing up and down has the appearance of a public display of copulation.

If hydraulic pumps have made the Lowrider's car into an automated pogo-stick, they have also transformed it into a mechanical firecracker. When Lowriders first got into lowering they found that accidental scrapes with the surface of the road would send sparks shooting out from under the car. This unintended result of lowering soon became the basis of a deliberate nocturnal spectacle. Lowriders started fitting soft metal scrape plates under the front of their cars. By setting the car in motion and bringing the plate into contact with the road they could now make sparks issue in a fiery wake from the back. 'Throwing scrapes', as it is called, is one of the most spectacular antics of the Lowrider. The effect is especially dramatic when the back of the car is jacked up and the weight of the car is transferred to the front. When this is done clouds of metallic sparks tumble under the car and sweep out at the back, lighting up the night. As one Lowrider remarked, 'It looks like the car's just gliding on fire.'

The cult of the lowrider goes back to the 1940s when Californians first began to experiment with custom cars by stripping them of all exterior chrome. Chicanos refused to follow this vogue. Instead they remained faithful to the idea of the car as a display rather than a performance vehicle. Brightwork was therefore emphasized throughout, and anything that could be chromed was treated to electrolysis: door frames, handles, exhaust, you name it. Furthermore, if any part of the car was going to be lowered, it would either be the back, or both the front and the back; never just the front.

Even though the basic motif of the lowrider car has remained unchanged, Lowriders have managed to move with the times. The paint used on today's lowrider car is as modern, varied and immaculate as any found on a custom car. Deep candies, shimmering pearls and iridescent metal-flakes are common, and colors span the full range of the automobile rainbow. Whether a lowrider car has its top chopped or its lights frenched, and whether it is adorned with flames or pinstripes, it will always be unmistakable. Firstly, it will be low. Then it will usually display a chrome-chain steering-wheel and Tru-spoke or five-spoke wheels. In addition, a lowrider car may boast certain symbols of the good life, such as champagne buckets and cocktail glasses in the center console. Some even have chandeliers dangling from the ceiling and miniature television sets housed in the console. When he belongs to a lowrider club the driver places a bronze plaque of the club's name on the tray. The interior of his car is usually upholstered in crushed velvet. The total effect of a lowrider automobile is one of cool sensuality. The glittering exterior and plush interior conspire to create an image of voluptuous excess. But this is not the ostentation of the truly wealthy; it is instead the garish ostentation of an oppressed class. When the Lowrider decks his automobile out with such misplaced symbols of luxury as chandeliers and champagne glasses he overstates his case. His claim to wealth is really a denial, a mocking statement of a people dispossessed.

A lowrider car is a kinetic art form. But it is always an art form which obeys the constraints of the vernacular, so that when a young Chicano modifies his car and exercises his artistic and mechanical skills he simultaneously announces his personal tastes and the group to which he belongs. Owning a lowrider car allows him to declare his commitment to the values of the tribe and at the same time to express his personality. When his car is original and tastefully conceived he gains the respect of his peers; when it is flamboyant he also catches the attention and uninformed admiration of people on the street. A lowrider car is driven slowly so that its artistry can be shown off to full advantage and so that its occupants can see and be seen. The slow progress of a lowrider car through the streets is very reminiscent of a Mexican *paseo*, where young men and women walk slowly round the village square parading themselves, observing each other, flirting and making sure that they are noticed. When Chicano youths go out cruising they crawl through the boulevards, parading themselves and their cars. The luster of the paintwork, the high polish of the chrome and the stroboscopic glitter of the Tru-spokes – all these features draw attention to the occupants of the vehicle as they glide along, slumped in the tuck-and-roll, surveying the passing scene.

The Chicano's lowrider vehicle is more than simply a means of getting around the barrio and being noticed. It is also a lure for girls, a seduction pad on wheels, an investment, a focus for his energies, a topic of endless conversation, and a means of autonomy and escape. But most important of all, the car allows its driver to wear the badge of his people. It is to the present generation what the zoot-suit was to his father and uncle. It is his uniform, his means of distinguishing himself from Anglo

culture according to a set of rules which have been established
by his own society. Typically the Anglo drives a new model
which has been purchased from a showroom or a customized
street rod which has been jacked up in the back for speed. By
contrast the Lowrider acquires his car from a second-hand car
lot and then lowers it. The Chicano's car has none of the de-
personalized blandness of the production model; nor does it
possess the restlessness of the street rod with its backside in
the air. As a uniform, the Lowrider's car is the perfect antithesis
of the Gringo's.

The Lowriders, the Hot rodders, the bo-so-zuku and the
Raggare, have all existed on the fringes of society – the Lowriders because they are an ethnic minority, the Hot rodders
because they were working-class, and the bo-so-zuku and the
Raggare because they have failed to make it in the success
stakes. By adopting the automobile, members of these groups
have been able to acquire a sense of freedom and autonomy
which their working lives could never offer them. Each has
taken the car and fashioned it according to its own requirements, so that it has become a way of reasserting the group's
value and its separateness from the rest of society. For the bo-
so-zuku, the Raggare, and to some extent the Hot rodders, the
automobile has symbolized rejection of a society that would
not fully accept them. This, however, was never the case with
the custom car people, who, for the most part, operated within
and with the full acceptance of middle-class society. For the
teenagers who tinkered with custom cars, cars were simply a
part of growing up. The custom car cult, as it existed among
American teenagers, was therefore more in the nature of a
youthful interlude. It was dictated by the need to express oneself through the medium of the car, and by the need to show
that one accepted the values of one's peers. It was not condi-
tioned by any feelings of social rejection.

Hot rodders invariably abandoned their automotive uniform
when they graduated to better things. Today the same is true
of those bo-so-zuku and Raggare who find that they are too
old to tear around in fast cars. However, this has been less the
case with the custom car movement which is still enjoying a
great deal of popularity, and it has never been the case with
Lowriders. When the Lowrider gets married and has children

he usually becomes more conventional, but it is not uncommon to find him driving a lowrider car, even if it is no longer the one he constructed in his youth. Unlike the members of other automotive tribes, the Lowrider does not abandon his uniform at the first opportunity. In this respect, it is less a mark of his youthfulness than it is a symbol of his allegiance to a distinct ethnic minority.

Geographically the Lowriders, the Hot rodders, the bo-so-zuku and the Raggare are poles apart, but culturally they are extremely close. At first glance their shared obsession with automobiles appears to arise from a need for transport, but in reality it has a deeper psychological significance which stems from their need to assert themselves in the face of a society which has denied them a basis for self-esteem. The degree to which individuals value themselves has always depended on the extent to which they are valued by others. Those who are valued by society – the bankers, merchants and celebrities of this world – can always use automobiles to consolidate, and even to improve upon, the high regard in which they are held by others. Those who are not so valued, who have no social esteem to speak of, can only use automobiles to deny what they really are.

When individuals or groups of individuals find themselves rejected by the society of which they are a part, they can either respond by passively accepting the low estimation of their worth or by banding together to affirm a new and positive definition of themselves. But individuals who feel under-valued cannot simply go about protesting their true value. In order to convince others, not to mention themselves, they must provide some palpable demonstration, some symbol of their worth. Among the symbols that are available for defining one's value in society, none is more potent than the automobile. It is visible and mobile, and it is a currency which everybody understands.

The automobile has provided young people all over the world with a means of distinguishing themselves from the society of their parents. Recently, however, the car has also been adopted as the uniform of groups of adults who enjoy the camaraderie and sense of purpose that comes from owning the same make or the same type of vehicle. Although the custom-car craze had its roots in America it now has flourishing offshoots all over the world. Britain, for example, has several enthusiast magazines, and there are regular meetings where custom cars are exhibited, and where spare parts and stories are swapped.

The most famous of these meetings is the Chelsea Cruise which takes place along the Thames Embankment once a month, and which offers a glittering spectacle of souped up Morris Minors and padded wagons. The fans who congregate on these occasions are drawn together by their special affection for customizing and everything that this mobile art-form represents. An unreserved devotion to automobiles may also be found in the car clubs – such as the Rolls-Royce Enthusiasts Club, where the paintwork and chrome is as polished as the accents, or the Cheltenham and District Flying Dustbin club, where the din of revving 2CVs is matched only by the raucous conviviality of the car owners.

Because our society has given itself over to the automobile it is only natural that people should use cars to define themselves as individuals and as members of a group. Whether they band together to share their enthusiasm for a particular make or style of car is unimportant. What matters is the reassurance and sense of belonging that comes from wearing the same uniform.

6

FANTASY

WHEN people are asked to say what they look for in a car they usually talk in terms of factors such as economy, reliability, comfort and appearances. The received wisdom, certainly among contemporary market researchers, is that the choices people make about which cars to buy are organized according to some rational decision-making process. For some time now there has been a lurking suspicion that the answers people give when they are asked about their car preferences may be nothing more than their *theories* about how they perceive cars, and their responses may have very little to do with how they actually perceive cars, or with their real motives for choosing a particular model.

The notion that people's car choices may be governed by motives they cannot articulate came into prominence during the 1950s when the motor industry discovered 'motivational research'. This research was basically concerned with what is now called market segmentation. It set out to identify the distinct market segments in the population in terms of their needs and desires so that motor manufacturers would be able to produce models that satisfied the requirements of people in each segment. Motivational research was, however, also committed to the idea that people are not always able to say what their automotive needs are, and that it is therefore the task of the psychologist or the market analyst to identify what actually motivates different groups of people to purchase certain kinds of cars. Motivational research was founded on two premises: firstly that people fall into groups that can be characterized in terms of discrete automotive desires, and secondly that a large part of their desires is unconscious. While the first premise has fallen into disrepute, largely because it can be shown that the same people sometimes fall into different market segments, the notion of unconscious motivations still has a great deal to recommend it.

Unconscious Drives

The most striking illustration of the power of unconscious factors comes from a study that was conducted by Dr Stephen Black in London during the 1960s. Dr Black was a medical practitioner who also happened to be interested in cars and hypnosis. He combined these two interests by enlisting the assistance of people who were prepared to discuss their feelings about cars under hypnosis, but before he hypnotized them he put them through a series of questions about what cars meant to them. The answers that he elicited during this phase of the study were very much the kind of responses that are obtained during a routine market research interview. Most people said that they were satisfied with the design of cars, although they were critical of the quality of workmanship and the price they had to pay. When it came to the subject of road safety, the subjects reported that they were anxious about their personal safety, and they thought safety measures such as seat-belts were a good idea. After the interview Dr Black hypnotized each subject and repeated the process of asking what cars meant to him or her. He discovered that under hypnosis subjects appeared to hold an entirely different point of view. Now, instead of referring to danger on the roads as a source of personal anxiety, they spoke about the liberating sense of freedom that motoring brings and the feelings of exhilaration that comes from driving fast. While subjects had mentioned seat-belts as a good idea during their waking state, under hypnosis they dismissed such precautions as timid and unnecessary. One subject, a male medical student, said: 'I see myself driving fast on a warm day with the windows open. It is not a busy road, but busy enough to make the driving interesting . . . I have somebody with me to share the driving . . . It is a wonderful sense of freedom:

there is nothing between me and almost anything I really want
. . . I like to feel she admires me and the way I handle the car:
the sun, the sky and the road and that wonderful feeling of
power: it's the feeling of power I suppose.'

Also under hypnosis, another male student said: 'The pleasure comes from moving. I'm relaxed, but I'm moving. That's
the interesting thing: I have an impression of the world going
by, but I don't belong to it any more. I'm on a journey, outside
it all. I feel free . . . I'm driving fast and enjoying what this
means to me.' When asked what he meant by 'driving fast', he
explained: 'It's the power, a sense of superiority, a feeling of
being master of it all; it's a bit like sex really . . . you see you
have to be gentle too – and careful!' The most revealing comment came from a woman who, while in a waking state, had
been worried about the dangers of driving, but who dismissed
any such concern while in a hypnotic state: 'I can't pretend I
really mind it when I see a car accident. In a funny way it makes
a journey interesting. You pull out, try to pass and have to pull
back – you look such a fool when it happens. And then you
see some monumental pile up and the police and all that, but
it kind of justifies you for not having tried to make it after all.'

When hypnosis is applied to research on cars it provides a
startling picture, not only of people's dismissive attitudes toward the dangers of driving, but also of their secret dreams of
what a car should be. As part of his study, Dr Black asked his
subjects several questions about the 'ideal car' while they were
under hypnosis. Given an opportunity to express their concealed desires, they described fantasian vehicles that could go
anywhere and which were equipped with every imaginable
convenience. Their dream cars were fast, they could negotiate
any type of road, and some were even amphibious. According
to the subjects, an ideal car needed to be a status symbol and
it needed to offer the kind of amenities found in a luxury home,
but most important of all it needed to look like a car. For example, it should offer the comforts of a living room, the convenience of a kitchen, and the sumptuousness of a bedroom,
but it should not be a caravan or a van: it should remain a car.

The fascinating thing about the images of cars elicited under
hypnosis is that they bear no relation to the kinds of vehicles
that people encounter in their normal lives: they are the ideal-

ized constructions that people drive in their imagination rather than on the road. Although hypnosis uncovers images of cars that would be difficult, if not impossible to build, it provides a glimpse of the fantasy world of cars that people inhabit when their choices and preferences are not limited by the constraints imposed upon designers of real automobiles. The vehicles that we drive in our unconscious are not the cars that refuse to start in the morning or which collapse in the middle of rush-hour traffic. They are the cars that liberate us from our inadequacies and our daily cares – a means of spiriting us away from our worries and into a dream world where our secret desires are satisfied in fantasy.

The main purpose of fantasy is to satisfy our desires symbolically. All of us yearn for things we cannot achieve, either because we are not rich or attractive enough, or because what we want is either immoral or illegal. But achievements in the realm of make-believe are not limited by money and appearances, or by morality and the law. In the world of fantasy everything is possible.

The themes that most commonly appear in people's fantasies are those connected with power, success and sex – things most often denied to people, or which they would prefer to enjoy in some other form. As Freud put it, 'unsatisfied wishes are the driving power behind fantasies; every separate fantasy contains the fulfillment of a wish, and improves on unsatisfactory reality.' Because a smart car is seen as the justified reward for a successful career, it is the natural candidate for a fantasy symbol of success. But a smart car is much more than an end in itself; it is also a means to an end, where the end is either sex, greater success, or of course a sense of escape. The reason why automobiles figure so prominently in people's fantasies is that they are both a means and an end – they are a means of attaining those things to which most of us aspire, as well as a public demonstration that we have achieved them.

Broadly speaking, car fantasies can be divided into those which enable people to escape their present circumstances, and those which improve upon the car they are driving. Take the case of a young man who imagines himself in command of some racing monster while he is either sitting in class, gazing out of the window, or driving home from school in his battered van. The fantasy he creates while gazing out of the window owes nothing to his presence in class – in fact its purpose more often is to provide him with a means of escape from its drudgery. However, the fantasy he entertains while driving home does rely on the fact that he is driving, because it enables him to transform his clattering van into a vehicle which is closer to his heart's desire, and to imagine that he is the type of person who is usually associated with that kind of vehicle. The underlying motive for imagining oneself in a better car is so that one can pretend to be a different person from one's real self. The same is also true of car ownership in the real world. Because cars confer a social identity on their owners, someone who drives a smart or unusual car is usually taken to be the type of person who is identified with that kind of car, even if he is nothing of the sort. Owning a smart or distinctive car therefore provides an opportunity for two forms of pretence. On the one hand it enables the owner to pass himself off as a certain type of person, while on the other it enables him to persuade himself that he is that type of person, even if he is not. These two forms of affectation are nicely illustrated in Weesner's novel, *The Car Thief*, where the young hero, who spends his time playing truant and stealing cars, is described in the following way:

> In easy fantasies, imagining he was the owner of the car, he drove around the corners and fronts of the strange schools during their lunch hours, to let himself be seen . . . He intentionally parked his Chevrolet Bel Air or his Buick Riviera under their eyes. He was able to see himself in these moments as he imagined he was seen by them, as a figure from a movie, a stranger, some newcomer come to town, some new cock of the walk with a new car, with a plume of city hair.

The important point about cars is that they provide people with an opportunity to impress others, as well as themselves. In deciding whether or not to buy a particular model there are therefore two questions the prospective purchaser needs to consider – namely: how will he appear to others, and how will he feel about himself as the owner of that car? These two issues are not entirely unrelated, because the responses one evokes from other people by driving a particular car can have a direct bearing on how one feels about oneself. However, this need not necessarily be the case because it is always possible for the owner of an ordinary car to upgrade his self-concept, either through some form of selective perception or by resorting to fantasy. Instead of accepting the indifferent opinion other people have of his car, the owner can persuade himself that it possesses certain virtues which they have failed to recognize, which in turn may provide a basis for the way he views himself in relation to other people. Having decided that other people are incapable of appreciating the finer points of his car he may conclude, for example, that he is more knowledgeable and sensitive than they are, or that while they are prone to the whims of fashion, he is not.

The other strategy open to the owner of an ordinary car is to imagine himself as the owner of an automobile that is universally admired. In his mind's eye his clapped-out family estate may become the Rolls-Royce that has just glided past him on the freeway, or the red sports car he has seen in the showroom window. Alternatively he may envisage himself as being in command of a hotted-up street rod, with the music blaring and laughing girls piled in the back seat. The problem with such Walter Mitty excursions is that the dreamy satisfaction they provide only lasts as long as the fantasy. Nevertheless, these fantasies do allow the driver the imagined experience of being in a different kind of car, as well as the sensation of being a different person.

Of course the fantasies that most of us entertain about owning a special car are never likely to be fulfillled. But that does not concern us, nor does it deter us from living out our fantasies. As John Z. DeLorean remarked some years ago, 'buying a Pontiac is for most guys like thinking about making his neighbor's wife. He probably won't do it, but he thinks about it a lot.'

Dream Machines

Although fantasy can transform an ordinary vehicle into something special, there are occasions where it is unnecessary to exercise one's imagination, simply because the car itself guarantees a sufficient degree of unreality. This was especially the case in America during the 1950s, when the fantasy aspect of cars reached such baroque proportions that motorists were never quite sure whether they were seated in an automobile, a land-based dreamboat or an earth-bound aircraft. The chief architect of this confusion was Harley Earl. No single individual has ever had such a profound impact on the shape of man-made objects as Earl, and nobody since has been guilty of so many design excesses. During his thirty-two years at General Motors he was directly responsible for the design of 50 million vehicles, and indirectly responsible for the shape of millions of cars produced by Ford and Chrysler. By the time he retired his extravagant approach to automobile design had completely changed the face of America and the way Americans thought about themselves.

From the early days when he worked in his father's coach-works in Los Angeles, designing cars for movie stars, Earl had recognized the need for cars which incorporated the low, elegant lines of custom-made vehicles. When he arrived in Detroit most production line cars were box-shaped, with separate panels bent in a single plane or bolted together at harsh angles. Earl succeeded in changing all this. He lowered the car, widened it and gave it a long voluptuous appearance. He brought to the production line the techniques of the art studio and West Coast customizing, creating vehicles which were admired, not for their mechanical ingenuity and brass trim, but for their sleek silhouette and rounded contours.

When Earl designed the La Salle in 1927 the eye was treated to continuous lines and a unity of form in which the mud-guards, the driver compartment, the trunk and the running-boards were molded together to create a single harmonious design. Earl also began to experiment with glass and paints. He introduced wraparound windshields and electrically oper-ated windows. He dressed his cars in giddy combinations of colors, and lavished them with swathes of chrome. By the time he had finished the American car was no longer a dowdy box on wheels – it was the glittering stuff of dreams. While many of Earl's contributions to automobile design were practical and elegant, as many were gratuitous and tasteless. The most gra-tuitously tasteless was undoubtedly the tail-fin. During the war

Earl was invited to an Air Force base to view some fighter planes. One was the new Lockheed P-38, a top secret pursuit plane which boasted radical streamlining, a bullet-shaped nozzle, twin fuselages and twin tail-fins. Airplanes had always held a special fascination for Earl, but when he saw the P-38 he was completely taken aback by its exquisite lines; and even though he was allowed to approach no closer than thirty feet, he was able to take in most of the plane's details. After the war Detroit stopped producing jeeps and trucks, and started tooling up again for automobiles. Earl dusted off his notes and recollections of the P-38 and produced the design for the 1949 Cadillac. When it was unveiled it sported two modest tail-fins which rose above the fenders and housed the tail-lights.

This marked the beginning of the car's attempt to masquerade as a fighter plane. It was followed by the appearance of fins on the cars of the other General Motors divisions, as well as those of Chrysler and Ford. By 1956 tail-fins were on Buicks, Studebakers and Hudsons and Chrysler had welded them on to their Dodge, Chrysler and Plymouth models. Ford followed suit the next year. By 1959 all the major motor manufacturers had clambered on to the back of the tail-fin bandwagon, and virtually every car boasted a pair of shark-like protuberances. In this year fins were larger and more grotesque than ever before. Most were tall and upright – Cadillac, for example, had fins that rose full three and a half feet above the ground – but some, like the cantilevered scythes which adorned the '59 Chevrolet, were almost horizontal.

The Soviet Premier, Nikita Khrushchev, was visiting the United States in 1959, and on passing a Cadillac he pointed to one of the fins and asked, 'What does that thing do?' The answer to this mocking inquiry was that fins did nothing: they were simply a decoration designed to make the car look expensive. However, the fact that fins had no practical function did not deter the car advertisers from inventing implausible justifications for the yards of extra metal that they had bolted on to their wares. A De Soto advertisement, for example, informed the public that 'Sweeping finned lines . . . aren't just for looks', while Plymouth declared that 'True aerodynamic styling not only sets the pace for design but also makes a real contribution to your car's driving stability on the highway.'

No sooner had the automobile sprouted fins, than it began to develop other appurtenances of airborne travel. First came the wraparound windshield and the flight-deck control panel with its gratuitous switches and dials to persuade the driver that he was really a pilot. Then chrome rudders were fitted to bumpers. Fake gun-ports and exhaust scoops were set into the panels, and, to cap it all, the tail-lights were modified to look like flaming rocket exhausts – presumably to persuade the driver behind that he was following a fighter plane rather than a car.

By borrowing these motifs from fighter planes and liberally applying them to the automobile, designers were able to upgrade the cultural importance of cars and to offer the driver a sense of adventure that he had never experienced before. In the process they were also able to equip him with a set of tangible props with which he could more readily embark on a fantasy of modernity and escape. Now the driver could sit in his personal cockpit, surrounded by the symbols of the jet age, and imagine himself screeching through the sky. Everything around him, the knobs, the dials, the molded windshield, conspired to create the perfect conditions for an exercise in make-believe.

Normally the integrity of the fighter plane idiom would have been sufficient to transform the automobile from a vehicle of transportation into one of fantasy. But the designers of the 1950s were not content to stop there. On top of the basic fighter plane motif they grafted other images. They fitted the grille with rows of chromium dentures, bolted phallic ornaments to the hood, and added enormous breast-shaped protrusions – 'Dagmars' as they were affectionately called – to the bumpers. By the late 1950s the American automobile was awash with strange and sometimes contradictory symbols. Some, like the snarling physiognomy of the grille, were clearly intended as a subliminal form of threat display, while others, like the sensuous moldings attached to the bumpers, were patently erotic. However, in spite of this confusion the basic underlying theme of the automobile was that of airborne travel. The average American was now in command of an aircraft on wheels.

In 1957, just at the height of the car-as-fighter-plane extravaganza, Americans woke up to discover that Russia had placed the first *Sputnik* into orbit around the earth. The news caused a great deal of consternation. It led to a frenzy of activity at Cape Canaveral and, a few years later, to Kennedy's famous pledge to place a man on the moon before the end of the decade. The advent of the Space Age also had another important effect, which was to draw people's attention toward the skies and the dark spaces beyond. The recognition that space flight was now a real possibility instilled a new awareness, which in turn reinforced the public's acceptance of rocket imagery on cars. Although the average American still had no clear picture of what spacecraft would eventually look like, he did know that they were likely to evolve from those high altitude planes that the Air Force were testing over the desert, and he could therefore take comfort in the knowledge that the fins and flaming exhausts which adorned his automobile were on the right side of history. With the world poised on the edge of the Age of Intergalactic Discovery, he had additional reason to imagine himself in the role of Buck Rogers.

Selling Illusions

It is a cardinal principle of human nature that people are only content when they are able to exercise some control, or at least an illusion of control, over their own destiny. This explains why astronauts still 'fly' the space shuttle in an age when computers are better pilots than men, why psychologists are constantly dealing with depressed patients who feel that they have lost control of their lives, and why the car-as-fighter-plane motif was so successful.

After the Second World War refinements in technology were once again applied to the automobile which improved dramatically in its performance. Innovations like electrically operated windows, power steering and automatic gear change appeared on the latest prototypes and, soon afterwards, on the showroom cars themselves. The fact that this automatization and the automobile's transformation into a fighter plane took place at about the same time was no coincidence, because just as the motor industry was stealing control of the car from the driver with automatic transmission and power-assisted steering, it was giving it back to him symbolically with false gun-ports, rocket exhausts and fins – with the latest images of air-borne fantasy.

Nowhere was this symbolic compensation more evident than in the immediate view confronting the driver. Now, instead of facing a bland dashboard with a few pathetic dials and knobs, he was treated to a simulated vision of the cockpit. As Reyner Banham, the design historian, points out, 'the dash-board created an illusion of control – or if not control then the illusion that the driver was being informed of the state of the running machinery. But cars were getting to the point where the driver had less control over its basic functions, but still the illusion had to be fostered that *the driver is in control.*' Equally successful at creating an illusion of control was the wraparound windshield: '. . . that big piece of glass may be the most important symbol of the space-race, far more important than the seats, far more than all the controls and things, because in a whole set of movies like *Strategic Air Command* and *Conquest of Space* people had been thoroughly accustomed to views of the pilots under their perspex canopies, man with transparent material wrapped around him'.

If the first part of Earl's success lay in his ability to substitute an illusion of control for actual control, the second lay in his sheer talent for showmanship. In 1952 Earl organized the first in a series of Motoramas where he presented the public with General Motors' cars of the future. These 'show cars' or 'dream cars', as they were called, were intended to whet people's appetites for the products of General Motors, and to gauge their responses to design features which were on the drawing board. Many of the features unveiled at the Motoramas did appear on later models. Others, however, were so impractical and bizarre that there was no way they could ever reach production. One of the most bizarre dream cars to appear at a Motorama was Firebird III, which was the culmination in a series of extravagant creations that Earl had modelled on another fighter plane, the Douglas A4 Skyray. But for the unfortunate fact that it possessed a wheel at each corner, Firebird III was virtually identical to a jet fighter. The grille – or rather the air-intake – was low, long and narrow, exactly the kind of nose one would expect to find on the offspring of an illicit union between a jet fighter and a Cadillac. Instead of being accommodated together, the driver and his solitary passenger were housed under separate perspex bubbles, and to complete the impression of other-worldliness the vehicle was provided with no fewer than three upright tail-fins and four vestigial wings!

Dream cars like Firebird III were never meant to fly, nor for that matter were they ever intended for the road. Their sole purpose was to indulge all those car-crazy fans who milled about the Motorama exhibits, dreaming of the day when they too would take command of a freeway starship. In a moment of revealing candor, Earl once confessed that the two major influences on him had been Cecil B. DeMille and Al Jolson – from the former he claimed to have learned the art of theatrical extravagance, and from the latter the ability to judge one's audience. Earl certainly learned his lessons well because half a million people visited the Motorama each year, and for every person who feasted his eyes on the glittering cornucopia of automotive dreams, there were several more who took them-selves off to the showroom to buy the products of General Motors.

American automobiles of the 1950s reflected the vanity of the era, and they showed how it was possible to manufacture and sell cars in which function was totally subservient to ap-pearance. True, automobiles of the period did boast more pow-erful engines, but most of the extra horsepower was needed to shift the two-ton monsters and to haul the decorative metal and slathers of chrome around.

The auto business of the 1950s was notorious for its crooked dealing. The lack of attention that Detroit paid to matters of safety was matched only by the public's boredom with the subject. For example, a survey of drivers conducted during the 1950s showed that while one-third of the sample were prepared to pay extra for a seat-belt, only one-fifth were willing to pay extra for a collapsible steering wheel. By contrast, however, half the sample were prepared to pay extra for a radio or for air conditioning. The Machiavellianism of the car manufacturers also revealed itself in the unscrupulous schemes they intro-duced in order to create a vassalage of compliant car dealers. The dealers in turn used every type of sales trick to outwit the public which was eager to acquire the fatuous symbols on offer. As the critic John Keats saw it, the automobiles were 'over-

blown, overpriced monstrosities built by oafs to sell to mental
defectives'. The other members of this rogues' gallery were of
course the advertisers, whose task it was to spin a web of
suggestive associations between the product and some aspect
of the good life.

The rise in the importance of advertising was due to the fact
that there was more money in circulation, and models had
started to become indistinguishable from each other. As an
economy measure, different divisions within the same corporation had started to produce different models using the same
chassis, engines and sheet metal. This had the effect of creating
a situation where the manufacturers were producing models
which were basically the same, and which therefore needed to
be presented as distinct. In order to disguise the basic similarity
of their models – in other words, to distinguish Fords from
Lincolns, and Chevrolets from Cadillacs – the manufacturers
tried to give each a distinct appearance. Each model was given
its own shape, as well as its own exterior trim and interior
appointments, and of course the more there was on offer by
way of superficial embellishment, the more the customer was
expected to pay. Finally, in order to lure wealthy customers
into buying an expensive model that was basically the same
car as one which cost far less, the manufacturers resorted to
advertising. Now, more than ever before, advertising became
a form of psychological warfare, waged by the motor industry
against the public. The purpose of advertising was no longer
to espouse a car's mechanical virtues or to endow it with class
associations, but to create a collective sense of unease. Detroit
was no longer selling personal transportation. Instead it was
in the business of purveying images and dreams. It therefore
bombarded people with messages that were designed to create
a feeling of dissatisfaction by persuading them that their current
model was out of date. In many cases the new model on offer
was not mechanically more advanced than last year's – it simply
possessed superficial styling features which marked it off from
last year's model and created the impression that its owner was
able to keep up with the latest in automobile fashion.

Advertisements of the time tried to suggest that by buying
a particular model one would automatically enhance one's social standing, expand one's social horizons, impress the neigh-

bors, and acquire a new sense of adventure – in short one would become a new and better person. At its very heart therefore, advertising presented automobiles as a social palliative: cars were a form of psychotherapy. Nowhere was this more evident than in a television commercial which urged the prospective owner to 'drive it like you hate it . . . it's cheaper than psychiatry'.

Writing at the time, John Keats noted that automobiles were 'not marketed as reliable machines for reasonable men to use, but as illusory symbols of sex, speed, wealth, and power for daydreaming nitwits to buy'. Certainly, if the people who composed the advertising copy were trying to sell cars as a means of transportation, it was difficult to see how, because in almost every way possible cars were represented as forms of escape and vehicles of fantasy. Advertising copy suffered from an epidemic of dreamy atmospherics, aggressive hardsells and hyperbole which had little to do with the car's ostensible purpose as a means of personal transportation, and a great deal to do with its purpose as a means of personal expression. A classic example of this was the 1956 advertisement for the Cadillac Eldorado Brougham which promised its owner 'anti-dive control, a power train, outriggers, pillarless styling, projectile-shaped gull-wing bumpers, outboard exhaust ports, fully magnetized gold-finish drinking cups . . . an antenna which automatically rises to urban height [and a] sound wave opening for the horn.' John Keats identified the underlying messages of this advertisement as follows:

> . . . Cadillac's description of itself is not meant to be taken literally. Instead, it is designed to create the impression that the Eldorado is not an automobile at all. It is a graceful carriage from Lord Brougham's own carriage house. Your attention is directed to the dreams of Spanish conquistadores. You are asked to think of the thundering power of the Twentieth Century Limited, of Hawaiians skimming past sunny islands in outrigger canoes, of the intimacy of milady's boudoir, of sixteen-inch naval shells, of gulls soaring, and – apparently – bumping into each other. You are asked to don a white suit to enter a laboratory to measure sound waves with your fellow-physicists . . . In cases like

the Eldorado one is not dealing with matters of practicality. In fact what sells cars like these is styling . . . The point is we cannot compare the practical function of a machine with dreams – we must wonder instead whether cars like this are functional *as an inducer of dreams*. People who want to buy cars like the Cadillac Eldorado do not necessarily want to buy an automobile. What they want is a combination of illusions.

The use of fantasy and exaggeration in car advertisements continued into the 1960s, until, in Emma Rothschild's words, cars were sold 'with the frivolous extravagance of detergents or deodorants'. By the 1960s the advertising agencies had developed a whole armory of crafty visual tricks. Photographers were snapping cars against backgrounds of the same color so as to round off their edges, and they were deliberately posing small men and women in and around cars so that they would appear larger than they really were. Another trick was to depict the person behind the wheel slightly out of focus, or in the shade, so that the viewer would be more likely to project him or herself into the driver's seat. Here the message was, 'This could be you!'

During the mid-1960s the children of the post-war baby boom, now teenagers, began to enter the automobile market. Millions of youngsters were acquiring their driving licenses, they had money to spend, and they were looking for fast cars. In 1963 General Motors ushered in the age of the muscle car with the Pontiac GTO, a vehicle with more brawn than brains. To some extent the same was also true of the youngsters who bought these cars – or at least that appeared to be the assumption behind Detroit's thinking, because advertisements began to deal with aggressive themes that were more a part of the football field and *Animal House* than the suburban preoccupations of the intelligentsia. An advertisement which appeared in *Life* magazine, for example, compared the Buick Skylark to 'a howitzer with windshield wipers . . . which is almost like having your own personal-type nuclear deterrent'.

Many of the advertisements of the time began to reflect the folksy inanity and inarticulacy made popular by pop singers. The copy for the Plymouth Hemi offered the following downbeat advice: 'Ask our engineers what makes a Hemipowered anything the one to beat, and they'll probably give you a lot of talk about volumetric efficiency, heat dissipation, flame travel, gas flow and that sort of technical stuff. Don't believe it. You can't make an engine like the Hemi with figures and formulas alone . . . It's gotta be voodoo, baby!'

Advertisements for muscle cars were also full of post-pubertal clichés. An advertisement for the Plymouth GTX told the prospective owner that 'as the member of an elite group, you crave the finer things in life. You know, the beach in spring. The Strip. Miniskirts. Neat cars. Blood rare steaks. Things like that. Well we have good news for you. The Boss is back. Bossier than ever.' Sex, inevitably raised its head, as in the case of the Chrysler advertisement which depicted a girl leaning up against a Dodge Charger, suggestively raising the hem of her skirt and saying, 'Mother warned me . . . that there would be men like you driving cars like that. Do you really think you can get to me with that long, low, tough machine you just rolled up in?'

Although the 1960s introduced a revolution in sexual mores, it was not until some years later that the full potential of sex was exploited, both as a means of grabbing and holding the reader's attention, and as a device for imbuing the car with a sense of excitement. Few advertisements can match the suggestive *double entendre* of the Peugeot advertisement which appeared in *Playboy*, where the reader was asked, 'Do you leap into life first thing in the morning? . . . Take a large boot size? Have a silken feel and a pleasing exterior? . . . Does your mechanism respond to the faintest touch of a feminine hand?'

Over the past few decades car advertising has advanced tremendously in terms of its technical refinements. Its thematic concerns have also changed. Gone, for example, are the days when cars were represented as muscular monsters, as aspiring aircraft or as land-yachts moored to palatial mansions. Instead, today's advertisements are far more down-to-earth, almost matter-of-fact. That, at any rate, is the first impression that one gets when flipping through the magazines or watching television. But closer inspection of car advertising of the last decade shows it to be as fantasy-laden as it ever was. It may be more muted in its claims and more jokey in its tone, but it is still in the business of marketing illusions. Nowhere has this been more evident than in the 'Live the dream' advertisement for DeLorean's gull-wing sports car, which presented a low-angle shot of the car in the clouds, and a text which ran: 'Your eyes skim the sleek, sensuous stainless steel body, and all your senses tell you, "I've got to have it" . . . of course, everyone stares as you drive by. Sure, they're a little envious. That's expected. After all, you're the one Living the Dream.'

Even Volkswagen's highly successful series, which made a virtue of the Beetle's ugly-duckling appearance with disarming quips like 'Ugly is only skin deep' and 'Even the bottom of a Volkswagen looks funny', could not resist the temptation to further the legend of the car's reliability, which it did by showing Beetles braving the elements and floating on the sea. The most famous Beetle advertisement was the one which showed a Beetle driving through a snow storm, and which asked 'Have you ever wondered how the man who drives the snowplow drives to the snowplow?' This was an important advertisement because it set the stage for a new vogue in advertising, where cars were commended, not simply for their social cachet, but for their durability, and in some cases their indestructibility.

Advertisements began to allude to the tough side of cars by dropping them from great heights or by showing them in inhospitable settings. Television viewers were treated to scenes of Volkswagens bouncing off the studio floor, Fiats being driven over waterfalls, and MGs being tossed out of the back of planes with parachutes. Part of the attraction of these scenes lay in their sheer eye-catching quality, but their main purpose was to show that these cars could go anywhere and do virtually anything. Of course nobody really believed that a car could ride the rapids or endure a parachute landing. But the mere sight of a car performing one of these super-automotive feats was thought to be sufficient to persuade the public that it was indestructible.

Models And Metaphors

Every automobile age has its own set of assumptions about what persuades people to buy cars. If the 1920s and 1930s were the age of nuts-and-bolts advertising and appeals to snobbery, and the 1950s the age of the wet-dream sell, then the advertising age that we have just entered is one in which advertisements exalt cars for their efficiency and technical reliability. The reason why contemporary car advertisements make so much of these qualities is that they also happen to form the basis of the popular image of computers. If there is one thing which has changed our lives more than the car it is the computer. The arrival of the car completely revolutionized travel, so that distances which had once taken weeks on horseback or foot could now be covered by the motorist in a day. In a similar way the computer has revolutionized our ability to process large amounts of information and to make rapid decisions, so that calculations which once took a lifetime can now be completed in a matter of seconds. Although the car and the computer have changed our lives in quite different ways, they share the fact that they are both extensions of ourselves – the car provides us with a more powerful pair of legs, while the computer extends our central nervous system.

Given the enormous efficiency of computers it was only natural that, as soon as they became small enough, they would be included in automobiles. Several makes of cars already have their own on-board computers, and it is now only a matter of time before every car is controlled by a super-efficient electronic system which monitors the car's environment and regulates its engine, ventilation, pitch and camber. In fact it is likely that in the very near future computers will control every mechanical function of the car, short of its speed and direction, which will have to remain in the driver's control if he is not to become totally redundant. Already this shift toward the computerization of cars can be heard in the form of synthesized voices which gently remind the driver to fasten the seat-belt. Dashboards now bristle with diodes and warning lights, little electronic messengers which keep the driver informed about the machinery, and even the water level in the windshield reservoir. The facia that confronts the motorist is no longer a symbol of the mechanical, but of the computer age. It encapsulates the visual language and the fantasies of the new technology and tells the driver that the car is on the cutting edge of science.

The seeming intelligence and logicality of computers recommends them for inclusion in automobiles, and it is these same qualities which also make the computer the perfect metaphor for the cultural elevation of the car. The current metaphor of the car as an artefact of the computer age can be seen in the way cars have begun to appear in advertisements. They are now depicted in the pristine, business-like colors of computers, and the accompanying copy frequently contains the kind of technobabble that one would normally expect to find in a computer manual.

The marriage between cars and computers is of course a complex one, not only because cars have assimilated computers, but because computers now play an important role in the design of cars and, with the assistance of robots, in their production. As robots improve, their collaboration with computers is likely to affect our perception of the car, and the image that we now have of the car as a computer-on-wheels will probably give way to a cultural definition of the car as a motorized robot. The Fiat advertisement which showed cars being built by robots to the strains of Rossini's *Barber of Seville* managed to persuade us that robots can happily work to music, but it also foreshadowed the day when the descendants of these uncomplaining workers would help to drive the car. As robots become smaller and more dextrous and they find a place under the hood, we may very well begin to see them as creatures who keep the car moving, as friendly homunculi who diagnose and solve problems which in former times were rectified by greasy mechanics. It is more likely, however, that the robotization of the car will give rise to a new relationship between the driver and his automobile, one in which he is able to confer directly with the car, and where he perceives the car as having an integrated personality all of its own.

In a sense we have already accepted this possibility, if not in fact then at least in fantasy. For example, in the television series, *Knight Rider*, the hero's automobile is able to sense the presence of villains, leap over buildings, drive through solid walls, and perform various other feats of daring. It is also capable of holding a reasonable conversation with the driver, and, when he is not around, of driving itself – which naturally makes one wonder what the driver's role is anyway. Leaving that aside, the interesting thing about *Knight Rider* is the way it imputes to an automobile those qualities which we normally reserve for the likes of Superman. In the old days fictional cars like the Batmobile were simply a glamorized auxiliary to the hero's defense of the law. But today's fantasy car is no longer cast in a supporting role, because with films like *Knight Rider* we have at last admitted, if only in the realm of make believe, that car and driver can work together as equals, and, in those instances where the driver is temporarily incapacitated, that the car is perfectly capable of taking over the role of its human partner.

Throughout its history, the automobile has modelled itself on other objects. It began, uncertainly, by pretending to be a horseless carriage, and at various times since then it has adopted the imagery of boats, fighter planes and now computers. During each phase of its evolution the car has therefore been able to appropriate some of the romance and glamour attached to objects higher up on the cultural scale of values. Not surprisingly, the automobile has also lent some of its glamour to objects lower down on the cultural scale. This happened during the 1930s, for example, when such household appliances as refrigerators began to assume the smooth, rounded appearance of aerodynamic vehicles like Buckminster Fuller's Dymaxion and Carl Breer's Chrysler Airflow. Neither of these cars in fact managed to capture the public's imagination, although many of the objects which these and other aerodynamic cars inspired did.

A more recent, and rather unexpected, case of image borrowing occurs in the film *Star Wars*, where the hero, Luke Skywalker, appears as a kind of interstellar hot rodder, and his rough companion, Han Solo, as a moonbeam trucker. The fact that *Star Wars* leaned so heavily on cars for its imagery was no coincidence, because George Lucas, who created the film, was also responsible for that epic of automotive nostalgia, *American Graffiti*. As a general rule, however, automobiles have been modelled on objects which earn greater respect than the car, rather than the reverse. The major, if not the sole purpose of the mimicry has been to give the car an illusive character, to deny its ostensible function as a means of transportation and thereby to make it more than it would otherwise be.

Fantasies On Wheels

The main purpose of corporate styling is to imbue the production car with an element of fantasy, whereas the sole purpose of present-day customizing is to create vehicles which are totally fantasian. Ever since cars began to roll out of the factory gate there have been customers who were less than satisfied with what was on offer. In the days of the coachbuilders a prospective owner could always give substance to his tastes by selecting a particular body, a certain color and special accoutrements for his car. But with the advent of the assembly line and the disappearance of the great coachbuilders, the opportunities for self-expression and personal fantasy were greatly diminished. At first the new owners remedied the situation with simple embellishments. They would apply an unusual coat of paint or fit special accessories to their cars to make them look different, and in some cases to give them a sense of unreality. But it was only with the birth of the customizing movement on the west coast of America that cars were transformed from stock models into wholesale vehicles of fantasy. Many of the auto artists responsible for this development – George Barris, Ed Roth, Gene Winfield and Dean Jeffries – are still creating automotive dreams.

George Barris is known as the 'King of Kustomizers'. Even if he didn't take a leaf out of Napoleon's book and crown himself, this is certainly the kind of appellation that George enjoys. If you visit him at Barris Kustom Industries in North Hollywood he will probably hand you a flysheet about himself which begins with the question, 'Which came first, customizing or George Barris?' This is not the motor world's version of the chicken-and-egg problem. It is just George talking the language of his clients.

When George arrived in Los Angeles in the 1940s hot rodding was all the rage and the big thing was illegal street racing. About that time, however, the mood started to swing toward more elegant and attractive cars, so when George and his brother Sam opened up their studio in Lynwood in 1945 they already had a market. Very soon they had developed their own style of customizing which consisted of fade-away fenders, frenched headlights and the chopped-top.

George Barris now caters for the fantasy needs of Hollywood, customizing cars for the stars, and building them from scratch. His office contains the trophies of the world's most successful customizer. The walls are festooned with testimonials of his fame and the shelves are filled with scale model kits of some of his more imaginative creations, like the *Batmobile*, the *Munster Koach* and the *Beverly Hillbillies' Hot-rod*. In the adjoining room the files of his famous clients are stacked right up to the ceiling. The names on the files read like a guest list at a Hollywood reunion: Elvis Presley, Frank Sinatra, Sammy Davis Jr, Dean Martin, Jayne Mansfield, Clint Eastwood, Ursula Andress, Ringo Starr, James Dean, Herb Alpert, Trini Lopez, Liberace, Sonny and Cher.

Most of the people with whom George Barris deals are larger than life, and their automobiles need to reflect this fact. His task has therefore been to design cars which draw attention to his famous customers, and to provide them with a means of transportation which is as unreal as the lives they lead.

In most countries celebrities are permitted a certain degree of excess, but the displays of ostentation which are merely tolerated in other parts of the world are positively encouraged in Los Angeles. Here, to be famous, you have to be noticed, and one certain way of being noticed is to drive a distinctive car. But in Los Angeles it is not easy to drive a conspicuous car because virtually every car is conspicuous. It is a bit like being a peacock in a paintshop. You might pride yourself on your gleaming Cadillac or your racy Porsche, but the moment you turn into Wilshire Boulevard you are likely to find a hundred cars more flashy than your own. Here the streets are a permanent *Concours d'élégance*, and the automobiles offer such a carnival of shapes and colors, such a celebration of diversity, that only the most unusual cars ever get noticed. Philip Marlowe, the great Los Angeles detective, recognized this when he observed that 'In L.A. to be conspicuous you would have to drive a flesh-pink Mercedes Benz with a sunporch on the roof and three pretty girls sunbathing.'

So far George Barris hasn't welded any sun-porches on to

his customers' cars, but he's come very close. The Cadillac
Eldorado he customized for Liberace was fairly tame by most
standards – until, that is, you inspected the interior. The seats
incorporated a piano keyboard motif and the musical score from
Liberace's famous theme-song, 'I'll be seeing you'. The hood
ornament on the car was a miniature candelabra – a reference
to the one which sits on top of the grand piano during his
performances. The Cadillac limousine that Barris customized
for Elvis was even more extravagant. It was painted with gold
murano pearl. The hub-caps were gold-plated, and so was the
grille. When Elvis sat in the back seat he must have thought
he had the Midas touch, because wherever he turned there was
gold. The entertainment console was finished with gold friezes
and gold plating, and as if the auric theme hadn't been given
enough attention, the interior was decorated with gold biscuit
tufts and gold buttons, and the windows were covered with
gold frieze, lamé curtains. To cap it all the center seat had a
pull-down section with a gold telephone.

While George and Sam Barris were fashioning automotive
dreams, other artists were also at work with their welding-
torches and body-hammers. Many were little more than copy-
ists – the number-painters of the game – but a few succeeded
in introducing a totally unique vision into the new movement.
In the early 1960s, when the show car phenomenon burst on
to the American scene, thousands of people were introduced
to the car as a totally fantasian art object. They saw Joe Flowers
win the first Autorama competition with his *Venus*, an immac-
ulately customized 1956 Chevy which looked like a teenage
dream machine. They also saw early feature cars like Ed Roth's
Beatnik Bandit, Bill Cushenberry's *El Matador* and Andy Didia's
Bobby Darin Dream Car. These early pieces were as wild as their
titles, and in some cases as extravagant as the names of the
people who had built them. The *Beatnik Bandit*, for example,
dispensed with a supported roof and introduced a plexiglass
dome in its stead; and the *Bobby Darin Dream Car* offered a
swooping celebration of glass, candy red and chrome. These
and the cars which later appeared at the shows were pure
fantasy – not those scratched, oily and unreliable objects of the
real world. At the shows they were cordoned off from the public

with tape – just like the exhibits in an art gallery – and, as if to emphasize their other-worldliness, they were supported on clouds of cotton wool or angel hair.

The separation between customizers who simply wanted an unusual car that they could drive around and customizers who produced exhibits for the shows was not unlike the evolutionary process that takes place in the natural world, especially those cases where birds lose their capacity for flight and end up hopping along the ground. For example, in Madagascar, Mauritius and the Galapagos Islands there are species of birds whose ancestors once winged through the air but who themselves are confined to a terrestrial existence. This is exactly what happened to exhibition cars. As they became more flashy and over-decorated, they effectively lost their capacity for locomotion. True, many of them boasted powerful engines, but for all the gas that these motors consumed they might as well have been fashioned from silver paper. In fact the process went further because many of the cars did not even have proper engines. They sported carburetors and superchargers, but there was often nothing inside the engine – no pistons, no crankshaft, nothing to make the car go. Exhibition cars were not paraded through the streets. Instead most of them were stored in hermetically sealed garages, and when the occasion demanded they were loaded into covered trailers and escorted across the country to exhibition halls where they were wheeled out and pushed into position by hand.

Just as the search for speed had led from hot rods, which were used for all kinds of purposes, to dragsters which were only good for sprinting down a straight quarter-mile track, so too the pursuit of elegance had led from the early customized cars, which got around town and looked smart, to exhibition cars which were purely sculptural. As Tom Wolfe points out in his famous essay, 'The Kandy-Kolored Tangerine-Flake Streamline Baby', the streamlined appearance of customized exhibition cars is totally expressive. Aerodynamic contours are an essential feature of airplanes, but in cars they are not functional unless, as he puts it, 'you're making the Bonneville speed run'. The other point which Wolfe makes is that exhibition cars are not really cars, in the sense that they are not meant to be driven round the streets. But these showy creations are not necessarily impotent. 'They'll run, if it comes to that – they're full of big, powerful, hopped-up chrome-plated motors, because all that speed and power, and all that lovely apparatus, has tremendous emotional meaning to everybody in customizing. But it's like one of these Picasso or Miró rugs. You don't walk on the damn things. You hang them on the wall.'

Over the years the car shows have presented a fantastic array of cars – cars like Gene Winfield's *Jade Idol*, which introduced the technique of fade-away paint, and Bill Cushenberry's *Silhouette*, which looked as though it was breaking every speed limit even when it was standing still.

Alongside these serious creations, the custom car competitions have also seen various whimsical entries, such as Carl Casper's *Telephone Booth*, an upright telephone booth powered by an injected Chrysler engine, and George Barris's *Bathtub*, which is a mobile washroom, replete with marble tub, gilded taps and a toilet for the driver's seat. But the prize for the most bizarre folly must surely go to Steve Tansy's *Pool Hustler*, a full-sized pool table which can be driven around and played on when stationary.

In their attempts to outdo each other, the show car customizers have been forced to produce ever more original objects. This has led to a wild escalation of shapes and forms, some of which are so peculiar that they no longer bear any relationship to cars as we know them. This same process has also led to spectacular achievements in the design and execution of serious show cars, to tasteful combinations of automotive motifs and to new developments in paint, trim and upholstery. Today millions of people are involved in car-related pastimes, and this is reflected in the vast numbers of automobile buffs who visit custom car shows every year. For some it provides a chance to gawp at the scantily clad ladies who drape themselves in and around the exhibits and who talk about cars in the suggestive innuendos of the massage parlor. For many, however, it is simply an opportunity to escape into a fantasy world of cars.

Fantasy is also central to the image of the people involved in the custom car movement. Although this car subculture has attracted a fair amount of media attention, it has never been fully accepted by mainstream society and, like so many other fringe movements, it has attracted various myths and rumors about the people who build and paint custom cars. During the 1960s there were several fanciful stories in circulation about Ed 'Big Daddy' Roth and his legendary assistant, Dirty Doug. One of the rumors was that Roth had joined the Hells Angels, which was not true, because all that Roth had done was take a job as a sign painter at Knott's Berry Farm in Buena Park. Roth's reputation for eccentricity was probably helped along by his maverick antics, his weirdo T-shirt business, and his habit of appearing at the car shows in full tails and top hat. It could also have had something to do with the fact that he was an accomplished pinstriper.

Pinstripers are artists who paint ultra-fine lines on cars. Usually the lines extend along the side of the car, but they are also applied to the hood, trunk, roof supports, mudguards – in fact anywhere where they might enhance the car's lines or serve as an esoteric embellishment for the benefit of other car freaks. Pinstriping requires the manual dexterity of the miniaturist and the concentration of the calligrapher. Because it involves the most exacting of the painterly skills, pinstripers are held in great awe. They are regarded as true wizards of the customizing business, and, like blacksmiths in primitive societies, they are often surrounded with an aura of mystery.

The most famous, and certainly the most mysterious pinstriper is Von Dutch, whose real name is Kenny Holland. It is said that he came to be known by his present name because he went around telling people that he was an escaped German U-boat commander, von Deutsch. This got distorted to Von Dutch and the name has stuck ever since. Von Dutch is largely responsible for the current vogue in pinstriping. In the 1920s and early 1930s it was common practice for pinstriping to be applied to one-off custom cars. This practice was picked up by the early motor manufacturers, who also treated their models to a standard stripe or two. By the 1940s pinstriping had virtually disappeared altogether. But in the early 1950s, with the upsurge of interest in customizing, people started to look around for ways of personalizing their cars, and it was to artists like Von Dutch that they turned.

In his heyday Von Dutch was regarded as the high priest, the most elevated artificer in the cult of pinstriping. He produced the most inspired striped webbing and flying eyeballs.

Nowadays Von Dutch is no longer in the car scene, preferring to busy himself elsewhere, but the tales of his legendary accomplishments and his crazy antics are still doing the rounds. The apocrypha surrounding him now forms a standard part of any discussion about pinstriping, and whenever two or three customizers are gathered together they invariably end up swapping tales about Von Dutch – like the story about the time he covered some poor customer's entire car with stripes, or the one about the Fire Department in Arizona that brought its fire engine to him for some discreet, classical striping and had it returned with red flames painted all over its sides. As with all urban myths, the escapades of Von Dutch have become more extravagant with each new telling. Von Dutch is not entirely without blame for these stories because he deliberately courted attention – such as the time he appeared at the Motorama car show, playing a flute, with a false eyeball glued to his forehead and paint-brushes sticking out of his ears. In the late 1950s Von Dutch disappeared completely, and his whereabouts remained a source of endless speculation until recently when he emerged once again.

Why custom car artists like Roth and Von Dutch should be the focus of such wild rumors is something of a mystery. It could be due to their deliberate attempts to court notoriety, but it probably has more to do with the fact that they were responsible for the magical transformation of cars. If there is one symbol which captures contemporary aspirations it must surely be the car. Because it encapsulates so perfectly the ideals of progress, achievement and independence, any artist who deals in the medium of cars automatically touches something deep in the collective psyche. When the symbol is a dream object, as in the case of the custom car, the artist goes much further. He then gives substance to people's fantasies, and in so doing he becomes a kind of shaman, a magician who is not bound by ordinary conventions, someone who supposedly does all those wild and fascinating things that the rest of us would like to, but dare not.

7

ICONS

In 1895 the whole of Paris turned out to watch Émile Levassor win the Paris-Bordeaux-Paris motor race in his 4 hp Panhard. Although motorists had pitted their primitive, wheezing machines against each other on previous occasions, this was the first time that they had taken part in a proper, long-distance motor race. So when Levassor crossed the finishing line, he instantly became a national hero. Parisians were ecstatic. Here was a man who, singlehanded, had braved the rigours of the *routes nationales* and completed the journey to Bordeaux and back in just over two days. It was as though he had circled the globe.

Levassor was riding on a wave of popular support when he entered the Paris-Marseilles-Paris race the following year. But it all ended tragically when his vehicle hit a dog, overturned, and killed him. The public had known that motor racing was a dangerous business, but they were totally stunned when they learned that the new sport had claimed its leading exponent. A fund was immediately set up under the chairmanship of the Marquis de Dion to pay for a monument, and Aimée-Jules Dalou, a famous sculptor of the time, was commissioned to create a suitable memorial to the fallen hero. Dalou was at first hesitant about committing himself to 'a monument to a victim of automobilism', as he called it. But he soon warmed to the idea when he realized that it offered him a way of propelling sculpture into a totally new realm.

Fired by his new enthusiasm, Dalou embarked on a bas-relief in marble which would depict Levassor's triumphant entry into

Paris. This sculpture, which was completed by Dalou's assistant after his death, marked the point at which the automobile became an acceptable topic of the serious arts. The sculpture was erected at the Porte Maillot, near the finishing line of the great race which it commemorates. It shows Levassor and his Panhard passing through an imaginary triumphal arch, with crowds of enthusiastic well-wishers raising their hats and cheering him on to victory. Levassor is leaning at the tiller of the Panhard with an unassuming expression on his face, and both car and driver are cast in such bold relief that they seem to be on the verge of escaping the very marble from which they are carved. The motor car was about to become a new icon.

Worshipping The Car

Dalou's sculpture commemorating Levassor's victory was unveiled in 1909, the same year that the Italian Futurists published their manifesto. The Italians, like the French, were among the first to incorporate the automobile into the arts. In France, for example, Toulouse-Lautrec had taken time off from his dancers to execute a fine caricature of his cousin chugging down the boulevard. In this affectionate portrait Toulouse-Lautrec depicted his cousin in the typical motoring garb of the time – cap, goggles, leather mask and heavy coat – fully dressed to do battle with the elements. At the turn of the century, just as Ettore Bugatti was abandoning his paint brushes and easel to design his first car, other Italian artists such as Umberto Buccioni were busy painting automobiles in full flight.

The exhilaration afforded by the motor car so overwhelmed Futurists like Buccioni, Severini, Balla and Marinetti, that when Marinetti came to draft the first Futurist Manifesto, he placed it at the very center of the new program for the arts. The manifesto began: 'We intend to sing the love of danger, the habit of energy and fearlessness,' and then went on to state: 'We affirm that the world's magnificence has been enriched by a new beauty: the beauty of speed. A racing car whose hood is adorned with great pipes, like serpents of explosive breath – a roaring car that seems to ride on grapeshot is more beautiful than the Victory of Samothrace.' Photographers like Muybridge in America and Marey in France had already managed to freeze the movement of men and animals on photographic plates, but the Futurists sought to portray the dynamic sensation of speed. The fact that Muybridge had revealed the actual gait of a horse in full gallop, using a battery of cameras, did not particularly impress the Futurists because, as they saw it, 'a running horse has not four legs, but twenty'. What was important for them was not the properties of movement, but its subjective sensation to the viewer. In the motor car the Futurists found their natural subject and ally. It represented a fusion of science and art. It symbolized the new age because it admitted the motorists to a realm of experience which was not accessible with other modes of locomotion.

Exaltation of the car and speed was not lost on other artists of the time. When Giacomo Balla caught the Futurist bug he was already an accomplished painter in the conventional mold. But he immediately auctioned all his work and embarked on a frenzied program of experimentation in which he attempted to capture the subjective dynamism of speeding cars. His friends pleaded with him to give up this nonsense, and his mother begged the Madonna for help, but Balla would not be dissuaded from his destiny. He now signed himself as Futur Balla and set to work depicting the merging, stroboscopic images of the automobile in motion. By 1915 he had produced no less than twenty works relating to this subject – works with titles like 'Dynamism of an Automobile', 'Speed of an Automobile' and 'Speed of an Automobile + Light'. These pieces were composed of harsh planes, circles and whorls. Although they contained no explicit image of the automobile, and none of the shorthand tricks that artists use to depict moving objects, they nevertheless conveyed every impression of the sensation the viewer experiences when a car rushes by.

Writing on behalf of his fellow artists, Marinetti stated, 'We want to hymn the man at the wheel, who hurls the lance of his spirit across the Earth, along the circle of its orbit.' For the Futurists, and certainly for Marinetti, there was in the association between man and car a strong suggestion of man's primordial relationship to projectiles. For thousands of years man had been fashioning spears and arrows – objects which exceeded his own feeble pace and which enabled him to act at a distance. These projectiles were propelled by human force. But now there was a new kind of projectile, one which carried man, and which required no expenditure of effort on his part. No longer was it necessary for him to launch his projectile and stand helplessly by while it traced out its pre-determined arc. Man could now ride the projectile he had created – he could control its speed and direction while it was in flight. The Futurists saw the automobile establishing a new relationship between man and his handiwork. Previously the link in the collective unconscious had been between passive man and active projectile. Now it was active man and active projectile. Man and his transportation had been joined together in a new symbiotic relationship. This was not the half-man, half-beast of mythology, but the half-man, half-machine of the modern age. Man and machine had become fused into a mechano-morphic centaur!

The adulatory attitude of the Futurists was only one of the many lines people have taken on automobiles. In its time the automobile has evoked the full range of human responses. Some people have regarded it as an object of wonder, as a perfect welding of technology and art, while others have seen it as a vehicle of social liberation and individual fulfillment. Still others have regarded the car as a dangerous foible, or, even worse, as a tyrant which has enslaved and chained us to the motorways. For such individuals the automobile represents a modern-day version of Frankenstein's monster, an innocent invention that has turned against its creator and which now devours people in their thousands.

The fact that the car provokes such diametrically opposed and violent reactions is hardly surprising when one considers the prominent role it plays in our lives. Because it is both our servant and our master, we can adopt either a positive or a negative attitude toward it, and when these attitudes are taken to their extreme they become expressions of either love or hate. But like a servant or a master – or, more interesting, someone who occupies both these roles – the automobile can evoke a complex amalgam of emotions in which love and hate vie with each other. Our society is now deeply dependent on the automobile, and it is the recognition of this dependency which gives rise to the mixture of feelings we have about it and to the

various ways it has been depicted by artists. By examining the
ways in which the car has been depicted in art, we can gain a
clearer impression of its significance for society.

Cars On Canvas

Artists have embraced virtually all the attitudes about cars held
by the public, and a few besides. One group which used the
motif of the car repeatedly were the Pop artists. Although Pop
Art showed certain affinities with earlier movements such as
Cubism and Surrealism, it offered an entirely new philosophy
and an original way of seeing the world. First and foremost,
Pop Art was a populist movement. It was concerned with the
fact that we live in a world of mass production in which manufactured objects are identical to each other, and are expend-
able.

Pop Art recognized that our views of the world are filtered
through the media. Television, the newspapers and advertisements constantly bombard our senses with a diet of glamour
and hard sells. Instead of rejecting the world of popular images,
as previous artists had done, Pop artists deliberately incorporated them into their work. Using bright, brash colors they
expropriated the iconography of popular culture and set humble objects like soup cans and comic strips into their canvases.
They used techniques of expanded scale, photography, collage
and repetition to hold the viewer's attention and to present
familiar objects in a new light. Pop Art was unashamedly low-
brow. It was, as Claes Oldenburg put it, 'as sweet and stupid
as life itself'. In attempting to reflect the world of popular images, Pop artists were naturally drawn toward the automobile,
not only because it provided an opportunity for artistic virtuosity, but because the car was the most important cultural icon
of the time.

One Pop artist who repeatedly focused on the car was the
English painter, Richard Hamilton. His preoccupation with cars
is especially noticeable in a piece entitled *Homage à Chrysler Corp*,
where a girl is shown caressing the hood of a car which, according to Hamilton, is a compilation of Chrysler's Plymouth
and Imperial advertisements with some General Motors pub-

licity and a bit of Pontiac's thrown in for good measure. The picture deals with the relationship between girl and machine, and more especially the glamorous treatment that both receive at the hands of the media. In the picture the car is represented by a clearly discernible front-end and a suggestion of a jet intake, while the presence of the girl is implied by an Exquisite Form bra diagram and a disembodied pair of lips. The total effect of the picture is one of sensuality, in which the voluptuous contours of the girl and the rounded bodywork of the car merge together to form an erotic composite. As intended, the picture calls to mind the way that glossy advertisements employ girls to promote automobiles.

The girl + automobile theme also appears in Hamilton's *Hers is a Lush Situation*. Here again one finds the motif of the front-end, but this time there is a cut-out of Sophia Loren's lips suspended in the air and a collage of the United Nations building which also doubles as the windshield of the car. In this picture the focus is on the image of the car as sanctuary. The girl at the wheel glides through the streets, protected and cocooned from the bustle of traffic outside. Hamilton explains the painting as follows: 'In slots between towering glass slabs writhes a sea of jostling metal, fabulously wrought like rocket and space probe, like lipstick sliding out of a lacquered brass sleeve, like waffle, like Jello . . . Sophia floats urbanely on waves of triple-dipped, infra-red-baked pressed steel. To her rear is left the stain of a prolonged breathy fart, the compounded exhaust of 300 brake horses.'

In Hamilton's treatment of the automobile he uses media images like rockets, lipstick and Jello. By linking the car to these images he seeks to show how advertising has transformed it into an object of heroic proportions. This heroic feature is further underlined in his painting, *AHH!*, where the driver's forefinger is on the point of making contact with a slender gearshift which looks like a finger. The reference here is apparently to Michelangelo's *Act of Creation* in the Sistine Chapel – just as God makes man by touching Adam's finger, so too man releases the power of the automobile by reaching for the gear-shift.

Although Pop Art was representational, it showed very little interest in portraiture or the pastoral themes which had dominated figurative art up to that point. Pop Art was concerned instead with manufactured objects. It spoke in a language of common symbols, and the motifs it borrowed were taken from mass production and the media – things like soup cans, pin-ups and automobiles. Objects like these were part of people's everyday experience, so that when they appeared on canvas they automatically induced a sense of familiarity, even if it was one that had been modified by the scale of the image in the painting. The most compelling image borrowed by the Pop artists was that of the car. The car was loud and colorful. More important it was saturated with personal associations and with social significance.

When the American Pop artist, James Rosenquist, first arrived in New York, he felt he had set foot in a strange country – a country where even the cars were unfamiliar. He explains: 'I was brought up with automobiles in the Midwest and I used to know the names of all of them and I came here and spent some time in New York and I didn't know anything that was stylish, and I found myself standing on the corner, and things going by, and I couldn't recognize anything and that wasn't only automobiles.' Rosenquist began his career as a billboard artist. The experience of dangling hundreds of feet above Times Square, splashing gallons of paint over acres of empty space, had an enduring effect on his sense of scale. It also left him with a permanent interest in the peculiarities of looking at large-scale objects close-up.

When Rosenquist took up oil painting he began to experiment with the problems of peripheral vision and the way that the eyes focus on different planes. He also brought to his work some of the images which had surrounded him during his days on the billboard gantry. His paintings were full of references to food, parts of the body and automobiles. Rosenquist regarded the car as 'the most potent image of modern consumer society', which is why he included parts of cars in so many of his paintings. Sections of cars appeared in *Silver Skies*, which offered a medly of media images, and in *F-111*, which has the dubious honor of being the largest Pop Art painting of all time. Automobiles were also the centerpiece of *Ultra-violet Cars*, which presents a close-up, almost intimate view of two cars bumper-to-bumper, with one nuzzling up to the other as if it were about to deliver a chromium kiss.

The most profound visual statement that Rosenquist has made about cars is to be found in his painting, *I Love You with My Ford*. This deals with the three consuming passions of modern society, namely cars, love and food. Cars are represented, in the top panel of the painting, by an imposing view of the front-end of a Ford; love is represented, in the middle, by a couple's embrace, and food, at the bottom, by an unappetizing sea of spaghetti. By locating this trinity of obsessions within the same painting, Rosenquist manages to imbue each of them with some of the feelings we have for the other two, and by giving the automobile pride of place he is able to suggest that our attachment to cars is at least as great as our attachment to love and to food. This idea is also contained in the title of the painting which refers both to the support role that the automobile plays in courtship, and to the way that the car has become the major organ of our affections.

Pop Art's concern with cars and the media is also to be found in the prolific output of Andy Warhol. Warhol is best remembered for his unrelenting portrayal of Campbell's soup cans, Marilyn Monroe and the lowly Coke bottle. But his work involving cars has equal significance. In his *Death and Disaster Series*, Warhol focused on the media's treatment of disaster, and in so doing he chose the car crash. Warhol started from the premise that 'when you see a gruesome picture over and over again, it really doesn't have any effect', and he proceeded to articulate this idea in multiple images of the same car crash. When one looks at these pictures they appear as an assembly of identical images, where the important feature of the picture appears to be the tedious relationship of its parts, rather than the substance of each part. One's eye, in other words, is drawn to the seemingly whimsical device of repetition rather than to the horror that each image conveys when it is viewed on its own. In this series Warhol succeeds in luring the viewer into the same unconcerned response that the media elicits in all of us. The fact that he manages to achieve this effect with horrific images of car crashes speaks for the artistic device of repetition. It also illustrates the numbing effect that continual exposure to the misfortunes of others can have on our normal sensibilities.

Hamilton, Rosenquist and Warhol were not the only Pop artists to concern themselves with the symbolism of the automobile. In fact most of the major Pop artists have addressed themselves to the topic of the car at some point or other. Auto images can be found in the work of such painters as Lichtenstein, Phillips, Wesselman and Indiana, as well as in the sculptures of Rauschenberg, Oldenburg and Kienholz. Oldenburg is widely known for his soft sculptures of such everyday objects as hamburgers, lipstick and icebags. These were produced on an elephantine scale and executed in the unlikely mediums of vinyl and canvas, stuffed with kapok. In this way Oldenburg was able to challenge the viewer's perceptions of the size, texture and appearance of ordinary objects, as well as the situations in which they are normally found. Like so many of his contemporaries, Oldenburg developed an early passion for cars, except that in his case the love affair blossomed earlier than most.

When Oldenburg was a child his favorite toy was a scale-model Chrysler Airflow with battery-powered headlights. Years later, when he was looking round for images on which to base his sculptures, he returned to this symbol of his childhood. Oldenburg has always made a special point of using autobiographical images in his work (he once proposed erecting a gigantic Teddy bear beside the Thames!) The idea of basing a sculpture on the Chrysler Airflow took shape when he met Carl Breer, who had designed the Airflow back in the 1930s, and spent some time with him, talking about the car and poring over the original designs.

The 1936 Chrysler Airflow was a true classic because it was the first production car to be built on aerodynamic design principles. Its sleek lines placed it far ahead of other models which were still committed to the ideal of the rectangle, and its smooth contours immediately captured the attention of thousands of auto fans who were on the lookout for something new. Oldenburg produced relief models of the car in tinted Perspex, and inserted a drawing which imitated the original blueprint beneath each Perspex image. These sculptures were produced as a limited edition at the rate of one a day – a process which deliberately imitated the mass production of the original Airflow. In choosing the Chrysler Airflow as his model, Oldenburg found a motif resonant with personal and social significance. But his Airflow multiple did more than crystallize his own ex-

periences and those of his contemporaries. It also captured the
image of an important automotive archetype. By mimicking its
production, Oldenburg was able to appropriate the processes
of mass production and to co-opt them for art. Like most Pop
artists, Oldenburg had a basically accepting attitude toward
technology. Although he and other Pop artists believed that it
was necessary to come to terms with the environment created
by mass production, their acceptance of technology did not
preclude them from mocking its effects or ridiculing its excesses.

There were several instances where Pop artists set out to
deride the circumstances created by technology, and in a few
cases their derision was directed at the automobile. Probably
the most disturbing sculpture in this idiom is Edward Kienholz's *Back Seat Dodge '38*. This is exactly what it is. Kienholz
got hold of a beat-up Dodge, removed the entire driver's compartment and then welded the front of the hood on to the back
seat section. What remained of the car was then set on a patch
of fake grass, suggesting that the car was parked in the open
countryside, and one of the doors was left open to expose a
couple copulating on the back seat. The voyeuristic impact of
the scene inside the car was compounded by the fact that the
man on top of the woman was fashioned from chicken wire,
so that she could be glimpsed beneath him. When you look
inside the car you feel as though you have stumbled upon a
scene of drunken debauchery rather than an act of love, and
this cynical impression is reinforced by the presence of empty
beer bottles on the floor of the car and on the grass outside.

Kienholz was certainly not the first artist to satirize the automobile, and he is unlikely to be the last. In the 1950s Picasso
produced a bronze sculpture of a baboon and its offspring entitled *Baboon and Young*, in which he used a toy Renault as the
baboon's cranium. The baboon's eyes are set, like two plump
occupants, behind the windshield, and the upward curl of the
front mudguards produces the effect of an apish grin. Although
this piece does not exactly flatter the car, it certainly possesses
none of the outrage that can be found in more explicit anti-
automobile works of art. A classic in this genre is José Renau's
radical photomontage, *Autocracy*, in which a fat capitalist is
depicted with a menacing automobile for a head, while he sits

on top of a pile of miserable, oppressed humans. Renau's vision of the automobile probably represents the extreme position in a continuum of opinions which runs from unreserved adulation to outright condemnation of the car.

Somewhere between glamorization of the automobile and its total rejection is an artistic attitude which regards the car as worth portraying because it is an important cultural icon. It is here that the Photo Realist painters are to be found. Photo Realism appeared as a response to the successes of photography. By the 1960s it had become apparent that the single reflex camera was presenting a threat to representational schools of painting. Thousands of amateurs, armed with no more than a camera, were now capable of producing images as pleasing as any figurative painting. A small group of artists responded to this challenge by taking up their paint brushes and returning to their canvases with the intention of beating the camera at its own game. They achieved this by first photographing the scene they wanted to paint at various focal lengths, and by then selecting different photographs as the model for different parts of the painting. In this way the 3-D world could be compressed into a flat, two-dimensional representation that was perfectly focused and totally faithful to what the eyes would have seen had they been blessed with an infinite depth of field.

All the major Photo Realists have dealt with cars, sometimes to the total exclusion of other types of subject matter. Ralph Goings, for example, has produced several paintings of jeeps and pick-up trucks in empty parking-lots. These images are executed with the luminosity of color slides and with an attention to detail that is almost obsessional. The same attention to detail, use of sharp focus and absence of feeling is also to be found in the work of Richard Estes, Robert Bechtle and Don Eddy, who have produced pictures of somber automobiles standing alone in show rooms and breakers' yards or in front of suburban period architecture. One of the most striking aspects of Photo Realist paintings is their detachment from human affairs. Looking at Goings's paintings of pick-up trucks or Salt's images of battered cars overgrown with weeds, one is immediately struck by the total absence of people. These cars have been abandoned, cast aside and forgotten by their owners, who have presumably transferred their affections elsewhere.

Sacrificial Rites

If Salt's paintings record a world of cars that have been left for
dead, then the sculptures of Jason Seley, John Chamberlain
and Cesar Baldaccini represent an attempt to rescue them from
oblivion. Seley, for example, has scoured the breaker's yard for
glittering grilles and bright auto bumpers which he has then
welded into strange biomorphic shapes, and Chamberlain has
salvaged parts from the corpses of cars and combined them
into colorful shapes which have all the appearance of abstract
paintings. Baldaccini has also worked with auto parts, but his
tool has been the industrial crusher rather than the cutting-
torch. His technique was to select scraps of cars and then to
compress them in a crusher so that they emerged as bright
sculpted blocks of steel. In this way cars, which had started as
blocks of crude unfashioned ore, were returned to the shape
in which they began.

Themes of death and burial can also be identified in the work
of several other artists who have worked with cars. Wolf Vos-
tell, for example, has encased a Cadillac in concrete, and Armand Pierre Fernandez has embedded no fewer than 58 French-
made cars in a 65 foot-high tower of concrete. This sculpture
was produced by welding the cars together and by covering
the entire structure in concrete which was then chipped away
to reveal the cars. *Long-term Parking*, as it is called, is situated
at Jouy-en-Josas on the outskirts of Paris. From a distance it
looks like an enormous vertical traffic jam, a wry comment on
the problems of parking in Paris. If it does nothing else it must
surely discourage Parisians from leaving their cars unattended
when Armand is around.

A not dissimilar sculpture is to be found in the parking-lot
at the Best Products Complex in Hamden, Connecticut. This is
the work of a group of architects known as SITE. Their piece,
Ghost Parking Lot, was created by assembling twenty automobiles at intervals around the car park. The cars were set into
shallow graves, stripped of their exterior trim, and then the
whole parking lot, cars included, was covered with tarmac.
Finally, parking lines were painted over the surface. When you
drive into the parking-lot at the Best Products Complex you are

therefore as likely to find yourself competing for a space with one of these strange incrustations as with the other customers.

In 1973, at the height of the first gas crisis, the Los Angeles artist, Craig Stecyk, drove his 1959 Cadillac up to Bel Air and set fire to it on the street. This flaming sculpture was entitled *Ignition Problems*, and it was intended, he later explained, to be 'a sacrifice to obsolete technology'. Some of Stecyk's other work has dealt with the themes of death on the highway. A few years ago he embarked on an unusual endeavour which involved driving out on the motorway to look for dead animals which had been crushed by passing cars. he would then gut them on the spot, make a bronze cast of their inside, cover the cast with the animal's pelt and glue it to the surface of the road exactly where he had found it. These fur-covered bronzes were meant as a permanent monument to the fallen dead, to those unsung victims of the motorway.

A similar preoccupation with animal pelts is found in the work of Dustin Schuler, who is also based in Los Angeles. Recently Schuler has taken to the habit of 'skinning' automobiles. First he gets hold of some beat-up car, say an old Beetle, and removes the engine, transmission, wheels, axles and interior. Using a cutting-torch, he then dissects the outer body into sections and lays the pieces out flat on the ground as if they were an animal's pelt. These skinned autos are either exhibited on the floor or attached to the outside wall of a building – as if they had been pegged out to dry in the sun.

For as long as he can remember, Dustin Schuler has been struck by the similarity between automobiles and animals. 'On the freeways here in L.A. it's like the Serengetti Plain,' he explains. 'You've got the herds moving, migrating back and forth every day and then you have the lions, which are the highway patrol, and they move through the herd, picking off the weak ones as they make mistakes.' Schuler sees himself as something of a hunter and he has been hunting a few times. His chance to bag a really big trophy came a few years ago when he conceived of a sculpture which he called *Death of an Era*.

During the gas shortage of 1979, Schuler was wondering what kind of visual statement to make about the crisis, when he suddenly hit upon the idea of running a gigantic nail right through an automobile. So he bought a beat-up '59 Cadillac, rented an industrial crane, and, on the evening of a hunter's moon, set the car up on oil drums in the middle of a field. With the scene lit by floodlights, he hoisted a 20-foot nail 100 feet above the car. The dramatic moment came when he released the brake on the crane and the nail came hurtling down, piercing the car right through the center and embedding itself in the ground. He had scored a clean kill! Schuler left the nailed Cadillac in the field for six weeks. During that time people came from far and near to look at the car as it lay on its side. As they stood there, gazing at the spectacle, they must have been struck by the strange animistic quality of the car, and even if they could not quite articulate it, somewhere deep inside them they must have felt that strange mixture of feelings one gets when one looks at some proud beast which has come to the end of its days.

If you travel west out of Amarillo on Route 66 you will come across what must surely be the most astounding memorial to the American automobile. This is *Cadillac Ranch*. From a distance it looks like a row of tombstones leaning in the wind, but as you get closer you realize that what you are looking at is a row of ten Cadillacs with their noses buried in the ground. This is the work of Ant Farm, a San Francisco art collective who were invited by Stanley Marsh III to produce something unusual for his ranch near Amarillo. If you are ever near there, take the trouble to look for *Cadillac Ranch*, and you will encounter a truly haunting memorial to the evolution of the fin, from its shy emergence in 1948, through its grandiose heyday in 1959, to its virtual disappearance in 1962. This strange spectacle provides a window on an age in which the Cadillac encapsulated the Americans' view of the world and themselves. One moves from the post-war period, when America was cautiously emerging into the world, to the bombast and brazen self-assurance of the 1950s. By the early 1960s, with Kennedy in the White House, a more demure tone had been established. The idea that America was always right began to wane, and with it went the tail-fin.

Every artistic motif has its age, and while it flourishes it inevitably tells us something about that age. The sculptures that were produced in Periclean Athens tell us a great deal about that society's devotion to athletic virtues and the human form, just as the beatific images of the Madonna that came out of the Renaissance tell us about the role of the Church in those times. Today the visual arts use a wide variety of figurative motifs, but none is more revealing than the automobile. More than any other image, the car has become the icon of the modern industrial society. It is a kind of shorthand, a way of expressing our attitude toward the world in which we live.

Any analysis of contemporary painting and sculpture which omitted the car would overlook a crucial artistic motif, just as any discussion of the car which omitted its artistic representation would neglect certain important ways in which it has been viewed by artists who attempt to depict the times in which we live. Ever since the car emerged, coughing and wheezing into the world, it has captured the attention of artists. Painters have used the automobile, either to say something about society or the media, or to comment on the craft of painting itself. Sculptors have scoured the breakers' yards in search of shiny bits and bobs that could be assembled into glittering objects, or they have taken whole cars and nailed them, skinned them, buried them, encased them in concrete and set them alight. These treatments of the automobile are important, not simply because they are a form of artistic expression, but because they mirror the sentiments that ordinary people have about cars – feelings which range from adoration to hate, and from mockery to indifference.

8

WEAPON

VERY few people have ever heard of Mrs Bridget Driscoll. Nevertheless, she occupies a very distinct place in history. In August 1896 at Crystal Palace in south London, she became the first British person to be killed by a car. At her inquest the coroner said that he hoped that such an event would never happen again. In the USA three years later, Mr Henry Bliss had the similar distinction of being America's first 'auto fatality'. We do not know if the coroner in this case expressed the same wish as his British counterpart.

What was novel in those times was quickly to become commonplace. By the 1930s the number of road deaths had escalated to the point where they were no longer remarkable. In 1951 Mrs Elma Wischmeir, a 52-year-old worker in a Cleveland food processing plant, provided evidence of the increased destructiveness of the automobile. When she was run over and killed by Herman Dengal from Dearborn, she became the millionth American to die on the highway.

To get some idea of the universally lethal nature of the car, one only has to look at those seemingly dry statistics published by government agencies. For example, in the United States 37 people are killed for every 100,000 vehicles travelling the highways each year. This figure, however, is quite low compared with that for Belgium, where the car manages to dispose of drivers and pedestrians at over four times the American rate, and this despite legislation which makes the wearing of seatbelts compulsory. Germany is also near the top of this macabre ladder. It is Israel, however, which takes the 'Black Riband'

with over 200 deaths per 100,000 vehicles, closely followed by
Greece where the figure is 195. South African motorists have
a similarly bad record and in a country where most of the car
owners are white, the majority of people killed on the roads
are black pedestrians. Britain, in this context, looks relatively
safe with a death rate not too far above that of the United States.
Even so, six and a half thousand British people will die this
year, and many more will be seriously injured.

We have a special way of describing the lethal consequences
of cars. We refer to the deaths they cause as *accidents* – a suitably
dispassionate term which largely removes any sense of blame
from both cars and their drivers. The killings are taken for
granted and seen as inevitable. They are the price we pay, and
seem quite happy to pay, for our automobile culture. Even
when individuals are held to be responsible for crashes, their
offence is considered, in most countries, to be quite trivial. In
Britain, for example, a conviction for causing death by reckless
driving merits on average only a fine of about £200, even though
the law makes provision for prison sentences of up to five years.
In the United States a rather tougher line is taken, but penalties
imposed on 'killers at the wheel' are still well below those meted
out to people whose actions lead directly to the death of innocent individuals in other ways.

The reason for this judicial disregard for the victims of the
car is quite simple. Members of juries are ordinary people, and
therefore most of them drive cars. Very few of them on the
other hand are burglars, rapists or embezzlers. So, while they
might lack sympathy for the accused in a robbery trial, they
will certainly identify with the plight of the person who has
killed someone with his car. If the penalties are too high, juries
will simply not convict – they know that they too could easily
find themselves standing in the dock for the same offence. The
1956 Road Traffic Act in Britain, which established the offence
of causing death by dangerous driving for the first time, was
in fact a direct response to the high acquittal rate for drivers
charged with manslaughter.

This 'conspiracy' by car owners allows the automobile to be
used with relative impunity. We can behave recklessly, aggressively and with criminal irresponsibility, and yet we are
unlikely to be imprisoned even when we are caught. The lethal

and injurious consequences of automobile use may not be 'intentional' in any simple sense, but neither are they totally accidental. Given the current levels of technological sophistication and engineering standards, few crashes are the result of mechanical failure – they are the result of human actions. The frustrations, tension and anger that we all experience from time to time, especially on the road, find clear expression in the way we drive.

To be aware of the amount of raw aggression flowing along the highways we only have to reflect on our own feelings and reactions. What did we feel, and how did we react, the last time an overtaking driver cut sharply in front of us, or we found ourselves stuck behind some little car ambling so slowly in the middle of the road? Can we recall the mixture of anger and resentment we experienced the last time someone drove menacingly close to our rear bumper? In these circumstances we become, perhaps uncharacteristically, belligerent. Behaving in an aggressive manner is somehow more acceptable when people are in cars rather than in shops, theaters or bars. If someone bumps into you while you are walking on the pavement, you generally overlook the offence. The British traditionally go so far as to apologize to people who bump into them! When people are in their cars, however, they are different. They get irate about even the slightest contact. Yet it is here that the consequences of aggression can be infinitely more destructive.

A study in Scotland found that in the 17 to 35 age group, a quarter admitted to giving chase to drivers who had offended them in some way. Eight per cent had actually been involved in fights with other motorists. Although this age group stands out as being the most aggressive, and consequently the most 'accident-prone', automotive anger is by no means confined to the relatively young. Older drivers may have learned to control their aggression rather more effectively, but they still experience the same emotional transformation when they get into their cars. A similar study conducted in Utah came to the same conclusion. While Americans seem less willing to admit their motoring misdemeanors, the report concluded that there was a lot of irritation and anger on their roads and that this frequently led to 'overt aggressive responses'.

The products of increased anger and aggression can sometimes be quite bizarre. In the United States we find reports of drivers shooting each other during a quarrel over a parking space. The British, who have less access to additional weapons such as guns, tend to resort to items such as wheel braces, or they simply tear off doors, smash windshields or rip off radio aerials. Fist fights between drivers are common throughout the world.

For most of us, however, our anger is more commonly conveyed through expletives and insulting gestures. In Britain the V-sign generally makes the point, although it is lost on foreigners who assume that one is claiming some kind of victory. Other countries have their own symbols of hostility and displeasure. Italians, for example, with the largest repertoire of gestures in the world, will wave a *cornuta* at you with the first and little finger extending from a clenched fist. It means 'You are being cuckolded by your wife', although some of the force of the threat is lost in translation. More serious anger might be vented using the forearm jerk. The trouble with this gesture is that it requires both hands to be off the wheel – one to slap the biceps and one to form a fist which jerks toward the recipient of the message. There can be few more terrifying spectacles than a Neapolitan driving toward you in a battered Fiat on a narrow road using this gesture to indicate what he would do to you if he was not constrained by being in his car.

The French and Belgians tend to opt for a less energetic version of the forearm jerk – the *bras d'honneur* – but in the south of France be careful not to mistake the ring sign made with the thumb and forefinger. You might think that it is the classic 'OK' sign. In fact it probably means that your car, or your driving ability, is 'zero' or worthless. This gesture can also cause trouble in Germany, where it is taken to refer to an orifice. Making an *Arschloch* at a policeman will result in a fine of about 1,000 Marks, as will a number of other gestures including sticking out your tongue, tapping your temple with the forefinger or screwing a finger into the side of your cheek. The 'thumbs up' sign, which is used as a friendly salute and even a request for a lift in Britain, is not at all appreciated in Greece or Australia. In these countries it is most likely to be perceived as a 'sit on this!' insult.

Americans use a less energetic but equally phallic gesture –

the middle finger jerk. This is one of the few signs which is understood internationally, perhaps because of its long history of use which dates back to the ancient Romans, who called it the *digitus impudicus*, or impudent finger. Present-day Greeks employ a similarly ancient gesture – the *Moutza*. This involves pushing an open palmed hand toward your rival as if to spread dung on his face. It usually evokes a strong reaction, so be careful how you ask for five gallons of gas in Athens.

A rather more bizarre way of insulting others from the relative safety of one's own car is the practice known as 'mooning' or 'pressing the ham'. Here, the bare buttocks are placed against a window and produce a startling effect on bystanders. This practice is quite common in the United States, and recently in England an unfortunate stranded woman motorist reported being shocked by the sight of two such buttocks inside a car which she thought was stopping to help her.

Gestures provide a very effective channel of communication between drivers. An additional channel is provided by the car horn, and this useful facility can convey a variety of messages, from a deferential 'beep' to a continuous expression of extreme anger. Like gestures however, horn honking styles, and their effects, vary from country to country. In Britain, honking is generally considered to be unseemly and rude unless used in an emergency. Elsewhere in Europe, on the other hand, using the horn is as natural a part of everyday driving as changing gear. The Italians, again, are the most expressive in this medium and even the modest Fiat 500 is equipped with particularly sonorous klaxons.

Cross-cultural differences are best illustrated by timing how long it takes for drivers to start hooting if the car in front fails to move when the traffic-lights turn green. Joe Forgas, a psychologist, drove a grey VW Beetle through Germany, France, Spain and Italy and changed the car's nationality from time to time by placing either a German or an Australian insignia in the rear window. In large towns he stopped at traffic-lights and, when they turned green, he simply waited. He found, firstly, that drivers were quicker to start honking when the car had a German identity, except in Germany itself. Secondly, there were marked differences in the delay before honking started in different countries. Germans were the most patient, with an average latency of over seven seconds. According to Forgas the Italians were the least patient, with an average delay of only three seconds. This last result is a little surprising because it is our experience that Italian drivers usually start honking *before* the lights turn green! Other 'honking' studies conducted in the United States have shown that men are quicker to use their horn than women. It has also been found that drivers are more inclined to honk if the car in front is displaying a provocative stimulus, such as an offensive bumper sticker, or has a rifle visible in the back.

It is clear that all around the world the car evokes more than its fair share of aggression and antagonism. Where does all this anger come from? What is it about the automobile that so radically transforms our feelings and behavior? In answer to these questions we could say that driving is stressful. We might also point out that to drive through a major city during a busy period you have to be more than a little assertive, but such considerations do not really explain the gut reactions that occur when people are frustrated in their cars. To understand these fully we have to return to the notion of the car as a special kind of *territory*.

The Territorial Imperative

Territorial defense is one of the prime reasons for aggressive behavior in man and other animals. Along with the striving for dominance and access to receptive females, the maintenance of territorial integrity is a major motive for threatening displays, intimidatory behavior and straightforward violence by men. When the territory of the automobile is invaded, or when some other car tries symbolically to dominate it, the perceived threat is sufficient to evoke almost primeval reactions in even the meekest of motorists. Women, by and large, express much less aggression on the road. But, as social roles change, they too are showing their capacity for hostility.

Because the car is a special territory, a 'home on wheels', our defensive reactions are aroused when it is threatened. The car also provides a protective position from which we can make threatening signals in relative safety. We can shake our fists and speed away unscathed, whereas we might think twice about being so bold when we are walking along the pavement. We have in the automobile both the motive for hostility and a suitable vantage point from which to engage in overt expression.

The territory of the car extends beyond the simple limits of the metal body shell in the same way that the personal space over which we claim jurisdiction covers a larger area than that occupied by the body. Normally, there is a zone of a few feet around our bodies which we feel we own, and we become very resentful when uninvited strangers invade it. This space, however, is not circular. It narrows at the side of our bodies and extends further behind us than in front. Which is why we feel particularly uncomfortable when people 'creep up behind us' or 'look over our shoulder'. Exactly the same is true for 'car space'. When other drivers come too close to our rear bumper, we feel edgy and defensive. They are inside the invisible boundaries that define our moving territory. If the situation continues for more than a few seconds, our anger will rise.

The link between body space and car space has been nicely illustrated in a study by Professor Crisp at St George's Medical School in London. His investigations suggest that people who see themselves as being fatter than they really are, tend to view their cars as being similarly corpulent when it comes to judging whether or not they can drive through a particular gap. People who think of themselves as being thinner than they really are, on the other hand, tend to think that they can drive their cars through narrower gaps. Thus, the people most likely to have accidents in such circumstances are those trying to deny the fact that they have put on weight and that their bodies are occupying more space than they would wish. Thin people trying to increase their weight would, in contrast, be expected to have the best safety records.

Whether our perceptions of body and car space are accurate or not, there are, of course, some circumstances in which we suspend defense of our territory. We do not object to invasions made by, for example, a person of the opposite sex whose attentions have been sought. Nor do we express hostility toward others temporarily pressed close to us in an elevator. On cross-Channel ferries we are quite relaxed about the fact that cars are parked within inches of our own. It is when the in-

vasion of either our body- or car-space is seen as unwarranted
that aggression is an inevitable consequence. The concern felt
by drivers about unreasonable invasion of the space immediately behind them is particularly strong and is illustrated by a
number of common bumper stickers. 'If you can read this, you
are too close' is one that can be found in several countries. One
which illustrates the similarity between car space and personal
body space reads: 'Don't come too close, I hardly know you.'
Another which has to be read with a mock Mafioso accent,
threatens: 'Toucha my car, I smasha your face!'

A common, but exceedingly dangerous, response to tail-gating is to dab a foot on the brake pedal. The following driver,
seeing the light flash red, will often respond with panic braking
– his skidding and weaving producing a smirk of satisfaction
on the face of the driver in front. In more extreme cases drivers
have become so enraged by the car near their rear bumper that
their own fierce braking has resulted in multiple shunts. Perhaps the most bizarre over-reaction to tail-gating occurred recently in Houston, Texas. Oscar Salinas, whose car suffered a
partial brake failure, tapped the rear bumper of a pick-up truck
in front. The driver of the pick-up let Salinas pass and then
followed him. Having drawn level again, he thrust a gun out
of the window and shot him dead. Lieutenant Massey of the
Houston Police Department, and a master of the understatement, commented: 'There's just a lot of unfriendly driving going
on.' Clearly, Texans have not heeded too well all those signs
which line the highways of their State and which exhort people
to 'Drive Friendly'.

Making contact with the automobile itself, rather than in-
vading its symbolic space is, of course, an even greater affront
to dignity. Even simple touching is enough to arouse our ire.
Observe your own feelings the next time a cyclist, working his
way along the inside of a stationary row of cars, puts his hand
on the roof of your car to steady himself. Most people get quite
indignant about this innocuous piece of behavior. A female
journalist, who also cycles, warned *Guardian* readers recently:
'One thing . . . a cyclist should never do is *touch* a man's car.'
She went on to remind them of the potential consequences:
'. . . there are those who chase offending bikes (usually only
those ridden by men) and force the riders off; . . . drivers who

leap out and start brawling, others who deliberately drive too close to the curb to let a bike past on the inside.'

Another type of territorial invasion which arouses considerable anger, is that which occurs in the frontal zone. This is most commonly caused by drivers who overtake and cut in too quickly in front of us, or by those who pull out into our path. In many cases the actual risks of the maneuver are less than those which result from the reactions to it. To prevent overtaking cars getting into the frontal territory, drivers will frequently close up the gap between themselves and the car in front. This leaves the overtaker with two options. Either he brakes and tries to return to the space he started from, or he keeps going, hoping that nothing is coming the other way. Both types of action can have lethal consequences.

This particular form of territorial defense shows how quite modest aggressive actions can have very damaging consequences. There are few occasions in our lives where we can cause the death of other people with such ease and impunity as when we lose our temper on the road. If the overtaking driver crashes headlong into an oncoming car because we have denied him space, the blame will very rarely fall on us. We may rationalize our behavior and say that we were driving 'normally', but in these circumstances our cars are quite literally weapons. We can, and do, get away with murder.

While territorial defense is largely a male prerogative, it is young men in particular who make most use of the car as a weapon. In many cases this is because the automobile is their only personally owned territory. In Europe and America, getting one's own car is an important step on the road to independence. The family home is a territory dominated by parents. The car, on the other hand, is one which the fledgling adult can control and master himself. Because it is so closely related to self-definition, the prospect of its being ferociously defended is greatly increased. Later on in life, when other territories such as a home or one's own office are acquired, the significance of the car in this respect becomes slightly diminished, although it still remains a space to be defended.

The territorial component of the car helps us to understand the cause of the very high rate of car crashes involving young men. Male teenagers, in particular, account for a disproportionate amount of death and injury. In the United States they are responsible for five times as many crash deaths per thousand drivers as those in the over-35 age group. The picture in Europe is very similar, although there are generally fewer teenagers with cars than in America. In addition, young male drivers are ten times more likely to kill someone with their car than are females in the same age group. Although the overall casualty rate has fallen in Europe and America as a result of nationwide speed restrictions and seat-belt legislation, the differences between the age groups and between the sexes have remained constant.

Various attempts to counteract the problems caused by young drivers have been made through the introduction of driver education courses. Ironically, such measures have been largely counter-productive. They simply encourage more teenagers to obtain licenses without noticeably changing their belligerent style of driving. When the State of Connecticut cut funding for such courses, there was a significant drop in the number of injurious automobile crashes. It is clear, therefore, that such driver education courses must do more than simply teach young people to drive. They must also be concerned with ways of encouraging control of emotions and highlighting the grave consequences of territorial defense on the road.

Traffic Wardens are another regular target for the wrath of drivers. Although drivers have jurisdiction over their cars, there are circumstances in which the space it occupies is controlled by officious pedestrians. Wardens directly challenge the integrity of the automobile's territory, claiming that the space it occupies is not defensible. They also do things such as touching the car, sticking plastic bags to the windshield and dispensing costly parking tickets. Because wardens are not *real* officers of the law, occupying a hazy role somewhere between the police and the milkman, they are reviled all the more. The high levels of aggression directed toward them have resulted in cries for their protection. In New York, traffic agents have been seeking 'peace officer' status, which would allow them to carry guns and generally even up the odds in their running feud with motorists. They also want the offence of assaulting a traffic warden to be made a felony and argue that they are a special class of people, deserving more legal protection than the ordinary citizen.

British traffic wardens have demanded danger money rather than weapons. At a recent conference in London, their delegates told of how they had been pelted with eggs, spat upon and drenched with water. One warden told how a motorist had driven a car straight at him and three of his colleagues. Not content with this tactic, the driver made a U-turn and scattered them all again.

The Dominance Drive

On our home ground we feel more confident in our dealings with other people. We resent anybody who tries to 'lord it over us' on our own patch. Similarly, in our cars we assume that we are in charge. Our feelings of dominance and authority are increased, but they are also made vulnerable. When a car accelerates away from us at the traffic-lights, we are forced into a more submissive role. It is not just a matter of someone else having a faster car or the slicker gear change. It is a slight to our own sense of automotive omnipotence.

Speeding away at the traffic lights is a kind of automotive gauntlet throwing. It presents a challenge to other drivers. The manner in which one responds to such challenges, however, depends very much on the fragility of one's ego and sense of dominance. For many individuals, driving a car is one of the few opportunities to escape from a life of routine submission. On the anonymous highways they can be 'kings of the road' like anybody else. The car is, for them, a technological leveller, physical strength no longer being a requirement for successful duelling. Challenges, which might elsewhere be avoided, can be taken up and symbolic battles won. In contrast, those whose ordinary lives provide a reasonable degree of authority and recognition are less in need of opportunities to demonstrate their dominance over others. As with chimpanzees, those at the top of the pile have to fight less often than their subordinates.

Dominance contests are often seen in circumstances such as

narrow streets where there is only room for one car to pass. The contest to decide who should reverse can take on all the characteristics of a lengthy, aggressive ritual. In many countries, quite energetic signals and displays are employed, Italians being particularly fond of involving passing pedestrians in the dispute. The British, in contrast, usually opt for a more dignified waiting game, headlights sometimes being switched on to show the earnestness of their claim.

Headlights themselves are potential triggers for aggressive encounters. Even the most passive of drivers is likely to become enraged by oncoming cars with undimmed lights. Blazing headlights certainly impair forward vision and are distinctly uncomfortable. But this is not the whole reason why people become angry. The bright headlamps are the automotive equivalent of the hostile stare. Fixed, wide-open gaze has a long evolutionary history as a signal of hostility. It is used by chimpanzees eager to climb up, or to defend their position in, the dominance hierarchy. In human cultures it serves exactly the same function. 'Looking daggers' is an apt description of this feature of non-verbal communication. In the case of the automobile, however, 'looks' can literally kill. The car with the lights on high beam is a hostile stranger in the night – an immediate threat which arouses primordial fears and gears us up for retaliation. Recently, one British driver was so angered by the undimmed lights of another car that he immediately turned round and pursued the offender. Having caught up with him and forced him to stop, he proceeded to smash all the lights on the car with a jack handle.

Directly related to the need for achieving dominance through one's car is the desire to be seen as a 'good driver'. It is an essential part of feeling, and being seen to be, in control of the automobile environment. In order to dominate and defend one's territory, one has to be competent. So it is not surprising that very few people (and, again, men in particular) will admit to being a bad driver, even though their track record of crashes and mishaps might lead one to conclude otherwise. In virtually all the studies that have been conducted in this area, an overwhelming proportion of drivers think that they are at least 'average', and most put themselves in the 'above average' category. To confess to being a 'below average' driver is clearly difficult and very different from saying that you are not very good at tennis or cannot get the hang of carpentry. It is more on a par with admitting that you are lousy in bed.

Because people tend to think highly of their own driving abilities, they also assume that the risks they face on the road are not as great as they really are. Equally, they construe their own maneuvers as not constituting a danger to others. One often hears, for example, comments about safety measures such as: 'High speeds are quite safe for a skilled driver'; 'Good drivers don't need to wear seat-belts', etc. In one of our own studies conducted in five European countries, we found that over 70 per cent of male drivers thought that their chances of being injured on the roads were less than that of the 'average' driver. Fewer than 7 per cent thought that the risks they faced were above average. This misplaced arrogance stems directly from the emotional changes which the automobile produces: defense of territory, striving for dominance and an unrealistic self-assessment – the combination of these forces is deadly, and yet we still call their lethal consequences 'accidents'.

The belligerence which has become so much a part of driving a car is reflected in both the styling and naming of automobiles. With the contemporary emphasis on safety and economy, certain bodywork features are no longer quite so hostile in their presentation as they used to be. But a distinct sense of aggression is still designed into today's cars and the way in which they are marketed reinforces this symbolic aspect. Gone are the fighter plane tail-fins, the false gun-ports, the gun-sight hood ornaments, the bullet-shaped chrome incrustations and the menacing radiator grilles which gave cars like the 1950 Buick the air of a ravenous predator. Today's more aerodynamic products, however, and even the tinny 'econoboxes', have not allowed us to forget the car's weapon-like potential.

Car names are particularly illuminating. The *Jaguar*, for example, is named after the ferocious South American beast of prey, and throughout its history the styling has reflected the deadly sleekness of this successful predator. The mixture of opulence and threatening appearance has ensured it a secure niche in the market-place, appealing most to those seeking to make a strong impression. Similar connotations are evidenced in the American *Mustang*, a modern-day reminder of the feral horse of the prairies – a wild untameable beast. Other fast and violent animals, real or imaginary, are used as designations for cars such as the *Cougar*, *Bronco*, *Panther*, *Firebird* and *Thunderbird*. The vicious hornet has also been used as a name for both American and British cars. Sharp-edged weapons constitute another group of aggressive names. In Britain the *Scimitar*, *Rapier* and *Dart* will be familiar to most people. The Triumph *Toledo* even manages to remind us of the Spanish town where such deadly instruments were manufactured. Similarly, in the United States we find *Le Sabre* and *Cutlass*. The *Magnum*, in a different category of weapon, sounds even more explicit. The violent phenomena of nature are also captured by both European and American models. Think of the *Fuego*, *Duster* and *Tornado*. Cars like the *Corsair* may sound quite innocent, until one is reminded that it refers to a particularly maneuverable and deadly fighting ship.

If you look through any world encyclopedia of cars you will find numerous examples of cars with bloodthirsty names. The important thing is that these names are not accidental. Car manufacturers go to great lengths to ensure that a particular nomenclature evokes the appropriate imagery, and consequently to sell the product. Symbols of predation, weaponry and war machines are clearly very successful in this regard.

Car advertising also succeeds in communicating aggressive imagery. The brochure of the O'Gara Coach company proclaims: 'Within every Mercedes is the soul of a hell-raiser.' Another advertisement from the same company describes the Porsche 935DP as: 'So dynamic it looks illegal just standing still – A turbo-charged lean and mean muscle machine.' The implications, when you consider that the 935DP can leap from 0 to 60 mph in 4.2 seconds and reach a top speed of 212 mph, are chilling.

Less ostentatious advertising in Europe conveys almost identical imagery. The turbo-charged Renault Fuego, for example, is presented as being 'Aerodynamite'. Even the Renault 5 Gordini is said to be 'faster than a speeding bullet'. The Ford Sierra XR4 does not have a dashboard, it has a 'cockpit' – a boon for all those with fantasies about being a fighter pilot.

Mazda suggest, only half jokingly, that their RX7 should be

fitted with an 'adrenalin gauge', presumably to enable drivers to monitor their state of aggressive arousal. Other Japanese products are advertised in an equally direct fashion, and the names of some of them are equally revealing. Take the Colt *Starion* for example. Presumably this is intended to communicate the image of a virile male horse, but the Mitsubishi marketing people, like most Japanese, had trouble with their 'l's and 'r's. Toyota, however, have recently had to tone down their more aggressive advertising after some of their street posters, showing one of their cars as a bullet, were 'vandalized' and the driver transformed into a skeletal figure of death, complete with scythe.

Some experts believe that the use of violent imagery in car advertisements is partly responsible for the death and destruction caused by the automobile. William Haddon for example, who is head of the Insurance Institute for Highway Safety in Washington DC, points out:

> There is . . . the glaring discrepancy between the need of societies to reduce motor vehicle casualties . . . and the images of violence and machismo with which many of the vehicles are sold – images which it is reasonable to believe increase the occurrence of motor vehicle death and maiming in the societies where they are used . . .

In Britain, similar fears have been expressed by the Friends of the Earth group. They have referred numerous advertisements to the Advertising Standards Authority – including those for Ford, Renault, Saab and Toyota cars. FOE claim that the advertisements break the Authority's code of practice, part of which states that an advertisement should not encourage defiance of the law, violent or anti-social behavior, or refer to dangerous practices. It would be interesting to know whether an advertisement which shows a car being shot out of a pistol with the caption 'the trigger is under your right foot' could be within this code of practice.

The car is a weapon in the hands of those who choose to use it as such. The driver rattles his symbolic sabre and announces himself as lord of the highway. His inflated sense of confidence

and his appreciation of the deadly features, both real and symbolic, transform his emotions and his behavior. In a car, even
the meekest of men has, like James Bond, a license to kill.

Automobile Armor

The inherent violent symbolism of the car has been taken up
by several writers of novels and film scripts. One of the dead-
liest automobiles ever to appear on the cinema screen was James
Bond's Aston Martin DB5 in *Goldfinger*, equipped with fan-
tastically lethal gadgets. Ian Fleming returned Bond to a rather
less murderous Bentley Mulsanne Turbo. When, however, John
Gardner took over the role of perpetuating Bond's adventures
after Fleming's death, he equipped him with a specially customized Saab 900 Turbo. In *Licence Renewed* we discover where
all of the Saab's lethal equipment comes from:

> The click of the lock came almost at the same moment as
> one of the shadowy figures closed on the car. It was time
> to test CCS's special fittings. Working quickly, Bond un-
> locked the two hidden compartments, threw the Browning
> onto the ledge above the instrument panel and grasped
> the spare pair of Nitefinder goggles . . . It was then that
> Bond hit the tear gas button. One of the safety devices –
> standard equipment on the CCS 'Supercar', as they call it
> – consists of tear gas ducts placed near all four wheels. At
> the press of a button, the gas is expelled, enveloping the
> car and anyone attempting to assault it.

Communication Control Systems is a real company operating
in London and New York and is run by a charismatic and affable
man called Carmine Pellosie. In addition to selling a wide range
of counter-espionage gadgets, CCS specializes in armored, bullet-proof cars – ostensibly for defense and self-protection, but
also with a number of distinctly aggressive features. The standard 'Supercar' has gun portholes and reinforced, ram bumpers
which are quaintly described as being for 'defensive driving'.

Carmine Pellosie sells about one or two of these conversions
a week from his New York office but he is understandably coy

about who buys them. Mostly they are bought by 'foreign dignitaries and ambassadors', he said vaguely, adding that after the death of John Lennon, a few pop stars had expressed some interest in protecting themselves with one of his automobiles. For $100,000, CCS will take your standard Mercedes, or some equally suitable car such as a Cadillac, and turn it into a Level IV military-standard, bullet-and bomb-proof cocoon. Pellosie readily admits that some of the ideas for equipment in these vehicles come from B-movies – like the spray attachment at the rear which covers the road behind with a slippery film of diesel oil. But what really captures the imagination is the 'Armageddon' button.

The Armageddon button is a self-destruct device. If someone tries to use the car, without knowing the complicated sequence which disarms the mechanism, a lump of C4 plastic explosive blows everybody inside to pieces. This would be rather unfortunate if you were being kidnapped in your own mobile fortress. As Pellosie says, 'You'd be history.' The ejection seat is a better alternative if you are being held at gunpoint by an unwelcome front-seat passenger – especially since none of the CCS cars has a soft top! The triple cannon fitted under the front passenger seat could also be used to give one's assailant an unforgettable ride.

One gets a strong sense of unreality when discussing such equipment with the people who make and sell it. It is too close to the Bond stories for comfort. Fact and fiction, hype and deadly seriousness, merge uneasily. The talk of bullet-resistant Kevlar, emergency oxygen supplies and half-inch-thick windows makes one wonder why the people who buy such cars do not just stay at home. But that is to miss the point. The reason for having a Supercar is to be seen about in it and to be able to talk about it in hushed tones with one's friends and colleagues. Although these armored fortresses don't look very remarkable from the outside, they provide a subtle status-kick for the owner. When you are tired of your Cadillac or your Porsche, you can indulge your fantasies or paranoia and ride around in a CCS special. After all, if you need all that expensive protection, you must really be *somebody*.

Having heard about cars that had been sold to Arab potentates and to people on the pre-revolution Iranian hit-list, we suggested to Pellosie that his product might suit an aspiring gangster very nicely. After all, Al Capone spent $30,000 in 1928 having his Cadillac lined with quarter-inch boiler plate to frustrate the Feds. Pellosie, however, denied knowingly supplying villains – 'The first guy who comes in here and tells me he's the head of the Mafia – well I'm going to roll him down the stairs!' – although he did confess to being a little worried by Wall Street lawyers who come in to buy armored cars on behalf of unnamed clients and pay cash. That, apparently, happens a lot.

Across on the other coast of the United States, The O'Gara brothers are also in the business of building armored cars. They bought up the Hess and Eisenhardt company which was responsible for building special cars for American Presidents and, inevitably, unpopular Arab princes. They combine this operation with their up-market customizing business, but unlike CCS do not advertise their more lethal wares. Tom O'Gara, however, believes that selling armored cars, like any other area of automotive retailing, is really a 'whore's business'. 'People lie, steal and cheat . . . Even in the armored car end of the business, people have tremendous stories to tell. They can tell a story so well . . . the car that James Bond rode in, that's a lot of hype. But that's not what it's like. It's not what you can do, it's what you say you can do. It's not what you are, it's what you look – and cars are a very important part of that.'

O'Gara has a good grasp of automobile psychology and of the make-up of people in the business. He is scathing of what he calls the 'less serious' competition who sell to 'guys off the street', and is keen to emphasize the legitimate, governmental nature of his work. Any violence associated with the Hess and Eisenhardt cars is 'official'.

In Britain, the armored car business has suffered a number of set-backs. When one Arab leader took the precaution of getting a squad of ex-SAS British bodyguards to test out his bullet-proof cars they drove one into the desert and sprayed it with machine-gun fire. It immediately blew up when one of the emergency air cylinders ruptured. Another Head of State conducted a similar test and found his vehicles to be more lethal than standard models. The special glass disintegrated when hit by a bullet, sending jagged fragments through the interior.

Some of the rejected cars were eventually sold to families who wanted something a little bit out of the ordinary to amuse their grandchildren.

What happened to these cars illustrates the fact that an armored vehicle provides little real defense against a determined assassin. Sending one's chauffeur on a special defensive driving course is also unlikely to be of much practical help. The real reason for all the Kevlar, and that perhaps not so bullet-proof glass, is to defend one's sense of importance, not one's life. The armored car offers only an illusion of safety and security, but as a theatrical boost to one's ego, it is peerless.

Fatal Fixations

The fatal fixation that we have with the car has repeatedly been captured by movie makers. No longer do the principal characters in films slug it out together beside the rails of the saloon with *dépassé* John Wayne grit. Instead, they batter each other with their cars in sado-masochistic frenzies. *Death Race 2000* is a particularly good example of this genre. Its director, Paul Bartel, commented: 'In American films, action is a very important ingredient, and a car provides that beautifully . . . fast driving and lots of crashing.'

In an even more bizarre film, *The Car*, the automobile takes on the title role. Here we have a driverless vehicle (one hinted at in an earlier movie called *The Duel*), but more important, one with a genuine personality – an agent of the Devil. It appears out of nowhere, kills a number of hitch-hikers and cyclists with ruthless efficiency and goes on to lay low policemen and local townspeople and 'nice kids' in a school parade. A black car with black windows – a true demon.

The Driver, in contrast, is very much about *human* activity. Ryan O'Neal plays a getaway driver, but much of the film is occupied with his ability to use his automobile so skilfully as a weapon that pursuing police cars are reduced to crumpled junk metal. The fate of the occupants, as in most movies of this kind, is rarely shown and it is basically inconsequential. It is the cars that matter. The same is true in most American and British films about cops and robbers, each with their compulsory chase sequence involving ever more fantastic stunt work. Few car chases can compare with the famous sequence in *Bullitt*, and few cars in movies can compete with Christine – the 1957 Plymouth in the film of the same name. Christine is a jealous mistress demanding the undivided devotion of her owner. Rivals are swiftly dealt with, asphyxiated by exhaust fumes or crushed up against the wall. Those foolish enough to tamper with her body become bloody corpses. She is deadly, but also immortal, rebuilding herself to cover up her murderous exploits. The plot is essentially pure rubbish, but the fact that the star is an automobile, and a pretty one at that, makes this otherwise fantasy film an attractive one.

A mixture of fantasian sexuality and violence is also present in J.G. Ballard's sinister novel *Crash*, where the main character drives around the M4 interchanges near London's Heathrow airport fantasizing about the death and destruction of anticipated car crashes. He imagines the maimed and bleeding bodies of women and the tangled wrecks which enclose them. Ballard explores the melancholia of highway junctions further in *Concrete Island*, a story about a group of people condemned to almost stone-age lives after having crashed into the pit of a clover-leaf intersection. The perpetual din of the traffic above prevents their cries from being heard. The books are shocking, but they highlight with an unusual vengeance those aspects of cars and highways which are at the core of our fatal fixation.

Films about car racing constitute a genre of their own and manage to highlight every aspect of mortality in this most aggressive of sporting activities. In John Frankenheimer's *Grand Prix*, starring an exceptionally gritty James Garner, we observe cars diving into the bay of Monte Carlo and being smashed to pieces on the side of a cliff. *Bobby Deerfield*, unkindly described by one critic as '. . . little more than one long Martini commercial', also brings out the frequently lethal consequences of driving fast racing cars. This peculiar fascination with a glamorous, macho death-wish has now reached a new peak in Britain on the video juke boxes to be found in some pubs and bars. For 50p you can play *The Greatest Crashes in Motor Racing History*.

The fascination of the Demolition Derby, on the other hand, has less to do with the mortality of the drivers, but with the physical durability, or lack of it, of the cars themselves. Here the whole idea of the so-called races is for cars to crash into each other as they rumble round a figure-eight track. The winner is not the driver of the fastest car, or necessarily the most skilfull. Rather, he is the one with the most powerful weapon and the most protective suit of armor. The Demolition Derby is, in effect, rather like a modern-day jousting tournament, but with noticeably less order and chivalry than in the days of the medieval knights. The heroes and villains are no longer human, having been replaced by reinforced stock vehicles which carry not the colors of noblemen and squires, but the advertising messages of scrap dealers and butchers.

Prurient interest in highway fatalities is also reflected in films such as *Accident* and in those movies where the automobile has an otherwise minor supporting role. French movie makers seem particularly keen on illustrating the gory end-products of automotive weapons, thus setting the scene for maudlin tales of unrequited love. We find a similar fixation in the lyrics of Bruce Springsteen's songs:

> Last night I was out driving
> Coming home at the end of a working day.
> I was riding along through the drizzling rain
> On a deserted stretch of a county two-lane
> When I came upon a wreck on the highway.

Springsteen goes on to tell how the image of this crash haunts him and of how he imagines the police arriving at some woman's house in the middle of the night to tell her that her husband has been killed.

This morbid fascination with automotive death, whether it be in the chic context of the Grand Prix circuit or the lonely misery of the highway crash, reflects our fears about the awesome lethality of the car – fears which we largely repress or conspire to deny. In order to live with the automobile, and reap its social and personal benefits, we have to maintain our belief that road deaths are 'accidents'. Only in the movies can we admit otherwise. Here we can show the raw aggression, the battles for macho supremacy, and the daring duels. We can turn them into gladiatorial spectacles, even make fun of them. It is a well-tried cathartic technique for releasing tension. Just as pornography flourished during the sexually repressive age of the Victorians, images of violence now dominate the media of countries which have developed the technological sophistication to annihilate themselves. The automobile, as weapon, has become a natural part of that imagery.

Like any weapon, the car can not only be used to kill others; it can be a vehicle for suicide. Some automobile deaths are clearly in this category. Each year thousands of people – solitary men and women, lovers with death pacts, even entire families – put an end to it all while sitting in a car, breathing the toxic monoxide gas. But what of other deaths in cars – those inexplicable crashes where no other cars are involved? Did they fall asleep, or did they do it deliberately?

Until recently we could only hazard guesses. With no driver left to interview there could be no hard evidence. In Austria, which has the third highest suicide rate in Europe, police estimate that around 50 motorists a year deliberately kill themselves while driving. This estimate, however, is based only on those cases where suicidal tendencies were known to exist in the first place. More detailed research at the University of California, San Diego, gives us good reason to suppose that a significant proportion of single-vehicle crashes are, in fact, intentional suicides. It is now fairly well established that the publicity given to suicides prompts others to kill themselves. The phenomenon is known as the 'Werther effect', after the literary hero created by Goethe whose suicide was imitated by others. When Marilyn Monroe allegedly killed herself, the suicide rate rose for a time in the USA by 12 per cent. Detailed statistical analysis has shown that newspaper reports of suicides are followed, three days later, by a significant rise in other suicides in the newspaper's distribution area. During this three-day period depressed and desperate people dwell on the model provided by the report, and eventually imitate it.

Professor Phillips had the idea of looking for similar links between reports of suicides and subsequent increases in traffic fatalities – particularly those where there was only one car involved and where there were no obvious signs of mechanical failure. If a proportion of these 'accidents' were, in fact, suicides, then an increase in their frequency at the end of the three-day period was also to be expected. Using the libraries of the *San Francisco Chronicle* and the *Los Angeles Times*, as well as smaller Californian papers, and the traffic statistics for the corresponding areas, a strong link was indeed found to exist. Suicide rates, of course, vary from month to month and according to the day of the week. Automobile fatalities also vary in frequency according to weather conditions, time of day and so on. To conduct a scientific study it is necessary, therefore, to work out how many road fatalities might be expected on a given day, and then check whether there are significantly more following a publicized suicide. Using this careful approach, the research shows that, on average, fatal single-car crashes increase by just over 30 per cent three days after newspaper reports of a suicide. A further study conducted in Detroit found an even bigger increase of between 35 per cent and 40 per cent.

The implications of these studies are very disturbing. Other findings from Phillips's research, however, give us even greater cause for concern. As well as looking at reports of straightforward suicides, the researchers also examined what happened following publicity given to cases where suicide was combined with murder. Here they found an increase not in single vehicle crashes but in those involving several vehicles where other drivers and passengers were also killed. It seems very likely that there is again a direct link between the model in the newspaper story and this combination of suicidal and murderous driving behavior.

Suicide, sometimes coupled with murder – it is not what we normally think about as we drive along. Rarely do we ponder on the prospect of such a gratuitous employment of the automobile's lethal potential. But it happens behind the screen of another 'vehicle fatality', another 'accident'. It also happens alongside all those other deadly examples of territorial aggression, the striving for automotive dominance and the false sense of invulnerability that drivers feel in their motorized environments. Death has always been associated with the car. Indeed, this has led to part of its mystique and its sinister attraction. At the same time, however, the greatest effort is being made to reduce the destructive aspects of the automobile. Most countries in Europe, for example, have legislation to compel the wearing of seat-belts – Italy being a notable exception. In America similar moves are being made toward legislation to prevent the horrific injuries that occur when cars collide. Here, though, perverse concerns about the freedom of the individual make it less likely that drivers will be forced to strap themselves in. Instead, it is more likely that manufacturers will be obliged to fit such things as air bags which explode into the driver's face when he runs into the car in front. But despite all this concern, and the hundreds of journal papers and articles that are published each month on highway safety issues, the real psychological causes of death on the road have received relatively little attention. There are learned theses concerning patterns of driver eye-gaze at different types of road intersection. There are also long reports on reaction times and the judgments of braking distances. But there is scarcely a mention of drivers' emotions, frustrations, anger and feelings of omnipotence.

Before the seat-belt legislation was introduced in Britain we undertook some research comparing drivers who voluntarily wore belts and those who did not. One of the surprising things we found was that those drivers who always wore their belts had a lower perception of risk and dangers on the road than those who never wore belts. We would have expected that the non-wearers would be the people who thought that driving was safe, and therefore did not bother wearing a belt. In fact, they were those who thought the whole business was the most dangerous. The finding was a difficult one to deal with. We were, and still are, convinced that wearing seat-belts saves lives. The figures on this are really quite incontrovertible. But do they prevent crashes? We warned at the time that seat-belt legislation, in the absence of any other education to remind belt wearers that they were still at risk, might unwittingly lead to an increase in collisions with other cars and with pedestrians and cyclists. People might feel even more invulnerable and take even less care, or feel free to act aggressively with greater impunity. Sadly, our predictions seem to have been right. The number of drivers killed in crashes has fallen dramatically, proving the protective value of belts. But the 'accident' rates have gone up by more than would have been predicted on the basis of the pre-legislation figures. Motor cyclists, pedal cyclists and pedestrians seem to have fared particularly badly.

Seat-belts, or any other protective device, do not stop us becoming aggressive or charged with other emotions. The basic psychological forces which are primarily responsible for many deaths and injuries on the road are not attenuated by any of the safety features we build into automobiles. They may rescue the driver from the products of his belligerence and irresponsibility, but they don't make him a better driver, and they rarely affect his state of mind. To tackle the problem more effectively a radical rethink is called for. And this must begin with a concern with the true causes of crashes, with the human factors which presently render the automobile driver the most deadly of our species.

9

THRILL

SINCE Kenneth Grahame wrote *The Wind in the Willows* in 1908 generations of young children, and not a few grown-ups, have been captivated and enchanted by the exploits of Mole, Rat, Badger and Toad. Of the four characters it is the incorrigible Toad who is best remembered, not only for his brushes with the law, but for his complete fixation with motor cars – a fixation which began when he and Rat were forced off the road by a passing motorist. Whilst Rat denounced the 'villain' driver who had caused his cart to end up in a ditch, Toad gazed in demented rapture as he sped away into the distance. 'Glorious, stirring sight! . . . The poetry of motion! The *real* way to travel! The *only* way to travel! . . . O bliss! O poop-poop! O my! O my!'

It was this first encounter with a car which prompted Toad to equip himself with his own machine, bright red in color and appropriately reflecting his status as the owner of Toad Hall. His three friends, feeling that only financial ruin or an early grave awaited the motoring Toad, were determined to prevent him from taking to the roads in his new-found dream. Such was the strength of Toad's obsession, however, that he stole, on pure impulse, a car he found in the yard of an inn:

'I wonder,' he said to himself presently, 'I wonder if this sort of car *starts* easily?'

Next moment, hardly knowing how it came about, he found that he had hold of the handle and was turning it. As the familiar sound broke forth, the old passion seized

176

on Toad and completely mastered him, body and soul . . .
He increased his pace, and as the car devoured the street
and leapt forth on the high road through the open country,
he was only conscious that he was Toad once more, Toad
at his best and highest, Toad the terror, the traffic-queller,
the Lord of the lone trail, before whom all must give way
or be smitten into nothingness and everlasting night. He
chanted as he flew, and the car responded with a sonorous
drone; the miles were eaten up under him as he sped he
knew not whither, fulfilling his instincts, living his hour,
reckless of what might come to him.

In England at the time when Grahame was writing, it was not
unusual to find members of the aristocracy and even the House
of Lords being arraigned before the bench for exceeding the
speed limit, and the Chief Constable of Huntingdonshire was
forced to complain to the Home Office about the difficulty of
policing the roads. His main problems were that motorists refused to stop when signalled to do so, they gave false addresses
and they tried to bribe officers of the law. The police began to
set traps to catch speeding drivers, and they were assisted in
the courts by magistrates who disliked cars and who were happy
to impose fines on the most slender of evidence. There was
even one motorphobic Justice of the Peace in Surrey who made
a habit of pelting passing cars with refuse from behind his
garden wall!

In the United States the public's resentment of motorists led
Woodrow Wilson to comment that nothing had done more to
spread socialistic feeling than the use of automobiles: 'To the
countryman they are a picture of the arrogance of wealth, with
all its independence and carelessness.' This kind of preaching,
however, did nothing to diminish the love that motorists had
developed for speed, nor did the zealous activity of the police
do anything to persuade them to obey the law. Very soon
drivers discovered a new pastime in the sport of outrunning
the police, and at this point the car-chase was born. Vanderbilt,
for example, would regularly go careering through the streets
of New York in his enormous red tourer, with the police in hot
pursuit, until he suffered the humiliation of driving into a swamp
in Harlem.

At the turn of the century roads outside the towns were unpaved, cars were mechanically unreliable and very few were designed to offer protection from the elements. This meant that the out-of-town driver had to contend with the costs of repeated breakdowns, as well as the discomfort of dust and biting winds. Driving in the open country was like sitting in a freezing dust storm, tearing up ten–dollarbills. That did not bother motorists, because they had acquired not only a means of defining them-selves socially, but a new kind of thrill.

The fascination with cars in the early part of this century, so eloquently captured in *The Wind in the Willows*, persists with equal intensity some seventy-five years later. Such is the strength of the longing that the sight of cars evokes in many people, young men in particular, that some become, like Toad, incur-able automobile thieves. In Britain, the lure of 'wheels' is so great for the young that over two-thirds of all car thefts are carried out by those under 21 years old. Some of the car thieves are 13 and even younger. They are not stealing for profit, and often they have never stolen anything else of real significance before. They are stealing to joy-ride – to introduce excitement into an otherwise dull and unrewarding life. Like Toad, they steal not to get from one place to another, but to gain access to a quite different world – a world of speed, pumping adrenalin and a sense of control over one's personal destiny.

The same is true in America. The perpetrator of the standard auto-theft is not the typical delinquent. He does not necessarily come from a 'disadvantaged' group. Factors such as social class or race are only very weak predictors of this type of crime. Like his British counterpart, the American who steals an automobile is searching for that special 'kick' which comes after knowing how to 'hot wire' a car and elude the police. He seeks the experience of escape described by Jack Kerouac in *On the Road*: '. . . the never-ending rhythm of the tarmac and the sublime joy of motion – but not of arrival.' The joy-rider is not trying to get to a particular place. He revels in the thrill of simply going somewhere in a car.

When people get behind the wheel of a car they become seemingly stronger and more powerful. Completely new op-portunities arise for mastery, enclosed within a private space that shields the driver from the concerns that ordinarily beset his or her life. People report a sense of freedom, a condition where they can shut out negative experiences and simultaneously admit new pleasures. The only contact with the world is through the vibrations of the steering wheel and the sight of the landscape rushing past – a psychological experience of detachment, but also of special involvement.

Speeding To Ecstasy

The precise nature of the thrill of driving is difficult to define. Few people can describe in words the mixture of sensations they experience, but for some the effect is so psychologically intense that no other experience can match it. To understand what lies at the root of this sensation requires first of all an appreciation of the physiological effects of driving – what happens to our bodies, particularly when we are moving at high speeds in a car.

As a human body accelerates, certain things happen to it. Nerves in muscles all over the body react instantly. Signals are sent through the spinal cord which in turn increase muscle tone – particularly in areas such as the neck which are most affected by the acceleration forces. The result of this is a vastly increased state of arousal throughout the body which, when detected by the central nervous system, is translated into a number of emotional experiences. For some people, the physiological effects are experienced as pure fear. For others, however, this basic emotional state is modified to give a sharply tingling experience which is perceived as intensely pleasurable. The fear, and the state of alertness, are still there – but they have been mastered. Acceleration is under one's control, and the result is a flush of bodily sensation that some people liken to a sexual orgasm.

When the acceleration forces are particularly strong – one needs a souped-up Porsche, a Ferrari or an Aston Martin Vantage for this – the gravitational forces start to have a significant impact. Not only is the skeletal and muscular frame jerked back, but the G-forces distort and flatten areas such as the face and stomach. Balance is affected because the liquid in the semicircular canals of the ear is compressed. Now the visceral system, the guts, reacts – adding to all the activity triggered off by the nerves in the muscles.

As acceleration gives rise to speed, quite different sensations are experienced. The initial rush of excitement is replaced with peculiar perceptual distortions. Cruising along at, say, 70 mph, produces a satisfying sense of getting somewhere pretty quickly. At around 100 mph, however, things begin to change. This is because the brain cannot cope with some of the rapidly changing signals coming from the eyes. What it does is to ignore the information coming from the edges of the visual field where the world is changing most quickly. Normally we can take in signals from an arc of about 160 degrees, but at high speed the effective arc is very much reduced. Things to the side of us become just a meaningless blur as the brain concentrates on what it really needs to know. The direct consequence of these perceptual changes is a kind of tunnel vision. The road in front is clear. So are the controls and dashboard of the car. Everything else, however, is effectively lost. Concentration increases naturally as the focus of attention is narrowed. The car and our control of it are all that we can really take in. We are at the center of a much diminished world, and this gives a greater accentuation to the experience of speed.

The third component of the thrill of driving comes from the risks we take, and adds to the excitement of acceleration and speed. There seems to be in-built into most people a desire to maintain a certain level of risk. This applies in all areas of our daily lives, but is particularly present when driving. We tend to avoid actions which put our lives in great jeopardy. Equally, however, we avoid circumstances which are completely safe. In so doing we aim for a balance between the two which keeps our level of arousal up but avoids producing the heart-stopping sensation of uncontrolled fear.

This balancing of risk-taking can be clearly seen on roads all over the world, and it raises serious problems for those trying to institute safety measures. If you make roads safer to drive on – add more lanes, improve the surface and reduce traffic density – people are likely to drive faster. Give cars better brakes, smoother suspension, reduce their noise levels, and you will achieve the same unintended effect. This is because when people perceive, even unconsciously, risks to be absent, they will alter their behavior in order to introduce an element of risk. Correspondingly, if people perceive themselves as being in a situation which is too risky, they are likely to change their behavior so as to reduce the element of risk without eliminating it altogether. To achieve a real improvement in safety it follows that it is necessary to make people think that they are still at risk, even if they are not – an approach which has received far too little attention from those in control of the safety campaigns.

'Self-pacing' of this kind is directly related to the level of emotional tension that a driver wishes to maintain. As we get older, we usually aim for less tension, but it matters little what car we are driving or which kind of road we are on. When we perceive the circumstances to be dangerous, we will slow down and concentrate. When we think they are safe, we will speed up until we reach what we regard as a manageable degree of risk. The trouble, of course, is that we frequently miscalculate the risks involved, and as the psychologist John Cohen has shown, we have a strong tendency to underestimate speeds in excess of 30 mph. These miscalculations are even more pronounced when we are under the influence of alcohol. We also fail to take the actions of others into account.

Experiments have shown that although people vary in their normal levels of arousal, they tend to keep their own level fairly constant when driving. This is the case when they go from safe roads, where there are few cars, to dangerous roads which are associated with high accident rates. They do this by making compensatory alterations to their driving habits – driving faster on safe roads and slower on dangerous ones. The same effect has also been observed in experiments designed to examine differences between day- and night-time driving. At night, drivers feel more at risk, and therefore drive more slowly, than they do during the day, maintaining the same level of arousal in both situations. These studies of arousal demonstrate that people are able to use their cars as means of regulating their own internal states. In this way a car takes on the properties of alcohol or nicotine. Just as one smokes a cigarette to cool one's nerves or to increase one's arousal, so too one can use a car to regulate one's sense of excitement. The car puts us in charge of our own emotions.

Acceleration, speed and emotional self-pacing, the three basic ingredients of the thrill of driving, coupled with all the other things that the automobile offers in the way of self-presentation and image enhancement, are at the root of the continuing success of fast cars. One particular strain of automobile which owes its existence to thrill seeking is the 'Muscle Car' – an action-packed machine which is capable of producing all the right physiological reactions and, at the same time, gives an image of masculinity.

Toning Up The Muscle

Muscle cars were born when Detroit suddenly realized that American youth had money to spend. In the late 1950s, as the post-war boom in car sales began to level out, the new breed of automobiles appeared with many of the features that had hitherto been found only in customized models. Large V8 engines and 4-speed stick-shift transmissions became the standard equipment of otherwise fairly unremarkable Chevrolets, Chryslers and Fords. The Chevrolet Bel Air Sport Coupe of 1955 was probably the turning point, heralding a new generation of cars for those who wanted to burn rubber in style. Its engine was on a par with those in competition racing machines, but it still had soft suspension and brakes which were better suited to a Sunday drive in the family saloon.

By the mid-1960s the Muscle car came of age in the guise of the Pontiac GTO (Gran Turismo Omologato, a designation appropriately borrowed from Ferrari). While European manufacturers had continued their successful production of out-and-out sports cars, the Americans stuck with their compromise between speed and comfort. It was the ill-fated John DeLorean who was the brains behind the GTO. He was fully aware of what Californians were doing to their cars by way of stripping and rebuilding them with modified engines and other special equipment. DeLorean followed the same principle, taking a basic Tempest and fitting it out with a massive engine, stiffer suspension, heavy-duty brakes and triple carburetors. This was not a car for the faint of heart. It was a thrill machine which captured the imagination and sold in numbers well beyond

Pontiac's most favorable predictions. Brock Yates, writing in *Playboy* magazine some ten years after the appearance of the GTO, summed up well the distinctive image that it projected.

> The visceral excitement of driving a Tri-Power GTO . . . was unparalleled at the time. The sounds – the harsh rumble of the exhaust, the howling of the U.S. Royal Tiger Paw Red-line tires on the pavement and the unearthly sucking noise of the air being sucked through the carburettors, coupled with the raw sensation of being bashed into the seat back by the forward thrust of the car – were enough to make every kid in America think he was the fastest, toughest driver in the world. The car was pure *macho*, filled to the brim with hokey gadgets like bucket seats, tachometer, hood scoops, wood-rimmed steering wheel, etc. to enhance the Mittyesque urgings of the grocery boys behind the wheel . . . 'Let's face it,' said one industry observer of the day, 'buying a GTO is like getting two inches added to your cock.'

GTO T-shirts and other ephemera were available almost as soon as the car was launched. Ronny and the Daytonas, at the behest of Pontiac's advertising agency, released a record called 'Little GTO' which captured the car's whining noise quite accurately. The GTO, later to be known as the 'Goat', was quickly followed by other equally powerful cars such as the Plymouth Roadrunner, Mercury Cougar Eliminator, and the Ford Shelby and Torino Cobras. Here were cars that were within the reach of the modestly paid American. They could go like the wind and they could also transport the owner to work and take the family on outings.

In contrast to the DeLorean approach at Pontiac, Lee Iacocca at Ford opted for a somewhat more stylish packaging of speed and thrill. In the early 1960s Ford Motor Company were developing a compact car to compete with European imports and with the VW Beetle in particular. The early prototype for this turned out to be too big and was also poorly engineered. It provided, however, the perfect basis for a 2 plus 2 sports coupé. In 1964 it appeared, after considerable modification, as the Mustang – a V8 notchback with most of the power of the GTO but also with a panache approaching that of a European 2 + 2 sports car. Although quite different in concept from the GTO, the Mustang shared the same market of Americans with $3,000 to spend. Here were thrills for everyone, not just the élite. While in Britain and Europe only the upper strata of society could aspire to Aston Martins and Jensens, or to Ferraris and Porsches, the Muscle car and Ford's *Pony* car liberated speed and thrill and made it available to the masses.

The Muscle car, in its raw macho form, had a relatively short history. For a decade, however, it brought the thrills of the race track within the reach of the ordinary young driver. It also killed quite a few of them. The manufacturers did much to encourage this association between their cars and racing by entering tuned-up versions on the circuits of the National Association for Stock Car Auto Racing, and in drag races. Stock-car racing, in particular, was big business, with annual prize money totalling over $5 million. The cars that were entered by the big manufacturers, however, although they may have looked like Dodges and Chevrolets, were somewhat removed from the models the customer could buy in the showrooms. They often had bigger engines and most of the other components were strengthened or modified to meet racing standards. Nonetheless, the public could see a strong resemblance between the track and road versions and Ford, GM, American Motors and Chrysler constantly featured the glamour of racing in their advertisements for Muscle cars. Chrysler, for example, showed a picture of its Dodge Charger with a braking parachute billowing behind it and the caption: 'Yet Dodge is more youthful than ever. Always experimenting. Looking for the action. And finding it. From the Daytona tri-oval – where a Dodge Hemi-Charger powered to the fastest 100 miles ever driven 170.77 mph – to the Tucson Dragway – where a Dodge Charger set a new S/FX record of 135.33 mph in the quarter-mile. That's the Dodge spirit. Young-Ho! It swings.'

The staccato style of the Dodge advert, with the speeds accurate to two decimal places, was typical of this mid-1960s genre. While cars one could buy from the showroom could not match the performance of the specially prepared racing versions, the standard model had sufficient power to hint at the thrills and danger of the race track but still serve as a means of regular transport. The strategy was successful because it made the world of modern-day heroes and kings of speed that little bit less removed from the lives of ordinary people.

Competitive speed has been a human preoccupation for much longer than the history of the modern automobile. Chariot racing, for example, was a particularly thrilling spectacle in the lives of people in the Roman and Byzantine eras. It lasted from the time of the Emperor Augustus, two thousand years ago, to the eighth century AD. Such was the interest in this racing, somewhat inaccurately captured in the film *Ben Hur*, that vast hippodromes such as the Circus Maximus were built which could accommodate more people than the Houston Astrodome and Wembley Stadium put together. The charioteers rode not as individual competitors, but as members of one of the four major teams. None the less, men like Constantine, Porphyrius, Scorpius and Diocles were celebrated for their courage on the track as much as their modern-day equivalents on the Grand Prix circuits. Like Fangio, Moss, Andretti and Lauda, their glamorous image came from the fact that they could cheat death in their quest to become the fastest men alive.

The use of the horse to achieve an exhilarating sense of speed remained a popular activity until the advent of the car. The Italians continued the tradition of the hippodromes in the medieval Palio of Siena, where the central square was used as an arena for races and the settling of old scores between the rival *contrade*. The Palio is still held today, although now as a tourist attraction. In the nineteenth century in England, even the modest horse and carriage was a source of thrill for some people. Samuel Johnson noted in his diary in 1777: 'If I had no duties, and no reference to futurity, I would spend my life in driving briskly in a post-chaise with a pretty woman.' The car, however, introduced the potential for speeds far in excess of those that had ever been experienced before. The early automobiles of Europe and America had, at the turn of the century, the means to travel at speeds which previously had been achieved only by a few predatory animals. In 1903, the latest Mercedes could reach 80 mph, and cars such as these were used by their rich excitement-seeking owners with arrogant indifference to the safety of others.

The French were among the first to channel the competitiveness of the first generation of speed seekers into organized racing. The Americans quickly followed and the Vanderbilt Cup Race of 1904, which was run on Long Island, was the high point of the society calendar. The British government refused to close public roads so that racing could take place, but were unable to prevent the Isle of Man from doing so. The first RAC Tourist Trophy for cars was held there in 1905. Two years later, Hugh Locke-King established a private racing track on his estate at Brooklands, and soon purpose-built circuits were to open all over the world. The age of motor racing had finally arrived, interrupted only briefly in Europe by the First World War.

Organized racing accelerated the technological development of the car. The introduction of a new 2-liter formula in 1922 led to innovations such as the supercharger, and improvements in tires, brakes, suspension and steering were developed to cope with the rapidly increasing speeds that racing machines could attain. As motor racing blossomed into maturity in the 1920s and 1930s it was not only the drivers who experienced the thrills of speed, acceleration and mastery in the face of danger. The spectators at the improved circuits could experience such things vicariously. While racing was now less suicidal than in the days of inadequate roads and uncontrollable cars, the prospect of death and destruction was ever-present, adding a macabre tingle of anticipation. The ancient Roman enjoyed both the chariot race and the gladiatorial contest. His descendants could now revel in a spectacle which combined the essence of both attractions.

In the 1950s motor racing reached what many people now regard as its finest decade. The cars were still built largely by factories which also turned out ordinary passenger cars and lacked much of the technological sophistication associated with today's Formula I machines. The Ferraris, Mercedes, Lancias and Maseratis still had engines up front and drum brakes, and the men who drove them wore little in the way of protective clothing and affected a reckless and devil-may-care image. They were true champions in the days before hard commercialism gained a stranglehold on the Grand Prix circuits. Unlike today's drivers, they were actually visible in their cars and could be seen struggling with the steering wheel on tight bends. A true drama of risk and speed was enacted, the price being a heavy toll in the lives of both drivers and spectators. At the 1955 Le Mans 24 hour race, eighty spectators were killed and many more injured when a Mercedes driven by Pierre Levegh scythed through a safety fence and into the crowd. Many were decapitated in this most horrifying of all racing tragedies. The race, however, went on. Two years later, eleven spectators of the Italian Mille Miglia road race were killed by the Marquis de Portago's Ferrari.

Such disasters, however, did nothing to diminish the appeal of motor racing. In fact, quite the reverse occurred. Increasingly, vast sums of money were poured into racing by way of sponsorship deals. The Grand Prix circuits became more like giant advertising billboards. The drivers themselves became less and less visible to the crowds, cocooned inside their high-tech machines and indistinguishable from each other save for the decals on their helmets. As safety standards at tracks increased and the cars themselves became progressively more stable, some of the glory associated with fatal crashes disappeared. Speed and thrill, however, remained.

Motor racing today, whether it be on the drag strips or the Grand Prix circuits, serves as a vicarious extension to the thrill of driving. The modern stars may be remote, and the things they drive even more remote from the cars that one finds on the roads. But it is here that the automotive muscles are most visibly and dramatically flexed. The driver of even a modest Escort XR3i can still identify himself directly with this most glamorous of worlds. The speeds he can never attain, and the risks he can never take, are provided for him – thrills in the safety of experience at one remove.

Courtship In The Car

The impact of the automobile on sex and courtship has been as profound as that of the contraceptive pill. From the time that Model T Fords and Bullnose Morrises first emerged from the production lines, cars have been cloaked in sexual symbolism. They have provided undreamed of opportunities for covert copulation, been labelled as vehicles of sexual emancipation and condemned as harbingers of promiscuity. Steinbeck, writing

about the early part of the twentieth century in America, said:
'Most of the babies of this period were conceived in Model T
Fords and not a few were born in them. The theory of the
Anglo-Saxon home became so warped that it never quite re-
covered.'

Today, such conceptions are less common because the means
to prevent them are more readily available, but the same activities go on in cars. More virginities, both male and female, are
lost on back seats or recliners than in any other single venue.
Every town has its 'Lover's Lane' or secluded but accessible
road leading to nowhere. In these quiet settings on Friday and
Saturday evenings you will find cars with misted windows –
their role as a means of transportation subverted in moments
of passion.

Although it is extremely common, sex in cars is illegal in
most countries. If you are caught *in flagrante delicto* in Britain,
you can be charged with an offence against public decency or,
if you are very unlucky, with gross indecency. Similar laws
apply in the United States, but different states enforce a variety
of more or less tolerant statutes. In most cases, however, the
police turn a blind eye partly because they themselves occasionally engage in such misdemeanors. Even in staunchly Catholic Italy, an appeal court judge has recently ruled that making
love in a car is permissible so long as the windows are either
so misted or iced that bypassers cannot see clearly what is going
on inside.

The fact that prosecutions are so few would seem to indicate
that we have largely accepted the role that the car plays in this
relatively liberal age of sexual emancipation. Boyfriends with
automobiles may arouse anxiety in the parents of teenage
daughters, but moral outrage about the sensual pleasure afforded by the car is quite muted. Not so, however, in earlier
periods of history. As car ownership became commonplace in
America in the 1920s, there was no shortage of puritans to
condemn its promiscuous function. A Juvenile Court Judge of
the period denounced the automobile as 'a house of prostitution
on wheels'. He went on to report that of the girls charged with
various sex crimes who had been brought before him, two-
thirds had committed their offences in cars. Preachers, Senators
and Congressmen added their own warnings about the moral

degeneracy that had been heralded by the automotive age.
Virgins were being driven at speed to debauchery by 'profligate
young heirs'.

A little later FBI Chief J. Edgar Hoover echoed the same
sentiments in his denunciation of tourist camps. These were
forerunners of the motel and had developed as a direct result
of car ownership. They consisted of rows of cabins in country
settings and their principal advantage was the lack of hotel-
style lobby. You drove straight to your own cabin and nobody
asked questions. Hoover, in an article 'Camps of Crime' in
American Magazine, concluded that they were 'little more than
camouflaged brothels' and 'dens of vice and corruption'. They
catered mainly for 'nomadic prostitutes', 'white slavers', and
'promiscuous college students' – an interesting collection of
enemies of the American way of life. Data from a study conducted by sociologists from the Southern Methodist University
were used to support this singularly negative view. They found
that 75 per cent of the patrons of these camps were not tourists
at all but local couples. One particular cabin had been rented
out to a succession of sixteen different couples in one night.

Hotel owners were also fiercely opposed to tourist camps,
principally because they were taking away a lot of their trade.
The President of the American Hotel Association therefore embarked on a smear campaign, dismissing tourist camps as cen-
ters of debauchery, disorderly houses and criminal hangouts.
Not only had the automobile become a vehicle for immorality
in its own right, but it had also spawned its own institutions
of similar degeneracy. Whether one sinned on the back seat or
on an over-used mattress in a wooden shack, by the side of
which the car kept vigil, the voice of the *censor morum* was
equally loud.

The sense of outrage reached its climax when the International Reform Society called on Henry Ford to 'frame legislation
that will stop the use of the motor-car for immoral purposes'.
Ford's reply to such an edict seems to have gone unrecorded,
but we know that he was concerned about the use to which
his products might be put. He allegedly designed the seats of
the Model T to discourage all but the most perfunctory and
uncomfortable sexual antics. He failed, however, to take into
account the level of ingenuity which has long been the stock

in trade of ardent courting couples. The Model T had so much headroom that all but the tallest of couples could achieve their pleasures standing up.

John Keats, in his epic study of the automobile, *Insolent Chariots*, pays considerable attention to the early days of sex and the automobile and to the new patterns of behavior that gave rise to puritan diatribes. He noted, 'Sex, of course, never need wait to raise its lovely head, and identification of the automobile as a sexual symbol was an instantaneous reflex action for America. Even before the first playboy squeezed the bulb of his Serpent horn at the first passing tart, village maidens deployed themselves at strategic intersections, pinching color into their cheeks trusting that a goggled millionaire would shortly appear to shower them with his welcome, illegal attentions.'

David Lewis, a professor of business history at the University of Michigan, has also taken an interest in the rapid rise of the car as a motorized bedroom. 'Autos were more than a means of transport. They were a destination as well, for they provided a setting for sexual relations including intercourse.' He describes how various modifications in automobile design made such activities increasingly feasible. Seats became lower and the interior was progressively enclosed, but even running-boards could be used quite happily for novel sexual exploits until the mid-1930s when they were phased out. Lewis also makes a point about sex in cars which is certainly appropriate to the present day. 'Early in the century many couples made love in cars because – in an era in which young men and women lived with their parents – they had no better place to copulate. But others made love in cars because they found it exciting, sometimes dangerously so, and a change from familiar surroundings.'

In the late 1930s an important institution began to develop in the United States which was to increase considerably the role of the automobile as a place for passion. This was the drive-in movie theater, which allowed a certain degree of cover for amorous activities. Young people now had an excuse for being out late at night in a car with a person of the opposite sex. Later on, such theaters opened up in other countries where the climate was suitable and offered similar opportunities for courting couples to be alone. In Australia, these drive-ins became known, rather irreverently, as 'finger bowls'.

In Brazil the function of the drive-in is even more explicitly sexual. Here the movie is discarded altogether and the drive-in consists of little more than a car park with a wall around it. Within the perimeters are small wooden garages into which the car drives – this being symbolic of what is to follow. Those without a car (they are luxury items in Brazil) can still make use of the facilities because drive-in owners keep wrecks in some of the sheds, which they rent out to promiscuous pedestrians. At one time these bizarre institutions were seen as a by-product of Brazil's tough line on moral standards and the stigma attached to sex outside marriage. These days, however, unmarried couples can openly sleep together and enjoy the more comfortable accommodation of hotels. Pornography is also freely on sale throughout the country. Despite these marks of liberalization, the drive-ins still flourish, catering for those whose romantic ideal continues to be sex in an automobile.

There is a constant demand for vehicles which facilitate courtship and this is currently reflected in the sales of vans, many of them 'customized' with special internal fittings which undermine their function as utilitarian forms of transport. Their potential payloads are diminished by plush interiors and they are seldom owned by people who need to move things around. In Britain, as in the United States in the 1960s and 1970s, they tend to be owned by unmarried males in their early twenties, and their true function is often revealed by corny stickers on the back. They are literally the 'passion wagons' that their nicknames suggest. They include mobile double beds in velvet-lined boudoirs, complete with hi-fi and drinks cabinet – all the conventional aids to seduction. Passion wagons offer a statement about the owners' availability and strictly heterosexual predilections. In a way though, they are also admissions of failure, because they are the cars of men who have to try that little bit harder than everybody else.

While vans may be rather unconvincing displays of macho potential, there is no doubt that they provide the most comfortable setting for all manner of sexual activities. They may be as tacky as cheap motel rooms, but for some people that adds a frisson of its own. Regular cars, on the other hand, make less obvious statements about a driver's sexual mores, or lack of them. They do not immediately advertise the sexual uses to which they can be put. Their concealed purpose is, however, so well established that there are even guide books which offer advice on which models serve auto-sex most effectively.

Richard Nichols, editor of *Custom Car*, provides just such a guide in his contribution to *The Book of Sex Lists*. 'If you know how to do it, you'll want to know where to do it', he claims, and there is no suggestion here that the automobile is just an emergency or second-best alternative. Fords are listed as being particularly suitable for sex. The now sadly discontinued Cortina is remembered for the role it played in shady parking lots, together with the hatchback Capri which featured both fold-down rear seats and reclining front ones. The more recent Sierra and Granada from Ford still await thorough road-testing.

Other models commended by Nichols include the Chevrolet Corvette. Here, however, it is al fresco activities on the external bodywork which are seen as the main attraction. Minis, Jaguars and, of course, MGs are also noted for their distinctive contributions to seduction. When the advertising agency people announced 'You can do it in an MG', everybody knew exactly what they meant. But perhaps the advertisements should also have given warning about the consequences of doing it in such a confined space.

More serious warnings about sex in cars come from a Marriage Guidance Counsellor called Zelda West-Meads. She warns of premature ejaculation in men and failure to reach orgasm in women. These can lead, she claims, to long-term after-effects and feelings of sexual inadequacy. Such claims may have substance, and it is certainly the case that some women are offended by the thought of having sex in a car, seeing it as somehow sordid and unromantic. But equally there are both men and women who claim that some of their best sexual experiences have occurred in these cramped but exciting conditions.

The Love Affair

The relationship between cars and sexuality has always been reflected in popular culture. In the early days it was the song sheets of tin-pan alley which highlighted the association most clearly. 'In My Merry Oldsmobile' was one of the all-time best sellers back in 1905 and is still known today. Written by Vincent Bryan and Gus Edwards, the song, while extolling the virtues of marriage, hinted at other less conformist pastimes with lines such as: 'You can go as far as you like with me in our merry Oldsmobile.' Such naughty intimations may perhaps have led other songwriters of the time such as Irving Berlin to warn innocent young ladies of the Edwardian era to 'Beware of the Man in the Automobile'.

Such kill-joy lyrics, however, were in a distinct minority. There was a rather dull tune called 'I'd Rather Go Walking With The Man I Love Than Ride in Your Automobile', but songs mostly celebrated the new-found opportunities for lovemaking. 'On the Back Seat of the Henry Ford' and a later song, 'Tumble in a Rumble Seat', hinted at some rather uncomfortable contortions. 'When He Wanted to Love Her He Put up the Cover' was a similarly honest reflection of what went on in the early days of motoring. Songs like 'I'm Going to Park Myself in Your Arms', 'Fifteen Kisses to a Gallon of Gas', and 'In Our Little Lovemobile', seem rather coy in comparison. 'Take a Little Ride With Me Baby', though, does have a ring of *double entendre* about it.

Such songs reflected the sensual novelty of the car. It was different from the horse and buggy, even though in the pre-motorized age such vehicles were regularly used by courting couples for activities which, when discovered, aroused considerable censure. As the novelty of the car wore off, popular songs made fewer references to love on the back seat. But the general theme has remained in other artefacts of popular culture. Magazines such as *Playboy* and *Penthouse*, for example, are full of allusions to the erotic potential of motoring. The letters pages of these magazines are particularly interesting. Some purportedly from driving instructors and RAC patrolmen, tell of quite exceptional good fortune that has come their way while they were pursuing their otherwise dull and routine jobs. Although many of these letters, one suspects, are made up by the magazines' staff, they clearly reflect what people would like to do in their automobiles, and usually the cars referred to are of the more potent and glamorous variety. A recent letter in *Penthouse* is fairly typical of this fantasy genre. It tells how the driver of a Jaguar XJS came to lose his license after meeting a forward

young girl called Fiona and engaging in acts which are certainly
not mentioned in the Highway Code. It was his car that initially
attracted this adventurous young lady. ' "Oh, I love fast cars",
she murmured as she ran her hands over the hood of my XJS
in such a sensual way as to leave me feeling jealous of my own
car. "They're a real aphrodisiac I find, don't you?" '. The aphrodisiac qualities of this particular car must have been quite
exceptional given the graphic explanation of what happened
while driving along in the fast lane before the police called a
halt to the whole escapade.

Such letters must be treated as projections of sexual fantasy
rather than accurate accounts. But the fact that cars figure so
prominently in them is an interesting reflection of the role that
automobiles play in people's sex lives, real or imaginary. Cartoons in this type of publication serve as similar mirrors on the
world of automotive sexuality. One features a man trying to
find a parking place who asks the clearly preoccupied occupant
of a stationary vehicle if he is 'pulling out soon'. In Britain, the
advent of seat-belt legislation provided *Mayfair* with the opportunity to devote three pages to cartoons dealing with the
sexual potential of this relatively trivial feature of the car.

Mayfair magazine has, in fact, gone further than most similar
publications in its exploration of sex in cars. Some years ago it
conducted its own research on the subject. In their 'Quest'
section, subtitled 'The laboratory of human response', the magazine examined 'the part the automobile plays in setting the
scene for female sexual stimulation.' The article concluded that
'the results show that the freedom which a motor car gives –
the total independence from home and social circumstances –
can precipitate petting.' According to *Mayfair* the research was
based on interviews conducted in Britain, fictitious names and
towns of origins being given to preserve anonymity. They included tables showing the percentage of women who had allowed their male partners to 'remove your bra', 'touch you
intimately', etc. One could not help questioning, however, why
no indication had been given of the sample size or any of the
other details one looks for in such a report. It was odd that
apparently only 20 per cent of the respondents had actually
had intercourse in a car, despite doing virtually everything else.
Other investigations have suggested that the proportion of peo-

ple who have 'gone the whole way' is rather higher. For example one very famous study conducted by Alfred Kinsey in the 1950s indicated that 38 per cent of women in their forties and fifties had engaged in intercourse in a car – the generation now thought of as being rather prim and proper!

While some of the respondents to the *Mayfair* study might have been more reticent with the interviewers than the magazine would have hoped, nevertheless, the conclusions drawn about the role of the car in sexual adventures, appear quite well founded. They point out: 'The motor car is not a sexual genie's lamp, yet it can represent a strong force in physical relationships.' They note how the car can free women from the pressures of their home and social circumstances. Perhaps most perceptively they reveal, 'within the confines of a car, a man has unchallenged control over a situation. In general terms, once a girl accepts that she will ride with a man in his car, she has accepted his authority within that car.'

Smutty picture postcards and Valentines are also among the ephemera of popular culture that reflect the erotic aspects of cars. Particular parts of automobiles lend themselves to risqué puns and innuendo – crankshafts, pistons and clutches all conjure up sexual imagery. This particular theme, however, is best explored in the more serious medium of poetry, and the classic example of the erotic car poem comes from the work of e.e.cummings, the celebrated American poet with a disdain of upper case. *she being Brand* is a clever exploration of the similarities between driving and the sexual act. Consider these few stanzas:

she being Brand

-new;and you
know consequently a
little stiff i was
careful of her and(having

thoroughly oiled the universal
joint tested my gas felt of
her radiator made sure her springs were O.

K.)i went right to it flooded-the-carburetor cranked her
up, slipped the
clutch . . .

. . . (it
was the first ride and believe i we was
happy to see how nice she acted right up to
the last minute coming back down by the Public
Gardens i slammed on
the

internalexpanding
&
externalcont racting
brakes Bothatonce and

brought allofher tremB
-ling
to a:dead.

stand-
;Still)

Cummings's poem is a classic – a tribute to those deep metaphors which shape our relationship with the automobile. In
another perhaps less well known poem by Karl Shapiro called
'Buick', the car appears not as a symbol of the sexual act but
as a goddess – a tempting, coquettish dream of nubility. Listen
to the affection and sense of excitement expressed in just a few
lines:

> As my foot suggests that you leap in the air
>   with hips of a girl,
> My finger that praises your wheel and
>   announces your voices of song,
> Flouncing your skirts, you blueness of joy, you
>   flirt of politeness,
> You leap, you intelligence, essence of
>   wheelness with silvery nose,

And your platinum clocks of excitement stir like
the hairs of a fern

Shapiro was thought by some people to be making a satire, an
ironic statement about the symbolism of Buicks. This is not the
case. In a letter to Laurence Goldstein, Professor of English at
the University of Michigan, he says quite plainly, 'It's absolutely
straight; a love poem to a Buick! A big fat Buick.' It is the Buick,
of course, which has one of the most blantantly erotic insignia
which, until very recently, was displayed as a hood ornament.
A silver ring pierced by a projectile – a symbol recognized
throughout the world for the sexual act.

In line with the poets' vision of sex and the automobile, visual
artists have similarly explored not only the phallic aspects of
automobiles but also the act of back-seat lovemaking. A drawing by John Held Junior from the 1920s, for example, is a witty
illustration of a 'flapper' with her legs wide apart, thighs revealed, being kissed by her consort whose attention has strayed
from the task of driving. A much more contemporary painting
by Kenneth Price titled 'Don't Think About Her When You
Drive' echoes the same theme, although in this illustration the
car is careering over the edge of a mountain road. Even the
salaciousness of the spark plug receives treatment by Mel Ra-
mos in his oil on canvas 'Kar Kween', where a naked girl presses
herself close to a tall, phallic version of this usually taken-for-
granted mechanical object made by AC. The American artist
James Rosenquist portrays, in comparison, rather more enig-
matic reflections of cars and sexuality. Crashes and the sex act
are fused into a single metaphor in 'Ultra Violet Car Touch'. 'I
Love You With My Ford', while making a fairly simple statement about the opportunities for sexual behavior that a car
provides, simultaneously hints at the awesome lethality of the
automobile.

It is, however, the three-dimensional work by Edward Kienholz that is the most explicit and celebrated of work in this
genre. *Back Seat Dodge '38* aroused a storm of controversy when
it was first shown in Los Angeles in 1964. The work was so
evocative of what really happens in cars, and what everybody
knows happens in cars, that there were serious attempts to have
the show closed down. Warren Dorn, who was running for

Governor of California at the time, seized the opportunity to demonstrate his own moral rectitude by leading the campaign against this apparently unacceptable reflection of the car's function. In the end a bizarre compromise was reached. The door of the Dodge was closed so that the activities inside could only be viewed voyeuristically through the window.

The erotic symbolism of the car has been recognized by novelists as well as artists. In Stephen King's *Christine*, the car, a Plymouth, is portrayed as a jealous, volitional and feminine machine which came to life under the attention of its owner, Arnie. The metaphor pervades the entire story and the relationship between Arnie and Christine, the car, is loaded with sexual symbolism. Arnie's girlfriend, Leigh, resents the time he spends tinkering with Christine. She wants his hands on her own body, not in the deeper recesses of the engine compartment. 'Cars are girls, she had said. She hadn't been thinking about what she was saying; it had just popped out of her mouth.' Such was the strength of her feeling that being in the car was like being in the body of another woman, so much so that she was unable to make love to Arnie in the car. '. . . Leigh did not feel that she *rode* in Christine; when she got in to go somewhere with Arnie she felt *swallowed* in Christine. And the act of kissing him, making love to him, seemed a perversion worse than voyeurism or exhibitionism – it was like making love in the body of her rival.'

While *Christine* extends the theme of car-as-sex-object beyond reasonable bounds of fantasy, the erotic symbolism of the car has featured prominently in the advertising and marketing of automobiles since the 1920s. Even the early posters for Michelin Tires showed no tires at all. Instead they featured women with revealed breasts floating above winged circles. The style was Classical, the message distinctly sexual. Similarly, the frontispiece to Filson Young's book *The Complete Motorist*, published in 1904, shows nymphs and satyrs in various stages of undress, cavorting on the roadside as a car approaches. European manufacturers at the turn of the century vied with each other to associate their products with the most elegant and sensual female forms that the poster artists could conjure up. While modern representations of the automobile may be somewhat more cautious, the messages conveyed are substantially the same.

They pay attention to the same subtle anatomical comparisons which, due to the evolution of the shape and style of cars, are inescapable.

Everybody knows of course that a long hood is really a phallic symbol. So commonplace is this comparison that there are untold jokes about it. The Germans, for example, will tell you that a man who drives a Porsche is a man with his fly undone. Psychoanalysts seize upon such imagery in dreams as decisively as Freud would have become excited at the mention of trains entering dark tunnels. The Id is revealed by the most significant metaphors of the historical era, and for us, most powerfully by projections of the car. But to see the car as little more than a motorized penis is to overlook the whole catalogue of symbolic features that have earned it a secure niche in the social history of sexual fantasy and behavior.

The shape of a car is not dictated by its function. There are limitless ways of attaching three or four wheels and an engine to a chassis which will accommodate up to five people. In fact, for true functionalism, Buckminster Fuller's Dymaxion came close to the ideal but, partly because it was built on functionalist principles, it looked terrible. It had neither hood nor fenders, and a pointed rear cowling which contained the engine and transmission. It certainly looked aerodynamic, but it was neither sexy nor aesthetic. The Dymaxion, built as a prototype in the early 1930s, shows up very clearly all those features of 'normal' cars which are built-in, not to serve a specific function, but to endow them with sexual imagery.

Sources of sexual imagery change over time as fashions and the idealization of the female form also vary. In the 1950s, for example, even fairly modest cars were equipped with a pair of pointed bumper overriders. These resembled bosoms so closely that they were known as 'Dagmars', after the over-endowed starlet of that name. They were, however, modelled on bosoms of the 1950s, forced into a pert, aggressive shape by tough and padded bras. Today's ideal breasts are gently enclosed, if at all, by light stretchy fabric which allows their natural shape to be evident. Thus, overriders, which don't have much real function, are now less clearly accentuated and are certainly less reminiscent of wire and whale bone.

Cowls over the top of headlights are another good example

of changing tastes in erotic symbols. Originally they gave the impression of mascara-laden lashes – coquettish but otherwise quite useless embellishments. Heavy mascara went out with the swinging Sixties, and so did cowls. The female beauty of today is slim and lithesome, curved but without bulges, with an understated but clearly communicated sexuality. Exaggerated decoration has given way to a quieter glamour, and while zany hair and make-up may figure in the glossy magazines, it is no longer there expressly to appeal to men. In fact it has become the hallmark of liberation. In the same way, the bulging protuberances of the 'fat fender' cars have been ousted by the new aerodynamic and decorum – an athletic, healthy beauty raised on aerobics and Jane Fonda.

It has to be said, of course, that some cars are distinctly lacking in sexuality. The 1970s were particularly lean years in this respect, due mainly to Detroit's commitment to the 'three box' design. Cars were rectangular and masculine – square-shouldered and reminiscent of three-piece suits. Nobody liked them much, which is why European manufacturers were able to gain a toehold in both the British and the American markets. The Europeans were making sexy cars – curvaceous Citroëns with their evocative hydraulic suspension, and upmarket *femmes fatales* in the guise of Porsche and Mercedes Sports cars – cars which simultaneously created images of beautiful women and embodied the virility and anatomy of the dominant male.

Ford in America has largely been responsible for turning mass-produced car styling back toward evocative imagery. However much they may deny it, they are beginning to build sexy cars again. They push technical excellence because they know that the public has a poor opinion of Ford's achievements in this area. But it is the new shape, rather than what lies underneath it, which will influence more powerfully and more subtly the decision to buy. There is, however, a warning to be made. As in all things to do with sex, an overly explicit invitation or display can become not an attraction but an offence, and Ford built just such a car in the late 1950s. It was called the Edsel and it was a disaster. The name (one of Henry Ford's sons) did not help, but it was the radiator which killed it. Shaped so uncannily like a female vulva, its labial explicitness would have been more at home in a gynecology textbook. It evoked images not of sensuality but of reproduction. Somehow threat and predation, not beauty, were the messages it communicated.

The ability of the automobile to convey both masculine and feminine imagery makes it a unique object. It is a modern hermaphrodite and thus appeals equally to men and women. For men the car can be both a phallic extension of their manhood and a mistress to covet. For women, the car serves both as an object of adoration and a reflection of their own sexuality. The female attachment to cars is nicely observed in Thomas Pynchon's novel *V*. Here Rachel Owlglass mutters lovingly to her MG: ' "You beautiful stud", she said, "I love you. Do you know what I feel when we're on the road? alone, just us?" She was running her hands caressingly over the front bumper. "Your funny responses, darling, that I know so well. The way your brakes pull a little to the left, the way you start to shudder around 5,000 rpms when you're excited. And you burn oil when you're mad at me, don't you?".'

Pynchon's perception of how females relate to their automobiles is an accurate one. The car works as a metaphor of the most basic aspect of human behavior for both males and females past the point of puberty. The symbolism evoked by its shape is fused with inevitable connotations of its mechanical functions. In the internal combustion engine pistons pump reciprocatingly in lubricated cylinders. So close are the parallels that they arouse embarrassment. To point out the details is to invite accusations of smuttiness, and so we avoid them in polite conversation. But the combination of evocative shape and symbolic mechanics can hardly be suppressed by mere etiquette. They, more than elementary considerations of privacy and concealment, are at the root of a particular aspect of the relationship with the automobile and our continuing desire to use it as a vehicle for sexual acts.

The variety and intensity of peak experiences that the automobile is capable of providing ensures it a continuing niche in the collective psyche of motorized societies. Some people, like Toad, are turned on by the sense of power and speed that comes through driving. Others may see the car as both a sexy machine and an environment for sexual pleasures. Few people are indifferent to the sexual potential of the automobile or to its sexual symbolism. They may suppress their feelings, but behind the wheel of a car they are different people with different emotions and unique experiences. They are in enclosed worlds which, from the very early days of motoring history, have been associated with pleasure and escape from the ties of the conformist world. For both men and women the car has given, and will continue to give, both the stimulus and the opportunity for thrills. Cars, speed, mastery and sex are all ingredients of a recipe that will ensure the survival of automobiles long after their ostensible utility as efficient forms of transportation has completely vanished. When automobiles can no longer compete with other rapid public transportation systems, perhaps then we will admit its real function. When people have no excuse for having a car, perhaps then we will own up to the real passions and emotions that the 'insolent chariots' instil. Gone then will be the techno-babble of the manufacturers and their advertising agents. Gone will be the contorted rationalizations that people use in order to justify owning and driving a car. When the guilt and dishonesty have finally been driven out, perhaps then we might confess that we knew all along what the Italians mean by 'donne e motori – gioe e dolori' – 'women and cars – joys and tribulations'.

EPILOGUE

FOR over thirty years people have been composing epitaphs for the car in anticipation of its imminent demise. John Keats, writing in the 1950s, for example, concluded that: 'The American's marriage to the American automobile is now at an end, and it is only a matter of minutes to the final pistol shot.' Such epitaphs were and still are far too premature. The automobile has kept her seductive charms intact and there are no signs that she is running out of suitors. Other writers, recognizing the mistakes of earlier crystal-gazers, have been rather more circumspect. Marshall McLuhan, for example, has suggested that the fate of the car will be similar to that which befell the horse. 'The horse has lost its role in transportation but it has made a strong comeback in entertainment. So with the motorcar. Its future does not belong in the area of transportation.'

McLuhan, of course, was clinging to the notion that, in the mid-1960s, the main function of the car was still as a means of transportation a view which was hardly sustainable given the weighty incrustations of chrome and useless ornamentation which characterized the models of that decade. He was right, however, in his observation that the car might have a future which is quite unrelated to its transportation role. Others, such as Lester Brown and his colleagues who wrote *Running On Empty*, still continue to rehash the old warnings about dwindling oil supplies and the negative impact of the automobile on the ecology, without so much as a thought for the quite different roles that the car plays. Both Brown and McLuhan, however, see the future of the car depending on the replacement of the internal combustion engine with an electric power source.

The idea of electric cars has been around since the 1920s and they have been manufactured in small quantities since that time. Despite all the obvious advantages of such machines, however, there has been remarkably little development in this field over the last fifty years. While the internal combustion engine has been the subject of quite radical technological innovation, we are still a long way from solving the problem of producing a light and efficient means of storing electrical energy. Apart from a few expensive prototypes, battery-powered vehicles are still only fit for humble roles such as the local delivery of milk.

Clive Sinclair's attempt to introduce an electric car resulted in one of the most dramatic commercial failures that Britain has seen for many years. The C5 was admittedly very crude, but it cost less than £400 and was quite adequate for local urban use and more comfortable than a motor cycle. It was also in keeping with the futuristic view of the car that has been championed for many years, a future in which pollution and the privations of oil shortages would be a thing of the past. So why did it fail so miserably, and why are other manufacturers apparently so reluctant to invest in the development of alternatives to the traditional source of automotive power?

A number of people have suggested that a conspiracy between the large oil companies and the car manufacturers lies at the root of the problem. This view is too paranoid. The real reason why the electric car is unable to find immediate acceptance lies in the psychology of the car owner. Electric motors and internal combustion engines have quite different inherent symbolism. The former are associated primarily with domestic machinery, such as refrigerators, vacuum cleaners and home tools. It is not that they are *women's* motors – although they have a less than masculine image – it is the air of homely domesticity which makes them quite unacceptable as the motive force for a car. The internal combustion engine, in contrast, has absolutely no associations with everyday household activity. It belongs uniquely to the automobile and has quite different symbolic characteristics. Its mechanical action conjures up images of sexuality and power, and the associations are with personal freedom and escape from the humdrum concerns of domestic life.

Clive Sinclair's disaster was caused by his failure to recognize the imagery of electric motors. He even let slip that the motor in the C5 was normally used in washing-machines and was manufactured by Hoover! Other would-be producers of electric cars will face similar problems. The Utopian dream of the ecologists and planners fails to take into account the fundamental reasons why people buy cars in the first place. In the same way that the early automobile manufacturers were forced to put the engine at the front of the car, to symbolize the power of the horse which the internal combustion engine replaced, a viable electric car will have to communicate messages similar to those conveyed by conventionally powered vehicles. That, however, requires a fundamental contradiction to be overcome, and even the most persuasive of advertising copywriters will find that an uphill task.

A popular alternative view of the future revolves around notions of much more sophisticated mass transit systems. The car, it is suggested, could be made redundant if public transportation were to be made more efficient and swift. Compromise schemes involve personal transportation being integrated with the mass transit systems by having cars controlled, not by the driver, but by signals transmitted from cables under the roads. The laudable aim behind such proposals is to reduce the number of individual vehicles, organize their journeys more effectively, reduce accidents and save fuel.

While such schemes appear to make good sense on paper, there are a number of psychological obstacles to their popular acceptance. First, cars and public transportation are not really in competition with each other. People do not drive cars simply because trains and buses are perceived as being inefficient. The automobile is preferred primarily for its expressive function and for the spontaneity of travel that it provides. Public transportation does not provide opportunities for self-expression and it requires forward planning on the part of the passenger. More important, however, the car allows individuals full control of their own destiny. Certain restrictions are placed upon their behavior through speed limits, traffic signals and so on, but within these constraints drivers are free to do what they please.

They can drive quickly or slowly, take risks or play safe. They can determine their own level of emotional arousal, express their personality through the car they own and the manner in which they drive it, act out fantasies and gain rare opportunities to dominate others.

Mass transit systems must be seen as serving a totally different function from that of the automobile. Trains, buses, or their futuristic equivalents can never *replace* the car. Their aim is to fill a role which the car has long since vacated, that of simply transporting people from one place to another. The present confusion only exists because the automobile manufacturers feel obliged to market their products *as if* they still served as viable alternatives to public transport. We are presented with quite absurd images of cars which are 'tough on the streets', speeding their owners through back alleys to their places of work, while other vehicles remain locked in the traffic jams. The problems of congestion are recognized, but the Renault driver still gets to the office on time.

Such imagery stretches credulity to the limits because it continues the false notion that the car is primarily a means of transport. If we can now recognize this falsehood, then our ideas about the future of the car must similarly be modified. Practical necessity will inevitably result in the growth of more sophisticated public transportation systems. It will also undoubtedly promote the development of alternative fuels and power sources. But the car will remain. The driving passion will ensure the survival of the expressive function for which it is really designed and which it so perfectly fulfills.

BIBLIOGRAPHY

Arias, Mrs, *Woman and the Car*, Sidney Appleton, 1906.

Banham, R., 'Detroit tin revisited' in T. Faulkner (ed.), *Design 1900–1960*, Sheffield City Polytechnic, 1976.

Barris, G. & Scagnetti, J., *Cars of the Stars*, Jonathan David, 1974.

Barthes, R., *Mythologies*, Editions du Seuil, 1957.

Basham, F., Ughetti, B. & Rambali, P., *Car Culture*, Plexus, 1984.

Bayley, S., *Harley Earl and the Dream Machine*, Weidenfeld & Nicolson, 1983.

Belasco, W.J., *American on the Road: From Autocamp to Motel 1910–45*, MIT Press, 1979.

Black, S., *Man and Motor Cars*, Secker & Warburg, 1966.

Bogart, L., 'The automobile as social cohesion', *Society*, July/August 1977, 10–15.

Bollen, K.A. & Philips, D.P., 'Suicidal motor vehicle fatalities in Detroit: a replication', *American Journal of Sociology*, 87, 1981, 404–12.

Brown, L.R., Flavin, C. & Norman, C., *Running on Empty: The Future of the Automobile in an Oil Short World*, Norton, 1979.

Brownell, B.A., 'A symbol of modernity: attitudes toward the automobile in Southern cities in the 1920s', *American Quarterly*, 1972, 24.

Cohen, J., *Behaviour in Uncertainty*, Allen & Unwin, 1964.

Dannefer, W.D., 'Driving and symbolic interaction', *Sociological Inquiry*, 47(1), 1977, 33–8.

———. 'Neither socialization nor recruitment: the avocational careers of old-car enthusiasts', *Social Forces*, 60, 1981, 395–413.

Dettelbach, C.G., *In the Driver's Seat: A Study of the Automobile in American Literature and Popular Culture*, Greenwood Press, 1976.

Di Sirignano, G. & Suzberger, D., *Car Mascots*, Macdonald & Jane's, 1977.

Drake, A., *Street Was Fun in '51*, Flat Out Press, 1982.

Flink, J.J., *America Adopts the Automobile, 1895–1910*, MIT Press, 1970.

———. *The Car Culture*, MIT Press, 1975.

Flower, R. & Wynn-Jones, M., *100 Years on the Road: A Social History of the Motor Car*, McGraw-Hill, 1981.

Fondin, J., *The Golden Age of Motoring*, Edita Lausanne, 1982.

Fox, M. & Smith, S., *Rolls-Royce: The Complete Works*, Faber & Faber, 1984.

Frostick, M., *Advertising and the Motor-Car*, Lund Humphries, 1970.

Gammage, G. & Jones, S.L., 'Orgasm in chrome: the rise and fall of the automobile tail-fin', *Journal of Popular Culture*, 8, 1974, 132–47.

Goldberg, T., 'The automobile: a social institution for adolescents', *Environment and Behaviour*, 1, 1969, 157–85.

Haddon, W., Jr., 'The safety of the automobile: an international perspective', Nordic seminar on the Safety of the Automobile, Sweden, 1983.

Harding, A. (ed.), *The Guinness Book of Car Facts and Feats*, Guinness Superlatives Ltd, 1983.

Hayakawa, S.I., 'Sexual fantasy and the 1957 car', in S.I., Hayakawa (ed.), *Our Language and Our World: selections from, etc: a review of general semantics*, Harper, 1959.

Heussenstamm, F.K., 'Bumper stickers and the cops', *Transaction*, 8, 1971, 32–42.

Hills, B., 'Vision, visibility, and perception in driving', *Perception*, 9, 1981, 183–216.

Huttman, J., 'Automobile addiction', *Society*, 10, 1973, 25–9.

Jerome, J., *The Death of the Automobile*, Norton, 1972.

———. 'The physiology of acceleration', *Car and Driver*, May 1983, 131–2.

Kaus, R.M., 'You'll get me out of my car when you pry my cold dead foot from the accelerator', *Washington Monthly*, Dec. 1979, 28–38.

Keats, J., *The Insolent Chariots*, J.B. Lippincott, 1958.

King, S., *Christine*, Hodder & Stoughton, 1983.

Knapper, C.K. & Cropley, A.J., 'Social and interpersonal factors in driving' in J.H. Stephenson & J.M. Davis (eds), *Progress in Applied Social Psychology*, Wiley, 1981.

Lee, R., *Fit for the Chase: Cars and the Movies*, Th. Yoseloff, 1969.

Lewis, D.L. & Goldstein, L. (eds), *The Automobile in American Culture*, University of Michigan Press, 1983.

Loftus, R., 'The idioms of contemporary Japan XVII', *The Japan Interpreter*, 11(3), 1977, 384, 394.

Lord, C., *Autoamerica*, Dutton, 1976.

McLuhan, 3M., *Understanding Media: The Extensions of Man*, McGraw-Hill, 1964.

Mandel, L., *Driven: The American Four-Wheel Love Affair*, Stein & Day, 1977.

———. *American Cars*, Stewart, Tabori & Chang, 1982.

Marsh, P. & Collett, P., *Seat-belts in Europe*, Report to the Rees Jeffreys Road Fund, 1984.

Medalia, N. & Larsen, O., 'Diffusion and belief in a collective delusion: the Seattle windshield pitting epidemic', *American Sociological Review*, 23, 1958, 180–6.

Montagu of Beaulieu, Lord, *Royalty on the Road*, Collins, 1980.

———. & McComb, F.W., *Behind the Wheel: The Magic and Manners of Early Motoring*, Paddington Press, 1977.

———. & MacNaughten, P., *Home James: The Chauffeur in the Golden Age of Motoring*, Weidenfeld & Nicolson, 1982.

Mumford, L., *The Highway and the City*, Harcourt, Brace & World, 1958.

Nader, R., *Unsafe At Any Speed*, Grossman Publishers Inc., 1965.

O'Connell, J. & Myers, A., *Safety Last: An Indictment of the Auto Industry*, Random House, 1966.

Parry, M.H., *Aggression on the Road*, Tavistock, 1968.

Pettifer, J., *Automania*, Collins, 1984.

Phillips, D.P., 'Suicide, motor vehicle fatalities, and the mass media: evidence toward a theory of suggestion', *American Journal of Sociology*, 84, 1979, 5, 1151–74.

Porterfield, A.C., 'Traffic fatalities, suicide and homicide', *American Sociological Review*, 25, 1960, 897–901.

Rae, J.B., *The American Automobile*, University of Chicago Press, 1965.

———. *The Road and the Car in America*, MIT Press, 1971.

Reser, J.P., 'Automobile addiction: real or imagined?', *Man-Environment Systems*, 10, 1980, 279–87.

Richardson, J. & Kroeber, A.L., 'Three centuries of women's dress fashions: a quantitative analysis', *Anthropological Records*, 5, 1940, 2.

Richman, J., 'The motor car and the territorial aggression thesis: some aspects of the sociobiology of the street', *Sociology Review*, 20, 1972, 5–25.

Roberts, P., *Any color so long as it's black: the first fifty years of automobile advertising*, David & Charles, 1976.

Rothschild, E., *Paradise Lost: The Decline of the Auto-Industrial Age*, Random House, 1974.

Sears, S.W., *The Automobile in America*, American Heritage Publishing Co., 1977.

Sheridan, M. & Bushala, S., *Showtime*, Promotional Displays Inc., 1980.

Siegel, J., 'An interview with James Rosenquist', *Art Forum*, 10, 1972, 30–4.

Silk, G., *Automobile and Culture*, H.N. Abrams Inc., 1984.

Stein, R., *The American Automobile*, Random House, 1971.

———. *The World of the Automobile*, Grosset & Dunlap, 1973.

Taylor, D.H., 'Driver's galvanic skin response and the risk of accidents', *Ergonomics*, 1964, 439–51.

Tubbs, D.B., *Art and the Automobile*, Grosset & Dunlap, 1978.

Veblen, T., *The Theory of the Leisure Class*, Allen & Unwin, 1971.

Williams, W.C., *Motoring Mascots of the World*, Motorbooks International, 1976.

Wilson, P.C., *Chrome Dreams: Automobile Styling Since 1893*, Chilton Book Co., 1976.

Wolfe, T., *The Kandy-Kolored Tangerine-Flake Streamline Baby*, Jonathan Cape, 1966.

Wright, J.P., *On a Clear Day You Can See General Motors*, Sidgwick & Jackson, 1981.